Personal A

Ascension

2012-2017

Second Edition

p. 304   you are a powerful infinite being

By Inelia Benz

Published by Ascension101 Publishing Inc.

Author contact details:
www.ascension101.com

ISBN: 978-1-329-07042-4

Table of Contents

See Working the Collective
— introvert
— extrovert

Introduction to the Second Edition

In 2010 we published the first edition of this book. It contained all the articles written and published by me on ascension101.com up until then. All the articles were available for free on the website, but several individuals asked for a PDF version, or book format version, so we published one.

When I got my personal copy of the paperback, I opened it randomly and to my great surprise the article talked about the exact thing I was looking at that day. It was such a big surprise that I decided to see if it would happen again, so I asked a question, held the book between by hands, and opened it randomly. It worked again!

I realized that the book could be used as an Oracle and Guide. So my suggestion would be that after you read it, to use it as an Oracle and Guide. It's the type of book which in a year's time you want completely covered in notes, highlights, bent pages and coffee marks… in other words, a book well used.

The plan was to publish a book per year, so seven editions to the year 2017, when I retire. But, other things become priorities, and before we knew it we were in 2015 and no other volumes had been published. We looked at what we could do and decided to simply publish a second edition which would include everything written on the website up until today (March 2015). And in 2017, we will publish a third edition, including everything I write up until the date I retire from public work.

Some articles have been edited to make it paperback readable, but the content is the same as the article library at ascension101.com

Enjoy!

What is the difference between Ascended Being and an Awakened Being?

An Awakened being is the person who has realized there is more to life than just the material world, has the capacity to see beyond the veil of forgetfulness and is in the process of ascension.

An **Ascended being** is living in a state of Oneness. There is no "individual", but a Oneness consciousness that uses the traits of their human existence to communicate.

It is practically impossible to live in a state of Oneness 24/7 and keep a normal lifestyle. That's why throughout the life of the Ascended person, they will need to continuously strive to do a daily practice of meditation, quieting the mind, and allowing Flow. The chapter titled Ascension Worker gives a very detailed description of what it means to live in an **Ascended state**.

Ascension and the Body

You have probably heard a lot of information about the importance of detoxing the body before attempting an ascension session.

This is both right and wrong.

On the one hand, your body will be able to handle the ascension whether you detox or not. On the other, if you are not physically prepared, you will get very sick.

The physical effects of doing ascension work without the detoxification of the body are not serious, but they are unpleasant. It's possible you will be nauseous, vomiting and with diarrhea for 3 days.

So, it's best to prepare the body :)

This is actually quite easy. Lower the intake of sugar, caffeine, meats, and all processed foods. Eat fresh, raw vegetables and fruits as much as you can, lots of water and other healthy drinks.

If possible make the food yourself using organic products.

If you smoke and or drink, try to cut them out for 24 hours previous to the exercise. I understand that smoking is problematic, and with this, cut down as much as possible if you can't go without for 24 hours.

Don't take any street drugs for at least a week (do try to stop taking them altogether and forever) and only take pharmaceuticals if your life and health depend on them. With regard antidepressants and other mind altering pharmaceuticals, don't stop taking them unless your doctor has given you the OK. With all medicines, ask your doctor for advice on whether you can or cannot stop taking them. There is no reason why you cannot start your ascension work while on meds but it is advisable that you search for and educate yourself on alternative medicines such as homeopathy, herbs etc... Don't self medicate.

I am not trying to make you think that if you do have to take medications the way will be as easy as someone who doesn't. This is not the case. However, all barriers to ascension are illusion. You are already in that space, you just have to tap into it.

Message to Indigo Children, Crystal Children, Rainbow Children and Diamond Children.

Yes, you have probably read a thousand websites telling you that you are special and that you are different. Something you know already. Unless you are a Diamond Child, in which case you have probably not found much information at all.

Why are you here?

To BE HERE.

A lot of you will have very special gifts, and some will have a very subtle one. The one I am talking about is not normally seen or recognized by people as easily as painting, signing, writing, science, dance and all the other forms of creative expression that we as human posses.

No, the one gift I am here to talk to you about is one that puts you apart from everyone else on Earth. Even Indigo, Crystal, Rainbow and Diamond Children. You are here because you need to BE HERE.

You do feel the same sense of urgency and need to fulfill your mission as all the other kids, but you know it is more than peace on earth, more than expression of love, more than changing society, all of which are beautiful and needed but just another expression of illusion. You may have multiple skills and abilities, so many in fact that there is not one that you can pick up and run with.

That's because your special skill is not even known to most of humanity. The one skill that you have brought with you my brothers and sisters is that of channeling the divine into Earth. For you to do this you don't need to write books, paint pictures, take photos or anything else. You can of course do these things and you will need to find yourself a career that pays the bills, but your special mission is to BE HERE.

BE HERE on Earth for as long as you possibly can. It will get difficult. But stick it out.

Near you, people will heal, they will harmonize, they will become more psychic, they will become more creative, they will blossom. This is because you skill, your mission and your invisible ability is to bring the light into the core of Earth and Humanity. By being part of this reality, and your Self having a direct connection to Oneness, you act as a path, a channel, a thread that links both dimensions.

If it is getting difficult come to present time and release fear. Don't forget that you are part human now and that means your body, mind, emotions and ego will need nurturing and looking after.

What does Ascension feel like?

Love is the nearest human word to describe the state of Oneness.

Pure and unconditional bliss in existing as Love.

Each person ascends to the place they are ready for. Each place is unique and precious. There are no two people who have the same experience. The place is not a time/space place, but a state of being who you already are.

The Ego and Ascension

Many spiritual and psychological modalities will demonize the ego.

Don't.

The ego is a necessary "body" we need to wear in order to live in and survive in the world. It can get out of hand and is the main brake on one's ascension process.

Yet it is necessary.

We can easily identify the ego when we feel a strong negative emotion. Whether fear, anger, frustration, intimidation... all these are felt by the ego.

When I trace the feelings, I often find them in one particular part of the physical body.

Next time you feel a strong negative emotion, trace it to a part in your body and then bathe it with love.

A lot of awakened masters have huge egos. This is reflected in the us/them mentality, "my way of doing things is the only way" mentality, and a huge resistance to try or learn any other "modality". They are often "healers" too, with a huge list of returning clients who "need" them.

The ego will battle and fight to survive.

Do I have an ego? Of course I do. All humans have an ego and I exist here on Earth as a human. Does it get out of hand sometimes? YES.

I can be arrogant, or feel a need to be "right", be ignorant of others feelings and outright needy at times.

And when I feel those things, I trace it back to the source and bathe it with love. Sometimes the feelings will bite me in the ass and I will do something stupid, like argue or feel hurt.

One thing though, the battles become silly and a waste of valuable time and resources. And the times of ego become smaller and less damaging, while the times of existing in Oneness become longer.

What does the process of Ascension involve?

This very much depends on where you are starting from.

Sometimes the journey is easier for someone who has not been on a spiritual or mystical path than for those who have. The reason is that inevitably, those who are on a mystical path usually will have modalities they are attached to, might be seduced by things such as psychic abilities, channeling information, talking with angels as well as more earthly skills such as telepathy, the law of attraction and such.

If you are working through one of these aforementioned modalities, and have been able to help yourself and other persons with it, then for you Ascension will first involve realizing that all of the above are as real as the ground you stand on. The skills do not make you superior or inferior to anyone else on Earth, and that they are as useful as any other skill held by anyone on the planet.

The first step you must take, whether you are in a mystical/spiritual path or not, is to start working of the following:

Release of Fear.

Release of Attachment.

Release of Being Right.

Flow of Love.

Silence of Mind.

Acceptance of your essence.

Become as much You as you possibly can.

The first three, those things you release, you must do using whatever modality you find that fits you best.

The one that works for me is to go straight for the Flow of Love and Flow Love to it and myself.

This is done by closing your eyes and becoming aware of the space that is our Heart Chakra. The space in the middle of your chest, just behind the breastbone.

Depending of where you are, this will either bring up big emotional responses to eventually feeling divine love flowing into you and through you, bathing you in bliss and ecstasy.

Silence of Mind can be achieved with any meditation modality. The one I use is the simplest and, in my opinion, most effective method of feeling the air going in and out of my nose. This works whether one is in a quiet space or in the middle of a mall during Christmas shopping.

Acceptance of your essence. You are divine. You are divine love, divine wisdom and knowledge, divine experience and divine consciousness. This is who and what you are. Human words cannot express your true essence, but you will know when you feel it.

Become as much You as you possibly can. This means warts and all. By accepting yourself fully, as a human being and divine being, you will be able to live in the state of ascension where ecstasy is your primary and fundamental experience of living. You will know that everything that happens in your life is an experienced to be experienced. You will know that loss is part of life, that negative feelings are simply messages to show you where you need to work a bit more and will know that everyone and everything around you is simply part of YOU.

How do I start the Ascension process?

The Ferrari of Ascension modalities is "Love".

If you want to take the fast way there, then start experiencing Love at every opportunity. This does not involve another person, except perhaps in reminding us what love is. This involves you.

You also need a daily practice of staying heart centered, meditation, quieting of the mind and allowing Flow.

To experience Love, you have to open your heart to receive it. Love is you and it is all around you. There is no lack of love in the world and no other person can give it to you. Love is you.

If you know what I am talking about, then start by becoming aware of your Heart Chakra, the spot in the middle of your chest just behind the breastbone. Be aware of this spot during the day and during meditation.

If you have no idea of how to experience Love because life has treated you harshly, then recall someone, a person, pet, or something that you loved in the past. Let that warm feeling appear and be aware of it. Now become aware of your Heart Chakra.

This is by far the best way to start your Ascension process.

After this, sit in silence, and allow Love to flow. This is such a strong and powerful experience that sometimes it can become overwhelming.

The person will often feel dizzy, release strong emotions through crying, will often become sexually aroused or nauseous.

The key is to go past these emotions and reactions and reach the state of Oneness.

It might take a weeks or months of practice to become completely comfortable in this procedure. Stick at it.

Also check out the Ascension Tools for MP3 (https://ascension101.com/ascension-tools.html) downloads you can use during the day.

Carnal Pleasures and the Ascension Process - Sex and Enlightenment

When we think of carnal pleasures, or pleasures of the flesh, the first thing we think about is sex. Of course there are other pleasures of the flesh, such as eating, drinking, enjoying nature, music, art, conversation... all the pleasures we gain from our physical senses, our body and our mind.

Carnal pleasures are not incompatible with ascension. In fact they can help. However, they are a two edge sword, just like any modality based in the body, mind or spirit.

For our existence on Earth, love and pleasure are closely related. Physically speaking, they create a lot of the same chemicals. We say things like, "I love to dance", "I love to eat", "I love sex."

I know I do.

Going without is not the answer. Indulging every pleasure can also become a trap. The way it traps is by sex or physical pleasure being hijacked by the ego, or small self.

Take a sexual union for example. Both parties fully aware that they are divine beings and want to create a sphere of divine love which is greater than the individual parts put together. It is a powerful concept. Intention is the key here. Enjoy and love each other fully. When the words start coming in such as "you are mine and only mine", "I don't want to share you", and other controlling and owning energies come to the surface, the flow is no longer what it can be.

Both parties can go into the ascension through pleasure relationship with an agreement to be exclusive to each other for as long as it takes. This is actually recommendable, especially at the start when both parties will be dealing with a lot of love flow and change.

However, the problem begins when it is not an agreement but a necessity due to insecurities, control, fear, anger or possessiveness.

Some of the people I have helped by providing an ascension consultation report become sexually aroused during the process. So an understanding of how the energy of love and that of sexual pleasure are linked physiologically speaking helps to get past this stage as it can otherwise be a stopping point for the person involved. The stopping point comes about because for a lot of us sexual energy and work of the spirit seem to be incompatible due to our upbringing.

The energy the person feels during the process, the one they become aroused with, is divine love. It is in fact themselves they are feeling. Their true essence. The key here is to let the physical feelings fully express themselves energetically and let them expand as much as they can, engulfing the body, the room and the entire Earth if needed. That energy is part of the person and has to be embraced by the person.

Sexual arousal and libido often will increase when traveling the route of love to ascension, which is why I often suggest to my students to get a boyfriend or girlfriend. Hey, why not enjoy the experience and take full advantage of it!!!

For a deep exploration of this topic, plus empowering tools and manifestations exercises get:

Sex, Love and Soulmates in the New Paradigm at ascension101.com

Leaving the Body - Ascension and out of the body experiences.

The concept of leaving the body or **having an out of body** experience is erroneous. You cannot leave the body because the body is **in** you.

What you can do is change your point of view. (I hear you saying AH HAH)

We live quite limited by having our viewpoint solely behind our physical eyes. When you learn to expand it to encompass not only your eyes but also your environment and the different dimensions, that's when you will fully see that the body is in fact inside of you, as is the world.

At this point, you can also move your viewpoint and, if wanted, create an energy body to explore other realms on Earth as well as outside of it.

As a young child I used to do a lot of astral travel. It really is a very thin line between our dimension and the astral one.

Gaia - apocalypse - 2012

I recently heard a person say that Gaia doesn't give a shit about us humans. That Gaia will continue to exist whether we are here or not. That it will transform regardless of whether that transformation will support human life or not.

Well, Gaia is an integral part of you as a human being. It is as much a part of you as your body is. Therefore Gaia transforming to become something different inevitably means that it is you who is transforming to become something different.

I was at a meeting of highly evolved and enlightened individuals and at one point a lot of fear was expressed with regard 2012 and what is going to happen then.

The feeling was that there is going to be a tremendous change, one that is already being felt by the apparent collapse of the financial system and extreme weather conditions throughout the world.

The fear expressed in the meeting was in the inability to survive, being burnt alive, lack of food for our children and much more.

Fear is the biggest stumbling block to ascension.

The truth of the matter is that those experiences have been happening on earth for thousands of years. People have been unable to survive here due to hunger, have died in the most horrific ways, have lost their children to starvation and more.

So what is the difference? Loss is loss, no matter if it happens to you or a person in the next continent. Chances are you have experienced loss in this lifetime as well as many other lifetimes. It is no big deal. You will not cease to exist.

The change will be experienced by each person differently. Some will in fact see no change whatsoever because they are not ready for it. Other will be burned alive because that is the experience they need to have. Others will transform into different physical beings, a change in DNA which will allow them to exist in a wider range of vibrational experience, having the physical body being a minor or non existent part of themselves.

Earth, Gaia, will change too, into whatever it is that you want it to. A heavenly paradise, a post apocalyptic adventure, or even, gasp, a continuation of what it is today... there is no limit. There is no judgment.

What is Ascension and What is Oneness

Ascension: movement in an upward direction. But unlike a movement up in a hierarchical sense, it is much more like one of two musical notes, one with a higher pitch than the other. Neither note is superior in any way to the other. They simply sound different.

Oneness: The state on non division. Perception of reality as one consciousness, one Being.

This blog is mostly concerned with Ascending into a state of Oneness. That place where Divine is All that there is. Experiencing life in this state is one of bliss, ecstasy and wholeness.

But are we all interested in this goal? No.

Therefore, reaching our personal state of ascension is when we stop moving "upward" in the vibrational scale because we have reached a place where we are happy, content and want to stay in for the next day, life, million years or forever. Is the state reached "Oneness"? Not necessarily. Is it a lesser state? No. There are no hierarchies in Oneness, that would be a contradiction in terms. And, the truth is that each one of us is already in Oneness. We just don't perceive it, or enter life from that oneness viewpoint automatically when we enter Earth.

We are here to play games, to have experiences and to BE in Present Time.

Ascension, then, means that a person moves from depression to a place of contentment. From enlightenment to a place of Oneness. From contentment to utter happiness. Is one superior to the other? No.

Why bother with ascension? Because we chose to. As the person ascends to higher vibrational awareness, their ability to do (power) increases. The game become more interesting.

The Permanency of Ascension

I have been asked by various individuals whether after going into an ascended state, experiencing it, will they come back to their previous state or whether they will be able to live their entire lives in that ascended state.

There is no set rule to this.

One person can stay in their ascended state for the rest of their lives and beyond. Another will have periods of ascension and then periods of their lives as an individual in duality. However, the more they allow the perception of their ascended state to exist, these periods will become longer and the periods of perception in duality will become shorter.

Why do we come back to a perception of duality when living in an ascended state is so much more desirable?

It is simple. We have perceived in duality for a long time. It is a well known and well traveled road. Our identity is often tied up with Earthly concerns and leaving that behind is difficult.

We are still in a world asleep, so if we fall into slumber it is not a big deal. It can be frustrating, but it is normal. However, we do have the tools to wake ourselves up again and if we do so, the state of Ascension can become permanent.

Suffering and Ascension

Suffering and pain is part of being human. Pain will happen with injuries and loss. These can be physical, emotional, mental or spiritual. Suffering is the attachment to that pain.

As a human being we have lived many lives and have suffered every kind of injury, death and loss that is possible here on Earth. We have had our spirit broken so many times that it would seem impossible for us to ever recover from it.

Yet we persist.

There are other beings who have lived full cycles of their existence in other realms. Although those realms will give them very particular experiences, they don't compare to what they can experience on Earth. Not that one is superior to the other. In fact many who have done their full cycles here on Earth will be born into those other realms to experience life there too.

When a very fine vibrational being comes to a very heavy vibrational reality such as ours, he or she will arrive with a full entourage to make the journey with him or her. His or her experiences here on Earth will be felt by the entire group, all of them learning what it is like to BE human.

A lot of the time the fine vibrational being will stay connected to his or her reality in the finer vibrational realms and will go through life from that perspective. They will see the differences between their experience of what life is and the experience of humans very clearly, but often will not delve all the way into the human experience. The person will always feel like an outsider, different and often "superior" to the rest of humanity.

At some point, the person might choose to delve all the way and to do this they have to lose all contact with their vibrational family and reality. Because they are not equipped to survive on Earth as an earthling, the person will often go into a deep and desperate cycle of loss and pain.

21

Is this necessary?

Only if the person wants to experience true duality.

The person's vibrational family will feel the loss as much as the person who has gone into disconnect. They cannot do anything to reconnect. Not until the person is ready and expands his or her perception back to a wider spectrum, a spectrum wide enough to encompass communication (in the form of presence, love, messages) from their vibrational family.

How can the person widen their spectrum? It can happen in an instant. It is done by becoming completely and utterly human NOW. Experiencing present moment fully and unaltered through his or her senses, the person is immediately connected to his or her entire being. Including that which is part of a finer vibrational family.

But a lot of people are not here from finer vibrational realities. They are here as humans and have been humans for a long time and many of them are addicted to suffering. These last ones think that if they don't suffer they will not evolve, will not appreciate beauty and happiness and will not grow.

Yet, all a person need to do to appreciate, be happy and grow is BE HERE NOW and APPRECIATE, BE HAPPY AND GROW. Feel the unconditional divine love which is the person's essence and simply experience life.

Like a skier going down a mountain, she doesn't hold on to the snow she slides on, she doesn't try to hold the fresh cool air that touches her skin, she doesn't hold on to the trees that speed past her and she doesn't wait to experience those things after she is done skiing. She simply experiences them in present time. If she tried to do anything else but be in present time, she would not really experience skiing, she would experience something else completely. She would experience suffering.

Suffering is the holding on of something past the event or incident. This includes waiting for something else to happen.

All a person gets from suffering is simply the experience of suffering. Nothing else.

A woman recently wanted me to honor and respect her path of suffering and gave me a lecture on how Mother Teresa, Nelson Mandela and other heroes suffered and how if they had not suffered they could not have done the work they have done on Earth. Well, I will not honor and respect her path. I accept it and understand it is important to her. But in my personal experience, suffering is a complete and utter waste of time and energy, unless one wants to experience suffering itself. In which case it makes sense.

In my humble opinion, I would say, that instead of suffering, experience life NOW.

Saving the Earth - Saving Humans

There is a distinct preoccupation with saving the planet, humans and animals on Earth. When we are born here, we are instantly responsible for our environment, which is after all part of us.

This is not the saving I am talking about.

People suffer.

Other people want to stop people suffering.

They want to stop people suffering even though the people who are suffering are actually doing so by their own choice.

Unless a person decides they have had enough suffering and want to stop suffering, there is nothing anyone can do to help them.

More, a great majority of individuals put a lot of value and treasure suffering like it was made of gold and diamonds. The gold and diamonds that will pay their ticket to salvation and heaven.

YOU are not here to save the world, and nor am I. We are not here to save anyone. We are here to BE HERE NOW.

If a beggar in the street asks you for money, you can do several things, one is to give him money and move on. Another is not to give him money because he will use it to buy drugs or alcohol and you judge that to be wrong. Another is to give him a lecture about his predicament. Another is to buy him food. Another is to try to save him by taking him to a shelter or addiction treatment center, or back to his family.

What is the right thing to do?

Well, any really. There is no judgment.

If you try to save him by taking him to a shelter or addiction treatment facility, you are wasting your time, but at least it will make you feel good.

Unless, of course, the beggar came to you in the street and said, "please help me, I am sick and tired of being an addict, I want to get my life back, please help me."

If this was to happen, I reckon that your actions will be very effective and the addict will recover.

How likely is that scenario to happen? Not very.

And there is the key and the problem. You cannot save every addict beggar in the street.

How does this compare to the rest of the population?

It is the same.

Ascension and Groups

It was Jesus that was reported to have said something in the nature of "For where two or three are come together in my name, there am I among them."

This sentence promotes a 3D group. A savior is needed, or a deity or person to focus one's love to, rather than existing as each individual being Source.

It is no secret, although to me it is a real mystery, that when two or more people of a high vibrational nature meet, their ability to affect their own work, lives, environment or visions, is much more effective than when only one person is there. It is almost as though by joining with others, the power generated is greater than the sum of the total individual powers.

For me this is annoying to say the least. This is because I do not work well with others unless I can come and go as I need, and often in groups others will project or require "savior", "need", 'co-dependence", "commitment" or their "love" to one person or each other rather than the temporary project we are working on.

However, when I am with others, one or more, to do a very specific session, or for a specific reason or project in a state of non-dependency, non-commitment except to stay through one's own choice because the work brings satisfaction, even if the reason is to enjoy a hike, it is a fantastic experience. I LOVE working in these groups. But I see them more as connections, networks, rather than groups. We come together temporarily to achieve a common goal which is inspiring, passionate and perhaps meaningful.

Even in my personal work, that of **channeling information and writing it** down afterward, I am much more effective when there is someone there asking me questions or tapping into their own streams of consciousness and databases or processes, that I can then have access to. So, I call for temporary groups to come join me in the co-creation. People come and people go as their own interest comes and goes. It is organic, it moves, it shifts and changes, it is rich and powerful, varied and colorful.

So groups are indeed very useful. Are they necessary? Not really. We can do the work on our own, as many, MANY, solitary workers will attest. But it is different. It could be said to be more effort involved at some levels and less in others in each configuration (alone or in an group).

To work in a group in present time (3D) there appears to need to be a group reality agreement. They have to agree to what is real, and new members have to agree to that reality for it to work. It is also the nature of human 3D groups to have a leader. Once these are sorted, working in a group can be very satisfactory for those involved.

For the group to work, if the members of the group connect to each other at a heart level it moves from 3D to a higher configuration. This means, connect from a level of **unconditional love** and open hearts. If it instead aligns to one specific person at a love level, need level, a specific external problem level, or issue level, or mission level, but not a HEART level, it causes a 3D group.

I work with people all the time, both on the phone and in person. The work is very specific, but without that **unconditional love connection**, it would be useless to say the least. IF that love connection becomes "conditional" in any form, such as exclusive, dependent, or needy, the work falters and falls. The agenda turns to "follow a guru," rather than, "lets co-create this in an organic manner".

Occasionally I will work with a person who really has "no business doing work with me" if looked at from a limited viewpoint. Not because they are "not worthy", but because they have no interest in staying in an **ascended sovereign state**. They will arrive to me through curiosity, or because his or her best friend had a session and he or she wants to get one too as the latest fad, or because they have projected their authority onto me.

These are the hardest ones to work with because they are not in the space from a **unconditional heart centered perspective**. It will take lots of sessions to get them to see **Oneness** even, let alone experience it. Then they go away and ask for advice on their **"path" to Oneness**. And they often return over and over asking for more, still projecting their authority and "needing Inelia". If I refuse, they feel abandoned and "left behind".

When this happens, it is difficult not to roll my eyes and sigh. It can be frustrating too, and there was a time when I would have done all these things. Yet the work stands. It is not a coincidence that they crossed my path. It is true that with the two of us working together at that particular time/space, they did indeed experienced a sense of the **state of Oneness**, albeit "conditional and temporary". Whatever happened to them afterward is their choice, but at least the seed remains. One day, perhaps in this lifetime, or maybe the next, that seed will sprout. When that day arrives, it will become clear that it was **not I** who planted that seed, but themselves... even out of all the "wrong" reasons.

So even in a group, whether small or large, that has only you as the person with the **open heart and flow of unconditional love**, the work you are there to do can still get done, but it is likely that sooner or later you will "become the leader" and others will start pulling at your energy, attention, and "leadership", or projecting their authority onto you.

If you find yourself in a group where a lot of the members are negative and have low vibrational perspectives, look for the nearest exit sign and run out of there as fast as you can. This is because the opposite is also true. A group of negative individuals is more powerful in their negativity than the sum of their individual negativity.

It is our human nature to join with others. We are all interdependent in existence. This natural aspect can, and has been, exploited through programming. One way to see if that is the case, is when we feel, or are told "we cannot leave the group", for whatever reason. Or if we do leave, we cannot come back. Or if we disagree with the "group reality" we will be thrown out and lose all our support, love and connection.

A higher vibrational group that comes and goes organically as passions for doing, or passions for projects arise, but gels in a sense of equality, not focusing their need or love on one particular person, God, being, or mission, but simply doing what brings the most joy at any one time, and each acting from a location of sovereignty, power and ability, that's a group that has moved into another dimension. It is hard to see how it can even survive as a "group" in present day society, and maybe that's the key, maybe it is no longer a "group" configuration, maybe the answer is simply **"two or more coming together to achieve a common goal"** rather than "when two or more come together **in my name**".

Ascension and Death

Death is painful for those of us left behind.

A person facing death can be in various states from extreme terror to ecstasy. But at the end of the day, our witnessing their state is going to end soon. For us, however, it is felt as a great and painful loss.

The pain of the loss can be so big we take years to get over it, if ever.

Often, and particularly with those we were very close to, we have a sense of continuity, we can feel the person's energy around us even after their body is gone. But it is simply not the same. We cannot touch them, hear them, share with them, hug or kiss them. All their items, their property, is now left behind and no longer have any meaning, except perhaps the residual energy from the person.

Death is such a loss in our society that we don't talk about it, we don't look at it, we don't even have the opportunity to process it with friends and relatives because they are also too busy repressing the pain of loss they feel themselves.

So how come death is such an important part of Ascension? Well, it is inevitable that we will die and it is inevitable that everyone we know and love will also die. Who goes first? No one knows.

Once in the state of Ascension, you will not suffer because of your own death. You will embrace it with as much gusto as you do life; seeing it as another adventure, an adventure as exciting as each day is in living.

You will, however, feel the pain of others dying. It is very likely that you will soon regain contact with those people who have passed away, unless they were in a very dark space when they died. The latter take longer to be aware enough to be able to contact the living.

Can someone Ascend after death?

Yes.

Non Duality and Oneness

What is the difference between "non duality" and "oneness"?

These two terms are very often used interchangeably. However, they are not at all the same.

Non duality actually means "not two". **Oneness** means "One"

To be "not two" means that the person has reached a level of awareness where they are no longer split into two. This could mean, "good and bad", "negative and positive", "light and dark", "divine and earthly", "right and wrong", "us and them", and many other ways we tend to split ourselves into two sides here on Earth.

Oneness means we are ALL. We are complete, whole, integrated. No sides. Not even a concept of sides.

Also, theoretically speaking, a person moving into non duality, could be said to be moving into a reality where only "goodness" exists. By the same token, another person could be moving into a reality that only "evil" exists. These realities would be non dual, however, they would not be in Oneness.

One of the most difficult concepts for a person to accept when moving into Oneness is that there is no judgment of actions or persons. In Oneness, Jesus and Hitler are equal and integrated. There are no "chosen people" in Oneness. No one is chosen to be lifted from Earth and taken to a heavenly paradise. Earth Ascension does not mean a move to a reality of paradise on Earth, or Angels coming down to gather the "good people" and save them from disaster.

Oneness is complete, fully integrated.

Sickness and Ascension

Does being in an **ascended state** mean your body will never get sick again?

The body will continue to go through sickness and death whether you are in a **state of ascension** or not.

It is much easier to cope with physical sickness when you are in an **ascended state**. This is because the vibrational energy you are functioning with is much higher, which means wholeness, healing, is achieved much quicker at a physical level.

Ascended beings still get sick and die. It is part of life on Earth.

It is also true that people who function in an **ascended state** very rarely get sick. And when they do, it is mild and passes quickly.

I get sick when I experience a block in energy. The blocks inevitably come due to ego issues that I have not addressed. So, for example, if I give myself a hard time because of a session not going as well as I intended, or because I don't like a certain person in my life, or because I am afraid of doing something, this will often turn into a physical condition very quickly. It is, for me, a great alarm system. If I ignore the problem I get very sick very quickly. If I address it, I stay healthy. Easy.

Do I suffer? NO.

Do I feel pain? YES.

When the sickness is painful it is extremely difficult to tap into one's core, and BE in present time, feeling the joy and ecstasy that the state of oneness is. It takes a lot of doing. However, it is precisely the moving away from that core that brings the sickness up in the first place.

Ascension and Diet

Many ascended masters will tell you that you need to become a vegetarian before reaching Oneness. Or any type of spiritual ascension.

Some will put other conditions, such as do not kill, do not take poisonous substances such as alcohol, drugs, tobacco, pornography or violent films etc.. And also many will tell you not to fool around if you are in a marriage or long term relationship.

Is this true? Will you not reach enlightenment and Ascension to Oneness if you carry on eating steak, drinking wine and sleeping with your neighbor's spouse?

Well, the moral conditions are there due to our personal sense of right and wrong. If we do wrong, we feel guilty, if we feel guilty we are not in a place of core center. And if we hurt others, then we will not feel good about it. Lying is actually very destructive to the liar's soul. Nothing good ever comes of it. Being completely and utterly true to yourself is always the best option.

Of course, if you already were unfaithful, being true to yourself doesn't mean running to your spouse and spilling the beans. Unless they ask you directly, don't hurt them. Of course if they ask you, then tell them the truth. And if you don't see anything wrong with being unfaithful, it will not affect you.

Eating meat is actually not essential. It does have a ton of toxins these days due to mass production, and does keep you down. So does a lot of refined sugar for that matter. As well as garlic and onion.

This does not mean you cannot achieve a state of Oneness if you carry on eating all these things. It does mean your journey will be long and arduous. More arduous than if you got rid of toxins of mind and body.

At a certain point you will find that all these things are irrelevant. Eating habits, moral habits, toxins, they can all be bypassed. But it takes a very strong spirit.

Personally speaking, I am not that strong. I had to detoxify and stop eating onion and garlic, stop drinking alcohol, cut down on sugar, caffeine, meat and chocolate.

Now, this is all to do with the body. The body houses our spirit and our ego is very close to it. The fastest and best way the ego has to put a stop to, what it thinks, is its retirement, is to make the body sick.

At the end of the day, to protect our body and make our journey a safe and fast one, it is recommendable to delete toxins of all kinds from our environment. This is an impossible task, so we have to simply eliminate what we can.

Eating fresh, local, organic fruits, vegetables, milk products, eggs and meats and no toxins does make your Ascension work easier. But that is all it does.

All this talk about how killing animals to eat them adds to your karma and how alcohol is the Devil's drink are simply ways to get the message across.

Yes, a lion does eat other animals, but you won't find a lion meditating to **achieve enlightenment and ascension** ;)

In short, yeah, all these ascended masters are onto something here.

If you do decide to detoxify, the rate you do it at is entirely up to you. I cannot recommend you do it all at once because most of us would suffer if we did that. If you are totally decided on this, then go ahead and do it. Otherwise take baby steps. Cut one item per week and give yourself six months to see if it makes any difference to you.

The toxins that are bad for me are the following and in order of worse to not so bad:

Garlic

Onion

Caffeine

Refined sugar

Meat

Alcohol

Eggs

Chocolate (probably due to all that refined sugar in it)

Go ahead and try them too.

After some research, I came across the biofeedback studies by Dr. James V. Hardt. In his book, "The art of Smart Thinking" he explains how he discovered that garlic and onion affect the energies on the right and left brain hemispheres, separating them (when meditating, we unite them). Refined sugar yielded similar results, but this time with the entire body.

Another way to go is to use some sort of divination tool, like a pendulum, and use it on the items before you decide to eat them. But if you do this, you cannot have an attachment to the answer.

We eat food in order to absorb energy. Our bodies are equipped to digest a variety of foods, including fruits and meats (we have canines), but not green leaves. Does this mean we stop eating green leaves? No.

Around the world there are people eating all sorts of different diets, none are right or wrong. At the end of the day, your best Ascension diet will be that one which is compatible with you and you alone. This will have to do with your cultural beliefs, what you personally think is right or wrong, how your body deals with human added toxins in the food and the weather environment you are in.

What is the highest level of Ascension we can achieve on Earth?

From my personal experience and also from studying various religions and occult teachings, I believe that the highest level of Ascension we can achieve here on Earth is that of Oneness.

Are there higher levels of Ascension than Oneness?

YES.

There are definitely higher levels of Ascension than Oneness.

Personally, I can only help you to the level of Oneness. After that you will need to find another guide or track a path yourself.

How do I know there are other levels beyond Oneness?

Two reasons:

1. When in Oneness, although complete and whole, I am aware of areas of existence that are beyond my comprehension as a human being. This would suggest that the Oneness we experience is not complete, but it is not like that at all. Oneness is all of existence in this universe. However, our universe is like a cell in a body. It is complete in itself, has all the information for the entire body, but it is not the body. There are other universes the nature of which we cannot imagine because it would be like a rock at the bottom of the sea imagining existing like a bird in the sky. The realities are so different.

2. Logic dictates that even our highest experiences of Ascension here on Earth are limited by the nature of creature that we are both on Earth and in all the dimensions of the Universe we inhabit. Therefore, it stands to reason that there are realities and levels of awareness we cannot reach from life on Earth.

I have not personally met anyone on Earth who has experienced Enlightenment or Ascension beyond Oneness. And most get stuck on Non-Duality, plus a whole bunch in just Enlightenment (in their light/God nature).

Who can start Ascension?

Unlike previous times in linear history, our time, the NOW, you are experiencing is a time of huge high vibrational energy. This means that anyone who wants to can start their Ascension right now, right here. No need for gurus, masters, initiation by a third party, going to a mountain top, entering a religious order or anything else. It is accessible to all of us right now, right here.

Become AWARE of now.

Detoxify your body (so it is a nicer and easier journey).

Quiet your mind, MEDITATE at least 2 hours a day.

Read and inform yourself on Ascension and self help, self awareness.

That is all you need.

If you want a leg up, then do the Ascension Course, rocket fuel ascension exercises and information.

What is the difference between an Ascended person and a Healer

It is true that when we are around an Ascended Master, we do indeed heal. Does this make all ascended masters into healer? Not really. Their higher vibration will activate our natural healing abilities, this doesn't make them healers. A healer has dedicated their life to heal and knows the ins and outs of healing in their particular module.

An ascended person can serve any purpose on Earth, including that of a healer. Healers, however, are not necessarily ascended or on their ascension path.

There isn't really a profession that is the sole activity of an Ascended Master. Once a person reaches a level of awareness where they want to stay, they can do anything they want with their lives. Sometimes the fact that they can do anything becomes a problem, they can do so much they don't dedicate enough time to one thing so their energy becomes dispersed.

It is important, if you are on your path of ascension, to decide on one activity and dedicate your life to it. Otherwise you will likely get bored.

Healing is indeed a very honorable profession. For as long as we are on Earth, will will get sick at one point and having a healer around is very necessary.

We, however, also need computer programmers, cleaners, cooks, engineers, mothers, fathers, gardeners, artists, farmers, and much, much more.

Let life unfold itself to you...

Forcing things is going to bring resistance.

A lot of our teachings and upbringing in the West have to do with working hard to get something out of life. However, to reach the ultimate goal of ascension, the opposite is true. You need to let go of results, expectations and hard work and allow life to unfold in the present moment. There is nothing you can do to change the present except change your mind about it.

The fastest way to reach your next level of ascension, or any goal for that matter, is to follow the road of most joy. Not expectation, excitement or adrenalin, but joy. The times when you think of a decision or a vision of what you want or want to do and feel joy in your gut. That's the right decision.

When meditating, which is vital for ascension, and there are a dozen things happening around you, meditate on those things. Don't try to lock them out of your consciousness in your attempt to "empty your mind". Instead, observe the things that happen around you with your mind, experience them in the present time without judgment and without expectation and without a running commentary.

Releasing control is one of the hardest things we can do. It means releasing what we think our present should be like. Releasing sadness and fear. Releasing needs and expectations. However, releasing these things will put you exactly where you are most powerful. It puts you in the flow.

The difficulties of Ascension - Spiritual Awakening

We live in a fast moving, modern society that does not encourage the expansion of awareness. We start our journey from the state of awakening into the realization that there is more to life than having a significant other, a job, somewhere to live, hobbies and interests. We have no tool, no knowledge, no information on what to do or what we will encounter.

The first few months are difficult because we don't know what we are doing, so the majority of us will go guidance shopping. This means we will buy books on self improvement, we will experiment with religions perhaps, schools of thoughts, yoga, tantra, meditation, chanting, visualizations, and on and on...

This is a great stage. The stage of learning and exploring, the stage of awakening. It is an adventure! And like any adventure, it has its dangers. We may fall victim to cults, to gurus, to religions, to ego, and lose our way for quite some time.

Eventually we come out of it. We look around and think, what next?

We still know there is more to life than the materialism we are surrounded by. We still know we have an expanded awareness and can see more than others. But we still have problems.

We may long for a meaningful relationship with an equal. We may long financial comfort. We may have a career goal we have not achieved, or health issues or psychological problems... the list can go on and on.

The miracles promised or implied by our previous teachers did not materialize, or if they did they did so very marginally and meant a loss somewhere else.

It's a difficult time.

So, where do we go from here?

We go back to the start. We shed all the tools that did not serve us 100% and keep the ones that did. Most importantly, WE MEDITATE.

It doesn't really matter what type of meditation you are doing. But the ones that involve a higher being are less effective than those that involve the quieting of the mind and bring you to present time.

When things get rough, don't try harder! Try less... do less. Just meditate at least 10 minutes a day and expand it to two hours or more if your present circumstances allow. If you are finding it difficult to start, go to the audio section and download some MP3 tools. They start with 5 minute exercises which we can all do.

If your brain is too active, write or draw, or run. Get into the flow. Get into the observer and move away from the running commentary of the mind.

Joy and Ascension

Joy is a conscious choice.

No matter how you put it, the way we feel is how WE CHOOSE TO FEEL. The concept that we are a victim to our feelings, our surroundings and our reactions is erroneous.

When we are in the depth of suffering or depression, or even anger or discontentment or frustration, it is very difficult to feel joy. However, dwelling in the negative emotion, no matter how much we deserve to be in that emotion, is not going to help us.

Say we lost a loved one. We have to allow the sorrow and loss to express itself energetically, overcome all our being. But we don't stay there. At some point, sooner rather than later, we have to become the observer, acknowledge the feeling and move our attention to something joyful. In this example, where we lose someone, instead of indulging in loss and pain, we move our attention to the moments of laughter and joy we shared with that person. Or imagine them in funny situations.

If we are suffering from poverty, instead of indulging in fear and lack become the observer, acknowledge the feelings as being real and move your attention to gratitude and joy. Find things to enjoy around you. Stop feeling fear and lack.

It is very strange, and fantastic, but sooner rather than later, your circumstances will change into the ones you are enjoying the most.

But this secondary effect is irrelevant. What is relevant is that we are much more aware, and able to ascend to greater awareness when we are in a place of joy rather than one of misery.

This method goes against modern counseling and psychological schools of thought which make you indulge and explore the things that made you miserable. So, if these modern methods worked for you, then you might have to take a leap of faith to use Joy as your new medicine.

41

Intimate Communication and Ascension

Sociologists say that we all have intimate conversations on a daily, or regular basis, with an average of four people in our lives. These include emails, phone calls, text messages and IMs as well as face to face interaction. Who you communicate with is a co-creator of your reality and a big influence on your ascension process.

That's not very many people. It doesn't seem to matter how many contacts a person has on their cellphone, on networking sites, or address book, the number stays very stable. Four people.

Like four pillars that hold up a building, or four legs on a chair, these four relationships are of great importance to your well being, your ascension process and your life in general.

So think of the four people that you communicate most with in your life. These are the people who are collaborating with you in the creation of your reality and also helping you in your ascension path. What types of conversations do you have with them? Are they heart based or ego based? Fear based? Anger based?

It is not many people and how we interact with them is of utmost importance. Why? Simple. Life on Earth is about communication. It is about joy and expansion. Life here is the school and ascension is graduation.

Make those four relationships into positive ones. If one of them is negative, change your perception of it, or get rid of it and replace it for a more positive one. Base those four relationships on a heart based connection. Communicate always from your heart.

When the Ego takes over

Ascension is the expansion of awareness, and Ego, if it takes over, will shrink one's awareness.

How can we tell if the Ego is taking over? There are signs. We become judgmental, we make others wrong, we become someone's victim, we get hurt and we hurt others.

Ego is a necessary body for existence on Earth and this article is not about "getting rid of it", "killing it" or anything of the sort. But it is about not letting it take over our existence.

A few examples of ego taking over.

Recently a friend of mine had a bad fall in his journey of discovery. He felt that he had to find his own truth and lead others to it. The details are personal so I won't go into them. However, I do want to mention this particular case because it is something that will happen to MOST OF US.

Basically, what happens, is that we get too wrapped up in our own importance. Especially so if our calling is one of leadership, education or dissemination, as was the case with my friend.

The call to lead can be very powerful, and does have with it, power. Power is the ability to do. The person with power has the ability to do what they want. This is a positive thing. Power, in the realm of the spiritual or enlightenment, has with it great responsibility. Responsibility is the ability to respond. Which in turn is power.

With this being the age of awakening, people are hungry for leadership of the soul. This, of course, is a contradiction in terms. People who look for leadership are simply looking in the wrong place. The whole thing about enlightenment and ascension is that the person does not look outside of themselves, does not ask others to provide answers.

I am not saying that a person should not seek wisdom of past and present masters, on the contrary. The more the person exposes him or herself to the wisdom of the ages the better. However, at the end of the day, the person will need to look at their inner self and experience their completeness within, he or she will need to find what is true for him or her.

My friend fell big time. He contacted me looking for answers, wondering what was happening, why this had happened to him. My answer, look inward. Stay heart centered and quieten your mind.

He felt bad that he had led people in his "truth" which turned out to be nothing but egotistical rumblings. There is no need to feel bad. People are divine beings each and every one. If one or more of those divine beings decides to follow another person in their spiritual growth, there is a connection there and lessons to be learned. There are no victims in life.

And you know what? Most people would not have even realised they were making a mistake, most people go ahead and live their truth and disregard other people's truths for the rest of their lives. He did not.

Signs that the ego is taking over:

We make others wrong

"You are wrong about that, it doesn't work that way."

"No, that's not it at all."

"If you do that you are a fool."

"NO, you have not had a good life, you've had a shitty life, a horrifying life. A life full of hardship. That's not a good life." I heard someone say this in a conversation.

When we make others wrong, we shrink their being. It is a way we cut them down and destroy them. Make someone wrong enough times and they will become depressed or worse.

Our feelings get hurt

Recently I traveled several thousand miles to spend some time to get to know someone better. This lady is someone I admire and have great affection for. When I got there, well, after a couple of hours, she basically let me know she did not want me in her space, mind, thoughts or feelings. It was honest, but the truth is it hurt like hell. Here I was, open wide to receive her. Spent hundreds of dollars to be there, traveled several hours to be there, and allowed her to be in my space, my thoughts and my heart, and she comes out with this... and really, this is someone I don't really know.

It is our EGO that expects to be expected, accepted, welcomed and loved. It is our EGO that looks for validation, approval and admiration. It is our EGO that expects to find something out there, in another person, that we should be looking for inside ourselves. But when we do this, we give away too much POWER.

DON'T GIVE AWAY YOUR POWER, and don't get so attached to your own TRUTHS that you can't see other people's truths, which are just as valid. But don't push others away to protect yourself. We are here to interact, to communicate, to experience closeness, friendships, love, connection.

Anything that shrinks our awareness, due to judgment, hurt feelings, accommodating others rather than being ourselves, second guessing ourselves, making others wrong, feeling important, and more, is most likely the ego taking over.

Strive for humbleness, openness of spirit, make yourself vulnerable, and allow life to teach you to grow, expand and ascend to your next level of awareness. Never become so invulnerable that no one can hurt your feelings or show you where you need to work in order to expand even more.

Humble Ascension

Being humble is a two edged swords. On the one hand, it is a positive state where the person concerned knows all is equal, everyone divine and life is wondrous, thus treating themselves and everyone and everything they meet with respect and acceptance.

This person doesn't need to be right, or wrong. He or she doesn't need to make you right or wrong, nor do they think you are right or wrong. A true ascended master is humble and non judgmental, simply because judgment, rightness and wrongness, do not exist in his or her reality.

On the other hand, there is the socially imposed righteousness of humbleness. Living a humble life, then becomes living a poor life. Being humble, then becomes being inferior to others or to God, and forcing humbleness becomes superiority over others. Religious zealots are usually found in this category of humbleness. And it is a road to ascension too.

I, while living my moments of ego inflation and judging from my extremely large soap box, cringe at the second type of humble person, while value the first greatly. This viewpoint, of course, is the antonym of humbleness and I laugh at my simple attitude, my personal mind chatter and realize, from a wider standpoint, that it is in reality an unimportant aspect of reality. It is, after all, the viewpoint of judgment, which is as necessary in everyday life as is breathing.

Therefore, I feel comfortable striving for the first type of humbleness, I believe that, while there, life is delicious.

Ascension is not a mental exercise

This site is dedicated to awakening and ascension information. By default we have to use our minds in order to absorb the information detail within this site. However, the mind is very much part of our ego body and not a tool that will facilitate our ascension in a practical way.

Yes, it will help us in finding out what **ascension is all about**, but on a practical level, it cannot help. In fact, the only way we can start our journey of ascension is by quieting the mind and centering our viewpoint, or point of attention, on our heart center.

It is very difficult to do this just through meditation, but we can help things along by practicing the art of heartfelt reaction to situations and people in our daily life.

This is how it works. Did you know that we choose how we react on an emotional level to everything that happens around us? This is not a voluntary reaction, but a programmed one. We are programmed to react to things in certain ways.

The way we react is very important because it is the vibrational blueprint that creates our reality. It is not about controlling our immediate reactions or burying negative emotions. It is about counting to ten and then observing our reaction to things. Afterward see if the reaction harmed you or healed you. If it harmed you, then remove yourself from the situation and look at it without judgment. See yourself as every participant in that situation, this is because in Oneness you are every participant.

Allow the emotions to express themselves, thank them then simply replace them with love, gratitude, and happiness.

Don't be afraid about forgetting or losing something, whether a situation, memory or learning experience. Keep the things you feel you must, but release anything that is hurting you and move on. If the negative emotion is too great, then simply breathe into your heart center for as long as it takes, taking your attention there, and looking out into the world from there.

Life is long and you will have ample opportunity to practice this exercise over and over again. The more you practice it, the easier it will be to expand your awareness.

Quieting the running commentary of the mind

Our culture is very much thought and mind oriented. This creates in us an overactive running commentary of what is going on around us and inside of us. We are continuously thinking. And we are almost afraid to stop, because if we do, we may lose our minds.

Sometimes the commentary is so intense that we need drugs or alcohol to quieten it down. Television to soothe it. Books to occupy it. Emotions and drama to feed it.

And if we let it take over, we don't have a chance at ascension. That's why throughout this page I always encourage you to meditate, quieten the mind, for even a few minutes every day. This is very, very important. It will keep you sane and on track. Check the audio download section at asecension101.com for useful MP3s that will help you, they start with a five minutes exercises, something we can all do.

Another thing that we can do that uses the mind's insatiable hunger for stimulation to our advantage is to focus it on a piece of art, a painting, picture, or photograph, that expands our awareness. It isn't about the picture, or the holiness of the subject. It is about bringing our running commentary somewhere productive. The picture could even be one of a ball of light. Or a flower. Or anything that creates a wow feeling for you. I use pictures I make myself with a person standing and a big star of light behind them. Some have light coming/going from their body to the heavens too. You can make one yourself with a few crayons, or just a pencil... it doesn't have to be a work of art, it is symbolism we are concerned with here.

Resolutions and Ascension

To resolve, to conclude, to reach a goal.

The New Year is an optimum time for resolutions, the type that mean we decide to do something, reach a goal. And in **Ascension Work**, there is no difference. We can decide to reach a certain goal this year. The only difficulty being that before we reach that goal, we don't know what it is, or what it is called, or what it feels like.

The best New Year's **resolution for ascension** is to determine to reach a step where we feel satisfied and happy with our progress so far.

In fact, aiming to feel satisfied, happy and content is one of the prime tools to reach any goals in life. We don't even need specific, physical, or spiritual goals! The field is left open for life to accomplish this feeling and free to achieve it any way at all. It, in fact, becomes the goal itself.

If you think about ascension, just like someone who has another goal, why do we want it? Why do we want to reach a level of awareness that encompasses more than we have now? Why do we want to live in a state of ecstasy? Of eternal wisdom? Why do we pull away at the veils of forgetfulness and want to expose the game? To be happy, satisfied and content.

Ascension Symptoms

Are Ascension Symptoms Real?

There is a lot of information out there with regard **ascension symptoms**. Well, **ascension** is NOT SOMETHING THAT HAPPENS TO YOU!

Ascension is something you do and there are no negative symptoms to it whatsoever.

There are, however, **resistance to awakening symptoms** when you decide consciously or subconsciously to begin your spiritual journey. These are due to the fact that your vibration and your bodies (mental, emotional, physical, vibrational) are changing.

The most common of these symptoms, which happens after you achieve a change in vibrational signature, and often happens after Ascension Sessions, or after Ascension Meditations, is a feeling of spaced out dizziness, nausea after eating toxic foods, sensitive skin, "burning" sensation at the crown chakra, feeling of a band around head, and ecstasy. These will pass after a few hours or days and are simply the bodies getting used to the new vibrational level.

Not everyone will get the so called **ascension symptom** when they start awakening. Some people will. The symptoms do include depression, cravings, sleeping too much, waking up at 3am every night, a sense of detachment, and the loss of friends, family and acquaintances who have been a negative influence in the person's life, tingling on the crown chakra and also physical feelings or illnesses of the other chakra locations, among other symptoms.

So, the trick here is, DO NOT USE THESE SYMPTOMS TO BECOME AN OBNOXIOUS SO AND SO! Do not use it as an excuse to get fat, lazy, procrastinate about your work, or as an excuse to have affairs... oh yeah, there's dissatisfaction with present relationships and sex.

Yes. I do like to capitalize strong points.

What YOU CAN DO is meditate, eat healthy food, drink lots of water (energize it first) and push yourself to read uplifting books and information (re-read some of the posts in this site for example), exercise every day, and keep a journal. Sounds too hard?? I said don't be lazy! Seriously though, it is up to you to lift yourself away from this crap. No one else is going to do it for you. And no matter what you read on other sites that tell you you cannot help it because it is part of **EARTH ASCENSION 2012**, it is still you and your choice. Anyone who tells you it's about the Earth and you can't do anything about it is DIS-EMPOWERING YOU. In other words, he or she is taking your personal power away from you. And if you read further, he or she will probably sell you a course, book, session, or whatever to help you through "this long and difficult period". In other words, it's a really good scam since It is the psychic who finds the curse, or negative being, on his victim who is also the only one who can lift it (after a small payment of $200).

The true ascension symptoms, in other words, the symptoms you will get once you start your ascension process, are:

- Bliss
- Ecstasy
- Happiness
- Contentment
- Completeness
- Creativity
- Wisdom
- Humility
- Heart Centered
- No judgment
- Good health
- Compassion
- Completion of your Soul Journey
- Oneness
- ... ok, so you will wake up at around 3am every night still :P

Ascension and the Art of Manifestation

It is no secret that a person will need to be fed, safe, and secure in life before they will start engaging in spiritual advancement. And I mean the basics, food in the belly, water, shelter of some sort and no wild animals or nasty weather killing his or her body.

On our modern society, it is often the person who is financially secure who then has the time and interest to begin on a **spiritual ascension path**. However, sometimes this security doesn't last. What to do then?

When we stay in a state of Oneness, or visit it on a daily basis, miracles happen. Things start going right for no apparent reason. Our wishes come true and life stabilizes. We really do not need to do much more than follow our inspiration and joy, and life works itself out for us.

However, we do also exist in a geographical area which is assigned to us for the time being, to a social karmic group that might be going through some rough patches, and so on and so forth. In other words we do not exist in isolation. Can we change those circumstances as easily as we can change ours? Yes, but not very quickly. It takes time.

There may come to be times in your life that you need to manifest wellness, whether financial, health, relationship or other, and do it quickly. This is what you do. You learn a manifestation module, such as The Law of Attraction, and stick to it! But my advice to you, do your meditation first, go to a state of Oneness first, then do the manifestation exercises. **WARNING:** Don't get stuck manifesting. Do it once a day, then go back to your natural state of ascension, follow inspiration and joy, stay heart centered, quieten the mind and allow the flow of universal energy to flow through you. You can find a great money manifesting tool with the Reconnect with the Spirit of Money MP3 in the audio section of Ascension101.com.

There will come a time when you will no longer need to manifest, because all that you need, and more, will flow to you easily and effortlessly simply by making Oneness your main priority in life.

Spiritual Guides and Ascension

We do not live in isolation, either physically or spiritually. Just like we have people around us that can provide us with good advice, teachings and wisdom on the material plane, we also live in spheres of existence at a **spiritual level** that are also populated with other **spiritual beings**. In fact, we come to Earth accompanied with a whole entourage, a support team, of **spiritual guides, teachers and helpers**.

These have been called different names by different cultures, angels, ascended masters, spiritual guides, Jesus, animal guides... the list goes on and on. The shape, identity or vibration the guides take is very much designed for our personal and cultural acceptance. Are they all the same entity? As much as we are the same entity as our neighbors, teachers, brothers, sisters, parents and acquaintances. We are indeed One in Oneness, but in our three dimensional reality we are separate and individual.

There are two main things to remember about guides as you look for them and accept them in your life:

1. They are not here to tell you what to do and to give you orders. I cannot tell you how many people have asked me, "what do my guides want me to do next?". They are not your parents and you are not a child. Asking them what they want us to do is simply a form of avoiding responsibility for our growth, life and actions.

Your guides are here to help you get where YOU WANT TO BE. And they have no judgment, so if your main preoccupation is the thought that you are poor, they will make sure you stay poor because the vibration you are giving is "I am poor". If your main preoccupation is to continue on your soul journey, they will put in your path teachers, books, tv shows, and people who will help you in this journey. And yes, the journey will be flavored with what you think it should be like. So if you believe you have to suffer to get into heaven.. guess what? You will be shown ways to suffer. They are energetic entities, live beings, not supernatural, God like creatures, or figments of your imagination. As such, they have their own evolutionary process to accomplish, part of which is to come to Earth and help with your soul journey or ascension.

2. The way to interact with your guides is on an equal basis, like you are going to meet a good friend who happens to have access to the Universal Library of All. You establish a relationship of trust, then ask for guidance on your latest problem. So, for example, it's not, "tell me what you want me to do next to become an evolved being." Or, coming with a shopping list of items such as, "Can you send me money for childcare, a new car, a beautiful house, my soul-mate, a new job." But, "When I try to merge with Oneness, I am afraid I will lose my identity. Can you tell me if this is going to happen or not?" In other words, be specific. Guides are here to guide us, very much like a Tour Guide on your Earth Holiday. We don't go to the tour guide and ask him or her what they want us to do next! No, we tell them where we want to go and they show us the sites and explain the history and what you can do in the area. But it is our choice of destination.

For example, recently I went to see the movie Avatar, which I highly recommend by the way, and I was reminded of the Interconnectedness of Earth and all that is on Earth, including us. Anyway, I went to bed that night wondering if this interconnectedness is as still strong today as it was when I was a child, or whether in fact we have "ruined" it for all of us through exploitation of natural resources. I asked Mother Earth for a sign, a message, anything, to let me know what the situation was.

The next day, I wake up and go downstairs, put on the kettle, then go to my computer to check email. My study has a very large window overlooking my suburbia garden. There are two large willow trees at the back, one directly in front of my window. Suddenly I see a huge, and I mean HUGE, Redtail Hawk land on this particular tree. My jaw dropped. You see, I am in the middle of the suburbs, and had never seen one before in all my years here. Some blackbirds, which were about the 1/3 of the size of this huge hawk, tried to scare it away, it just sat there watching them, and watching me too. Then a tiny little bird made it's way through the branches and stood right next to it, looking at it, had probably never seen such a creature in it's entire life. The hawk just looked at it, as they do, and then looked back at me. You know the feeling you get when you know an intelligent being is looking back at you? Well, that was the feeling I was getting.

I sat down, and instead of checking email, I did a search on the spiritual meaning of redtail hawks, and this is the first page I found:

"Part of the Role for the two-legged beside whom Red Tailed Hawk flies is that of Guardian of the Earth Mother. These are individuals who will possess an astute awareness of the concept of the interconnectedness of all things, and will have an inner reverence for all life."

Do you see how it works? It is simple, yet inspiring, motivating and full of wisdom.

By the way, I'd like to thank Mother Earth for being such a powerful and inspiring Guide and Teacher.

Ascension Worker

An Ascension Worker is a person who helps others through their ascension to Oneness. Oneness being the state of experiencing life as one Universal being, one entity, something that has been described as Nirvana, Ecstasy, Life Force, and many other names.

This ascension work can happen in stages and it doesn't necessarily go straight to Oneness. For example, a person might want to go from a vibrational signature of depression, to one of contentment. Or from Awakening to Enlightenment, or Enlightenment to Oneness. Enlightenment as being "in-the-light", and Oneness as "being-the-light".

There has never been in the history of humanity so many Ascension Workers and religious and spiritual leaders as there are today. A short google search on "spiritual ascension" will pop up millions of websites from dedicated workers who are here to raise the level of vibration of other individuals.

The difference between an **Ascension Worker** and religious leader, or spiritual leader, is that the first has no alignment to any religion and can work with the person within their own belief system, not invalidating what the person's spiritual truths are. The second and third, however, will normally expect the person to abandon their religious or spiritual beliefs and align with that of the religious or spiritual leader which are normally very specific. However, the **Ascension Worker** and the religious or spiritual worker are in the same line of work.

Whether you decide to be a religious or spiritual leader or an Ascension Worker really comes down to your detachment to yours and others spiritual beliefs and whether you are able to lead the person to their next vibrational level in a non-detached manner.

So, for example, on one session* you will be guiding a person through to **Oneness** and Jesus will appear in front of you, while in a second session the same day, another person's journey will take you both to another planet where beings are so different, you will have no words to describe them. Of course this all happens energetically, and is identified in your minds eye. If you were to judge either, the session would end immediately, and you could cause the client lots of damage. The reason is that both journeys are real and true and as valid as each other and as valid as your own.

The **Ascension Worker** will often be identified by the client as "the same as me". This is because, having lost all attachment and judgment, divine light, Oneness, can come through the Ascension Worker, making them a mirror of the client. The client is actually seeing themselves. The universal love, warmth, energy and completeness that the client feels, is their true vibrational signature. It is Oneness.

Ascension Workers live in normal modern circumstances. They have families and if they don't do this work full-time, they will have daily jobs, mortgages, pets, joys and pains, which of course they use in their **Ascension Work**. And because we lead normal lives, if we don't take care by meditating daily, quieting the mind, staying heart centered and allowing Flow, we can fall flat on our faces just like the next person.

The **Ascension Worker** can only lead another person to the highest level of Ascension he or she has reached themselves, which is why he or she never stops striving for a higher vibrational level. You never know, maybe one of us here on Earth will be able to go beyond Oneness!

When we stay in a state of **Oneness**, or visit it on a daily basis, miracles

happen. Things start going right for no apparent reason. Our wishes come

true and life stabilizes. We really do not need to do much more than follow

our inspiration and joy, and life works itself out for us.

* **Personal Ascension Session**: A session where the Ascension Worker creates a channeled "bubble" of Oneness. It can only be described as an extremely high vibrational energy that feels like pure, unconditional love, ecstasy, nirvana and where the person is safe and free to experience life as Oneness, tap into the Universal Wisdom, travel (like shamanic journeys) and see, feel their guides in their minds eyes. Pretty much what gurus in India have been able to do for hundreds of years, minus their strict religious beliefs. If the person is psychic, they will be able to expand their vision tremendously. The person can then tune into that vibration, or as close as they choose to go. There is a distinct feeling of "losing" oneself, which can scare the ego into stopping the session. Everyone who has a session will then go through tremendous changes in their daily lives as their life aligns with their primal soul journey here on Earth. If they are already in their soul journey, the changes won't be so severe.

Tools and Exercises for Ascension

It is sometimes difficult to change our vibration to a higher one, or expand our awareness when there is so much going on in our lives. That's why I have started a series of self growth tools that you can use in daily life to kick start the work.

On the Tools section in the top menu at Ascension101, you will find some MP3s that help you relax, some meditations and other Self Growth tools.

If you have not used relaxation audios before, start with the 5 min Relaxation for the Workplace one. Also start with this one if every time you try to mediate you fall asleep and also if you are going through stress and an overactive life and don't get much time to simply sit down somewhere and relax.

For the mediation audios, use the one you feel is most appropriate for you.

In February I will also be adding some videos explaining the basic concepts of Ascension as well as some tools you can use to fast forward your progress. If you are registered for the newsletter, you will get an update when this section goes up on the site.

These tools are not aligned to any religion or belief system. I do mention things such as elemental, Mother Earth, Spirit Guides and the like, so if you do not subscribe to these concepts they might pinch a nerve. I use these terms because there are no better terms to describe the energies we are working with at the moment. Remember, your beliefs are more important than anything written or spoken about in this website, so take from here what you find useful and discard the rest.

You can also rocket fuel your ascension process with the Spiritual Ascension 101 Course

Is Ascension only for Lightworkers or can Darkworkers get a bit of the action too?

Ascension is the expansion of awareness to the state of Oneness. Oneness encompasses all, everything, light, dark, male, female, night, day, all the polarities we have here on Earth are integrated, included in Oneness, and it doesn't really matter what path the person has taken to get there, we are all included.

Sometimes, the person who finds ascension the hardest will be the Lightworker, as opposed to someone on their soul journey who hasn't taken sides. This is because the lightworker, by definition, has taken sides. The person who does everything for the greater good, who goes out of their way to help others, no matter what this might cause to their own welfare, and who judges those who choose a path of destruction and fear as "evil", will find it extremely difficult to integrate their own darkness, acknowledge it, accept it, and let it expand with the rest of their Self. And darkness they do have.

A lightworker can be so set on his or her side of the fence, so set to save the world, so set to survive and "ascend" through 2012 that of course he or she are getting nowhere fast. They are very much attached to their healing, or lightworker, modality and seeing past it is near impossible for them. They think that to Ascend, they have to be "good". They think that "love heals all", and that heaven is a place where animals don't eat each other and that's where they are going to ascend to with the rest of their lightworker friends. I've heard it said that, "they are going to ascend to the new Earth with the other pure hearted and chosen people of Earth." See "the chosen" is highly hierarchical. Hierarchies are not inclusive, they are not Oneness.

Is there an opposite to the Lightworker? Of course, otherwise neither would exist. There is an erroneous belief that the Darkworker is someone who is dedicated to their own welfare, and only their own welfare. However, this is not the case. A Darkworker also has groups, and works for the greater good of the group, or their master. This includes keeping people as slaves of fear and ignorance so as to have "power" over them, and feed off them whether by feeling powerful, or being able to inflict pain, suffering and other manipulations over their slave population. It's a power trip. They "take" from others, whether it is life force, energy, hope, happiness or money, it doesn't matter, they take it. And what do they want for 2012? For everything to stay the same of course. Can they do ascension work? Yes. They can ascend to Oneness but their path is as difficult to the one the Lightworker has chosen. And the reason is that they too are polarized and find it extremely difficult to integrate their "light" side. They think that if they do, they will become vulnerable and lose power.

Both the lightworker and the darkworker function within hierarchies. Both have a very high sense of righteousness. Both will go to war defending their own side of the fence. And both think the other one is inferior and should be destroyed for their take on salvation.

The truth is, the greatest battle will always be fought inside ourselves. Both the lightworker and darkworker have each other inside themselves and, even if they are outwardly polarized, this only comes about by suppressing their opposite side inside of themselves.

Some believe that a person cannot get anywhere unless they do polarize, this is erroneous. The fastest and most powerful ascension occurs when the person integrates both sides fully. That is when the person becomes truly powerful.

Oneness can only be achieved by the inclusion, integration and acceptance of all sides of oneself and others without judgment or fear.

And FEAR is the key.

Each side is AFRAID of the other. And Fear is the one thing that can stop anyone from achieving Ascension into oneness.

Makes one wonder really, after all, just about everything that we see on tv, hear on the radio or read on the internet, causes fear inside us. Worry. We fear for our future, for our lifestyle, for our children, for our jobs, we fear... fear... fear. It looks like someone is trying to stop our personal ascension work, don't you think?

Anyone who tries to sell you fear as the way to heaven is working for the dark side. And that's ok. That side will get you to Oneness eventually too.

The thing about the darkworker is that once they have feared, taken, and done all they can to destroy others, the persons realizes it is as ineffective path as the work their opposite is doing, saving, giving and nurturing all and everything around them. Once each realizes the futility of the polarization, they are no longer afraid of the other side, and can integrate it into themselves, becoming whole and complete.

Soul Mates and Spiritual Ascension into Oneness

It is one of the urges of our nature to reconnect with Source, with Oneness. The closest we can identify this urge as in daily life is the complete connection with another human being. To be able to connect with another human being at this level, both parties have to have a very similar vibrational signature. When we meet another human being with whom we have a similar vibrational signature, we resonate with them. This often is called finding our twin soul, soul mate or twin flame.

It just so happens that when we do find someone like that we stop looking, and therefore the belief that there can only be one soul mate on Earth was conceived. But, fortunately, there are many other people on Earth with whom we can resonate at a vibrational level. And it so happens that if we change signatures through our soul journey work, if our soulmate doesn't do it too, we will eventually become dissatisfied and move on. This doesn't mean that our soul mate was not the "true one". It just means they are no longer vibrationally similar to the level we need for the connection.

When two souls meet and embark on Ascension work together, no matter what the modality is, fantastic results can happen. There are well known couples throughout history that have changed the course of human evolution and path due to their combined power.

It is said, in India, that the true couple doesn't look into each others' eyes, but in fact are looking forward in the same direction, toward the same goal.

Once you enter Oneness, and make it the center of your attention, the urge to connect with another human being at this level passes. This results in the ability to achieve just that, to find and connect, or reconnect, with a soul mate in total freedom and with no expectations or ego getting in the way.

Sacred Space and Ascension

Nearly every religion, culture, and spiritual or occult practice in the world will teach its' followers that he or she needs a sacred physical space in order to facilitate spiritual growth. This is old technology. Old in that it has been around for as long as we humans have. So, what does it mean to have a sacred space? Well, when religions became established it meant a special building where practitioners would go to worship. I'm not going to get into the politics of how this became part of the power game between leaders and followers of a religion because, honestly, it is irrelevant. The space is still sacred. Before that, it meant a special place on the territory that had a higher vibration, one more in tune to Source/Oneness/God/Goddess/Universal Love. At the same time, we created personal sacred spaces with altars at home, special groves in our gardens, by kneeling beside the bed, or by having a special mat where we carry out our our prayers or meditations.

It is still one of the most effective tools at our reach. Our personal sacred space can be a special mat, an altar, a chair in the house where we do our meditation. A corner where we keep what is precious to us.

There are things we can do to make this even more effective. It is part of the "cause and effect" law, as well as the concept of "intention". Firstly we need to empty the area, or choose an area in our home, that will be our sacred space. The spot we will go when we are going to meditate and tap into Oneness. If you live in one room, this could be a shelf or a small table if possible, it could be a corner of the room where you can put a chair, cushion or a mat. You need a wall and enough space for you to sit comfortably. Of course if your personal circumstances allow, it's best to have an entire room dedicated to your sacred space. Whether you do this indoors or outdoors is up to your personal affinities, your local weather and personal circumstances.

When you are clearing the space, and when you are putting your objects in there, you must have the intention that this is your will to reach a state of Oneness in this lifetime, and as soon as possible. Like, NOW.

Then choose an object, or objects that represent Oneness to you. In mine I have the picture above, it's something I scribbled quickly to represent Ascension into Oneness and helps me in keeping my mental conversation silent and helps in meditation. If you want to use it you can right-click on it, press "view image", it will open in another window, then you can print it on Ascension101.com (look for this article title in the articles index). You can also draw one yourself, it doesn't have to be a work of art, as you can see! A stick-man picture with the right symbolism for you will do. Other things that also help are incense, candles, water (bowls or fountains), bells, plants and crystals. Make sure you thoroughly clean anything before you put in in your sacred space.

Stay Heart Centered - what does that mean?

One of the main techniques we can use for ascension work is to stay Heart Centered. But what does this mean exactly? Well, it doesn't mean, "be good", or "be loving", or "be forgiving". Although these things might happen when we stay heart centered, but only as side effects.

To stay Heart Centered is an actual physical practice. It's like going on the treadmill to keep your physical body fit. This exercise is designed to move our awareness from our head center/ego to our heart center/higher-self.

The first thing to do is to locate the heart center. This the area behind our breastbone, up toward the jugular notch, and back to between the shoulder blades. This whole area is your Heart Center. It encompasses what are called the Heart Chakra, and Angel Chakra or the Shoulder Blade Chakra. It is your Core Self.

This center contains your physical existence, including emotional, physical and ego bodies, and your Higher Self connection, or connection to the Divine.

After you locate the Heart Center, you will become aware of it, the space it occupies in the physical realm, and breathe into it. As you breathe in, it fills with life force, as you breathe out, the life force expands into the rest of your body and your vibrational space.

At least once a day, move your "view point", where you imagine to be inside your body or head, into your Heart Center.

Simple :)

When you first start this exercise, you might get strong negative emotions coming up. They are coming up to be released. Thank them and release them. Eventually you will be able to stay Heart Centered in full joy and love.

Why do we get sick?

Note: this is NOT medical advice. For medical advice go to your doctor.

When we get sick during our ascension work, and I mean actively working on our Spiritual Growth, sickness is always a red flag. It is caused by a block of energy in one of our bodies. Our bodies are the physical body, emotional body, spiritual body, and ego body. And the main block is usually caused by fear.

It could be fear of failure, fear to see what is really going on, fear of our power, fear of becoming vulnerable, fear of being rejected, and more.

The way to work with the sickness and identify the block is to, firstly, locate it.

So, for example, if our stomach is the troubling issue, that's our solar plexus, the center of power and exposure to society. It can also mean that we can't stomach something that is going on.If our eyes are troubling us, it's usually because there is something we don't want to see about our life or someone close to us. Chest, has to do with our Heart Center and love and nurturing issues.Legs and feet have to do with stepping out into the world, or stepping into our independence.Urinary and sexual organ illnesses have to do with your connection to the world, sex and creativity. Throat and mouth, our communication is blocked, we need to say something and we haven't, or we are simply suppressing our voice. Head issues, migraines, head injuries, head colds, have to do with our spirit connection (higher self/divine/God/Oneness) to our present existence in a body... in other words, with our incarnation. And we need to be fully incarnated to do Ascension work.

You get the idea.

All the above will probably have something to do with fear. Other things will also block us, such as cultural conditioning, judgment and peer pressure. And during our Ascension work, it can come up for two reasons, one is that it is an area we need to address next, or it is an area that we have addressed and decided to unblock so all the negativity comes up to be released.

In order to heal, we have to understand that the process of illness is a release that will solve the problem that came up in the first place. We go into the pain, discomfort, or troubling area, we breathe into it, relax, breathe out, and allow it to exist and then release it. If we clear our minds, we may receive input from the area as to why we are sick. Then we can do something about it.

All negative emotions, visions, memories or feelings come up so we can release them. Then we concentrate on how we want to feel. Basically, we shift our vibration, into a positive one. Now, I personally have a very, very low pain threshold, so I know how difficult this part is. But it is essential to swap the negative vibration of pain and discomfort, to one of well-being and comfort. A good way to do this is through visualizing oneself well and doing something we love, then stepping into that vision and into the vibration of ourselves well and enjoying ourselves.

Remember, sickness is a red flag. The red flag has to be taken notice of. If we don't, then the sickness will return in the same or similar manner.

Of course, we also get medical and/or alternative treatment if necessary.

Find out what to do when dealing with sickness during your ascension process with the Spiritual Ascension 101 Course

When bad things happen. Is it our "fault"?

We have all gone through hardship in our lives. Sometimes it has been so bad that it may seem unbearable. The last thing we need to hear is that it somehow is our "fault" through "karma". Also, the fact that in Oneness there is no judgment, is often translated by someone that they can witness a child being molested and do nothing about it, because in Oneness there is no judgment on the event. Or that we should accept destructive and negative people in our lives because to judge is bad.

Bollix.

Sorry, but the above beliefs are superficial understandings of both karma and Oneness. If something bad has happened to you, recently or in the past, then it is **not** your "fault". Nor is it something you are responsible for (response-able). If you had been able to respond to it, then you would not have suffered so much over it, or still be suffering because of it. And that is the whole point of the karma thing.

Karma is not "fault" or payback. Karma are simply patterns we are stuck inside, programmings. If we are programmed, whether by experiences, upbringing and cultural beliefs in this lifetime or others, in a certain pattern, for example always getting romantically attached to abusive alcoholics, then that becomes part of our vibrational signature. It is ingrained in us and is part of our reality.

If no one out there saw that pattern as something negative, because there is no judgment, or because it is our "fault" due to karma, or that we "created our own reality", then it would continue to exist. Or, if that is all they could say, then we not only continue in the pattern, but also feel guilty and bad about it being our own making. And that is the point. We cannot be "response-able" when we are stuck in a programmed pattern. We need help to get out of the programming. We need someone, or something, to help us shift our awareness out of that pattern and make us able to respond to it in a constructive manner. Once we are out of the pattern, we are able to respond in a more positive manner. We are able to help ourselves.

So, if a child is being molested, help that child! And get the authorities on the perpetrator. DO SOMETHING. Painful patterns, those that cause suffering, only trap the person in fear and guilt. They do nothing for Spiritual Growth.

This belief, the "fault" belief, also goes into the other extreme. When a victim blames the other person or situation, for their suffering. Of course the other person, or situation cause the suffering, but staying stuck in the suffering because another person or situation made it happen is self defeating. Holding on to suffering without an effort to move out of it, is a huge spiritual trap. It invalidates our power and keeps us at a low vibrational signature.

When bad things happen to good people we often wonder why. Gandhi was shot in cold blood. Jesus was crucified. These things happened to stop their work. Not to save humanity. It was not their choice. And, seeing as they were not able to respond to it, they were not responsible for it.

Reality check... we can only "create our reality" when we take charge of our own game. When we learn the rules of the game and can take our power back from those who keep us asleep and as pawns in their games.

Will this stop us experiencing pain? No. But it is likely we will stop suffering. Oneness integrates joy and pain. It integrates all experience. But it empowers us, it gives us options, it gives us ways to respond to situations and people that will minimize the pain, suffering, and fear, and moves us back on track, back to our soul journey, back to our passions, missions and goals.

We are not playing the game of life on Earth in isolation but we can most certainly play a powerful game ;)

Natural Disasters, Armageddon, 2012, HAARP, Conspiracy and Ascension

One of the highest ever recorded earthquake on Earth was in Chile in 1960, at 9.5 on the Richter Magnitude Scale, that earthquake, and the tsunami that followed it, literally wiped out an entire city in the South of Chile. Today, February 2010, another earthquake hit Chile, this time at 8.8 on the Richter scale, again, one of the highest recorded on Earth. Following so closely on the devastating earthquake which hit Haiti, at a 7.0 on the Richter scale, and hours after the earthquake that hit Japan at 7.0, we can see how many will be increasingly afraid at the meaning of this world wide phenomenon. Tsunami warnings have gone out to several countries and islands around the world and emergency teams are on their way or on standby. **Is it natural, is it 2012, or is it HAARP?**

Anyone who is familiar with HAARP and Conspiracy theories will be nodding in agreement to how they are all related and how it is a certain group on Earth trying to eliminate millions of people from the face of the planet. Two things are not theoretical. One is that HAARP exists, and the other is that it's technology can cause earthquakes. What is questionable is, are they using the technology to cause all these disasters, so many weather anomalies around the world, and cataclysmic type "natural" events? And, are they trying to wipe out a lot of the population or are they simply trying to cause fear? Would you be very surprised if I told you that none of these questions, or the existence of HAARP are relevant?

That's right. Whatever it is that is causing these disasters, whether natural or man made, is irrelevant. The fact is that they are happening and are part of our lives. Yes, if people are causing so much devastation, we feel angry and upset far beyond the anger and upset we would feel if these were part of natural cycles. Especially seeing as we would have nothing, no one, we could pinpoint and hold accountable, or be able to stop them doing it again.

So, how exactly does this affect us and our ascension work? Simple. It is FEAR. Fear is the biggest block a person can encounter when doing ascension work. Whether this fear is brought in naturally, or drummed into us from every media outlet in our environment, it is still fear.

And that is the whole point of this problem. Whether the disasters are natural or not, the way they are put out there for our consumption, the core message, is FEAR. Followed closely by frustration and anger.

But why, we ask, would anyone want to stop people from Ascension in their personal lives? How would one person reaching Oneness affect the rest of humanity? Well, it's not just one person. And, if you want to see the effect, lets look at something that was very common in a previous Earth cycle and was brutally suppressed during the cycle that is coming to an end. It is called **Manifestation**.

Manifestation is a core "power" of the new cycle, the cycle we are entering, and the cycle that ended a few thousand years ago. It was kept alive by a few individuals and it was called "magic" or "witchcraft". I don't need to go into the details of what happened to people who used this power in recorded history. Now, however, it is not only in the human collective subconscious, but in full swing at the conscious level. Everyone has either heard of or has tried the **art of Manifestation**.

How is this relevant? Well, as a person takes on their personal Spiritual Ascension, one of the first side effects is their power to manifest. The time between "cause" or intention, and "effect" or manifestation, gets much shorter and the results much more accurate. And what will happen when a big portion of society has mastered the art of manifestation? Well, there will not be much point in a capitalist system, that's for sure. Nor will there much point in wars, or governments.

This might sound idealistic, but it isn't. I don't have any lofty ideals of what happens to society or Earth. It is actually irrelevant as far as I am concerned. What does concern me is that whomever chooses to do their personal Spiritual Ascension has the tools, information and freedom to do so.

In that spirit, therefore, before you act on anger, compassion, or in any other way, to respond to the people who need your help in these, and upcoming, disaster areas around the world, I ask you to release FEAR first. Release FEAR first, then reach for your checkbook, pen or keyboard as you communicate your response to others through monetary support, or words, audio, or video.

Do I personally think there is a group trying to eliminate a great portion of the population on Earth? No.

Do I personally think there is a group trying to stop personal spiritual ascension on a great portion of the population on Earth through chronic fear and post traumatic stress? Yes. **But this is not going to stop us or our Spiritual Ascension.**

Why being physically fit is so important during Spiritual Ascension

The physical body is the most important expression of our existence on Earth. It is our greatest ally and greatest tool. Without a physical body we do not exist on Earth.

The physical body is ESSENTIAL in Spiritual Ascension work. And thus should be placed as the first thing to address when we are embarking on our Ascension.

What does this mean? First, we need to detoxify the body to the best of our ability. This means, less sugar, caffeine and other stimulants, minimize food additives and processed ingredients, hormones, antibiotics (anti life), recreational drugs, and medications. Add plenty of fresh air, fresh water, sunlight, exercise every day for at least 20 minutes, lots of chemical free protein and fresh vegetables and fruit.

Next, reconnecting with our body.

When is the last time you felt your body, reached for it, without judgment or mental commentary? Do it now. Simply reach and feel your body. If any judgment or mental commentary comes up, release it. It comes up to be released. Then return to feeling your body, how does it feel? Let it express itself to you, let energies and feelings grow and expand as far as they can go. Observe and allow.

What is it's vibrational signature right now? Send it love, or light, and make it your will that you are going to reconnect with your body 100%

Aim to feel at home, safe, comfortable, happy and satisfied in your body. It is as much part of you as is your mind, feelings, ego, and spirit.

If you have a medical condition or are very unfit or overweight, consult your regular doctor, or alternative practitioner, before making any physical lifestyle changes such as diet, exercise or medications.

Setting Goals and Ascension

The setting of goals while working on our spiritual ascension is very important. The whole thing about the art of manifestation, including the manifestation of our own ascension, is knowing where we are going. Or having a pretty good idea. And... knowing where we are going is usually the hardest thing to find out.

I am often asked where a person should be going, what they should be doing, what their life journey is, what they should be dedicating their lives to. This question has come up in just about every coaching or reading situation I have ever done. And the answer is, not your guides, nor me, nor anyone one else can tell you that. No one. This is something you have to find out for yourself, and decide by yourself. To do otherwise would be a violation of free will.

Quantum reality is accepted by top scientists today. Why do I mention it in an entry about goals? Because what you will be doing 12 months from now could be many things, an infinite amount of things. There are some things that are more probable than others in this particular lifestream, but, according to quantum physics, they are all possible. Your probable future depends mostly on your present life patterns, your mindset, your skills and your decisions. In order to choose a future where you will be fulfilled, satisfied, happy and successful in every way, you need to have clear goals where to focus your attention.

One way to find out what your goals should be is to have a simple daydream, and do it often. In this daydream, you imagine yourself in 12 months time. This self of yours IS the most successful, most fulfilled, satisfied and happy you that resulted from this lifestream. When you see that self, simply ask him or her for information and clues on what you did to get there. What ascension work did you do? What do you do for a living? What is your life journey? Write the information down. Then step into their body and feel the love, joy, satisfaction, fulfillment and success that he or she is feeling. Remember that feeling. Remember that vibration. Then move back to the present time, bringing back that vibrational signature with you.

Do this exercise often enough and you will soon start seeing results in daily life. Your mind will become more focused and your life will begin to reflect your decisions.

[Note: this powerful exercise came from the Ascension 101 Course.]

Detoxifying your Physical Body - is it Necessary?

Extracted and edited for general release from the Spiritual Ascension 101 Course

Is it necessary to go on a **detox diet**? Well, not really. You can work on your ascension without detoxifying your body and while consuming large quantities food toxins, drugs and alcohol. But your progress will be minimal and very, very slow. Also, the chances that you will stick to your Ascension work is highly unlikely. The difference is like walking up a steep hill carrying 50 pounds of rocks on your back, versus driving a Ferrari up that same hill, with no rocks. So, what exactly are toxic foods and drinks?

If you regularly, or even occasionally, drink alcohol or take recreational drugs, I suggest you stop while doing your Ascension Work. You will have much faster results if you don't have these in your body. Of course, taking these things should not stop you from continuing, or starting, your Ascension Work.

Other high toxins are: refined sugar, refined wheat, artificial food additives, coffee, chocolate, meats (unless they are organic and free range), and, surprisingly, garlic and onions. We also ingest toxins from food and drink in the form of pesticides and hormones in vegetables, fruits and meat products. Sea fish now also contains high quantities of mercury. And of course there's the prescription drugs which are given out like candy these days. Talk to your doctor about cutting down on prescription drugs. If you can't cut down on prescription drugs, then you will have to do your Ascension work with them.

The process of detoxification doesn't have to be sudden and extreme. Although if you can do it overnight, doing a detox diet and sticking to it, that's about the best thing you can do. Otherwise what we do is a gradual process of elimination. So, for example, if you have a bottle of wine per night, then cut it down to half a bottle. If you take white sugar in your tea, use a less processed alternative or gradually cut back on the amount. If you drink 4 cups of coffee a day, cut down to 2. Anything in your toxic list that you can cut out of your life without a problem, do so straight away. Progress slowly cutting back in the next few weeks as you do this work. And if you don't manage to cut something out completely, don't worry about it. It will have to do. With regards the meats, the amount of chemicals used in the growing, processing, storing and packaging is the problem. So if you have access to organic and free range products, this is much better than battery grown animals and birds, the meat of which is full of stress hormones, growth hormones, artificial colors, antibiotics and other toxins. If you can't find organic, free-range animal products, then cut down as you do with other toxins. The same goes for vegetables and fruits.

If you find that the process of detoxification is too severe, or you have no power over what you eat because someone else provides you with food, then a good solution is to fast one day a week. Choose a day where going without solid food will not affect your work, and for 24 hours, don't ingest anything solid. Keep to water, herbal teas and a chosen fruit juice, such as apple or cranberry juice. Fresh if at all possible.

Tap-water is now also highly polluted with chemicals, hormones and additives. Get yourself an effective filter and use it for your drinking water.

At this stage, watch out for binge attacks! This is the sudden urge to consume large quantities of food or drink which is not good for you. This is the body crying out for what it is used to. Release the urge with love if you can. If you can't and find yourself stuffing your face with crappy food or drink, then simply say, "it is my will that I will no longer feel the urge to binge." Eventually the body will get the message and the urges will stop.

And last but not least, energize and feel gratitude for everything you consume before consuming it, whether it is an organic apple or a burger from your local fast food joint.

Check with your doctor, chemist or nutritionist before making dietary changes, including the taking of supplements and vitamins.

Are you too FAT for Spiritual Ascension?

Extracted and edited for general release from the Spiritual Ascension 101 Course

The title of this article is not just an attention grabber. Unfortunately, if your weight makes you suffer, then being too fat will stop, or slow down, your Ascension process. But this is something we can fix, no matter what the problem is. And the solution is not, as you might think, to lose weight. All we need to do is reconnect with our physical body.

When we first begin to reconnect with our physical body, it is very common to have a judgmental mental commentary throughout the whole procedure. Often, the commentary is not positive. Our aim is to be able to connect with our body, receive the information we need from it, and become One with it, without any commentary at all.

Our body is more than our Temple. It is an integral part of us. It is not a suit we wear for an unimportant lifetime, and will shed as soon when we die and therefore is unimportant. It is in fact, our own creation. It is the physical manifestation of our Self, our Soul, our Spirit and our Divine. It is as much part of ourselves as is our mind, our spiritual body, our ego and our emotions. And it is the most important part of us with regards existing on the physical Earth plane. Without it, we are not able to exist here on any capacity or form. Yes, we would be able to move around the different Earth planes without a physical body, and we do even now, but within the physical plane, and our daily lives, it is not possible to exist without the physical body.

Our physical body is not our enemy. It is not our friend either. It is our creation. And thus, it looks upon us for nourishment, protection, information and love. In return, it gives us feedback on everything we do here on Earth. It is by far the most sensitive and wise of our bodies when it comes to giving us unbiased information with regard everything we experience. It is also the perfect conduit for giving expression to our Earthly creations. It is what holds the paint brush if your are a painter, or clicks on the keyboard if you are a writer. Without it, we don't have a physical voice, cannot take in the beauty of a sunset, or feel our lover's warm skin.

Our physical body is our most prized possession, and the only physical expression we can really call our own.

Often hijacked by the ego, our physical body has had a rough time of it in present society. We punish it, we judge it, we starve it or over fill it, we use it for gain, or blame it for loss.

It is too fat, too skinny, too tall, too short, too hairy, too bald, too light, too dark, and look at those legs! And that waist! This part is too big, this one too small, if I was Native American the new age groups would take me seriously, if I was White society would take me seriously. If only this was different, then I would be able to succeed, be loved, be attractive, find my soulmate, be someone, speak my message and my message would be heard ...

And the irony is that our body is our most powerful communication device. Whatever it is that we are feeling or thinking, is perfectly reflected in our body. So, for example if you have a big message to deliver, but feel you are too bald to start delivering it, guess what, when you get on that platform and start speaking, people will at first hear your message, then will start looking at your bald head and think, what kind of authority are you if you can't even look good. And this is because under your message is the anxiety of being bald, and not being taken seriously because of it. Your body will express it by bringing attention to your bald head in various ways, your tone of voice will reflect uncertainty and your overall image will have a big and bright arrow pointing at your bald spot.

Yes, our body is our greatest communication and connection device, yet most of us are completely and utterly disconnected from it and unable to hear it shout.

Our body talks to us all the time, but we barely hear it, if at all.

But all that is about to change because the physical body is our greatest, and most important, Ascension tool.

A very simple, gentle and effective exercise you can start straight away is the following:

Say to yourself: "It is my will to reconnect with my body in a loving and healthy way."

Repeat as often as you can for the next few weeks.

To Eat Meat, or Not to Eat Meat, that is the question.

Extracted and edited for general release from the Spiritual Ascension 101 Course

There is a lot of feelings, judgment and attachment to the views of eating meat and also not eating meat in our daily diet. These are based on medical considerations, moral considerations, religious and spiritual considerations. What we are concerned with, while doing our Ascension Process, is whether eating meats will stop us from achieving our goal or whether it is irrelevant. Well, it is neither actually.

Yes, eating meat will slow our process down, but it will not stop it. The reasons are rather simple. Firstly, most meats, and animal products, are full of toxins. While the animal, or bird, is grown in our modern farms, it will be subjected to huge amounts of stress, unhappiness, and physical pain. All these leave a chemical and hormone residue in the fat content of the meat as well as smaller amounts of it in the meat itself. Apart from these naturally occurring chemicals and hormones animals and birds will generate in huge amounts while they are grown under these conditions, there are also additional toxins added to them in the form of food additives, growth hormones, and even colorants and flavor enhancers. After the animal or bird is killed, more chemicals are added during the cleaning and packaging stage in order to keep them "fresh" for a longer period. Some meats will receive an added dose of colorants and artificial flavors at this stage too.

Of course, if you only eat small, organic farm grown animal and bird meat and products, most of the above will not be present. So if you are going to continue eating meat, this is the best type for you to buy.

Secondly, if you have any moral attachment to eating animals or birds, or even fish, you will shower your food with negative vibration. Yup, you will pollute it. So, if this is you, stop eating it.

On a purely vibrational level, vegetables, even the factory grown kind, will have a higher vibration than any type of animal meat.

However, if you compare the ascension process of a person who eats from a burger joint every day, but is an extremely positive and feels gratitude for everything that he or she ingests, to someone who is a negative person who complains about everything and feels bad about eating in general, it is the person who eats processed burgers every day who will achieve their ascension goal first.

In other words, although eating meat does slow us down on our Spiritual Ascension, it will definitely not stop it.

Being a vegetarian will not automatically start or continue your ascension process. The physical body is imortant, but only one of many bodies that need to be detoxified and aligned in order to achieve a permanent vibrational change to a higher, more refined, more empowered level.

Shifting Dimensions

There's a lot of talk about the Earth and humanity going to the 4th Dimension, or skipping the 4th Dimension and going straight to the 5th Dimension, or about beings from the 9th Dimension channeling information for us to use on our shift to another, higher, dimension. So what does this mean exactly?

What it doesn't mean is that we are going to move planets. Nor does it mean that Earth will become all "good" and that all the "bad" people will suddenly disappear. Nor will creatures come from the heavens to lift us, chosen ones, up and save our lives from sudden death as apocalypse happens.

You see, we are already IN all those dimensions. We never left them. We are simply unable to become consciously aware or recall the different dimensions, and use them, in our daily life. It is like trying to become aware while we are living in a city when we are one year old what shops and services are there for our use and comfort. It really is not possible. At least, I personally don't know of any infant in history who was aware enough to know he or she lived in a city. Most don't realize they "live" in a "house".

The Ascension Process is simply a growth of awareness, as well as the capacity to function from that growth, making us more able to do things, create our reality as we see fit and live from that state of ecstasy which comes to us when we are able to allow that connection in a conscious way.

When a person experiences the 5th Dimension, he or she experiences the state of Connection with Earth and Humanity. The state of wholeness and a feeling of being, experiencing and radiating complete and utter Love. When a person experiences all dimensions, they experience the state of Oneness.

But as we do our ascension process, these experiences of the 5th Dimension, and Oneness, are fleeting and temporary. Mostly, they come during states of meditation and quieting of the mind, and are so intense that we are not able to function on a daily basis while in that state. For example, we are not able to drive a car, or have a conversation with someone else. The good news is, the more we practice our ascension process, the longer these periods of ecstasy become, and the more often they come, until we are able to feel it as a constant vibration in our being. It becomes the underlying feeling, being, sentiment, vibe, of our self, our body, and our daily existence. And at the same time, the intensity is such that we CAN function in everyday life. Not only that, we can function much better at daily life as we are unburdened of so much suffering, negativity, fear and confusion.

Will we still feel pain, loss or war? Yes. This is because, like it or not, we exist in a 3D reality too, and are not moving out of it. The 3D reality is rich with experience as well as a large shared game of opposites. Plus, the more people who exist here on the 3D reality and also consciously exist here in the 5th, or higher dimension, the faster and easier it is for everyone else to make that jump of awareness. The more we tap into the larger awareness, and the more of us that tap into that awareness, the easier it is for us to manifest an existence which is far beyond happy and to our individual taste. Don't worry, there are plenty of people who want to play at pain and war and they can play among each other. Leaving the people, who don't want to play that game, in peace. That's the difference between existing only in 3D and existing in a broader awareness. You get to choose what games to play.

Feeling Offended, the Skunk of Ascension.

Years ago, I read somewhere that if something someone says, offends you, it is because there is some truth in it. Otherwise, this piece of wisdom explained, it would go past you completely. If anything, it might be comical.

Well, I chewed on this for a while and it simply did not taste right. After all, if someone calls me a moron, I feel offended, but I know, and have no doubt, that I am no moron. And then it hit me. What offended me was the act of being attacked.

I went a step further and thought, well, if attack offends me, is it because I attack others? Is that what it is? And the answer was, again, "no".

Well, the universe has a wonderful way of unraveling mysteries to me and this is what happened in this case also.

There are many things that offend us. And a lot has to do with culture, upbringing and personal experience, and some things are universally offensive. So, for example, the smell of skunk is very offensive to just about every animal on Earth. When something offends us, we feel repelled. We want to either move away from the offensive person, situation, or object, or attack it. If all our senses are offended, then it's likely we move away from the offensive thing as fast as possible. Which means, the thing, person, or object's role in offending us, is for us to stay away, don't get close.

Then there are cultural offensive behavior, like body odor, offensive in some cultures and not even smelled in others. Foods even... some people eat snails, others would rather die than eat them.

And the list goes on forever.

But when someone insults us, and we feel offended, it can be because the action of being attacked offends us, or because what they said had a grain of truth, and that truth hurts.

When something hurts, it is a red flag. Red flags in ascension are things that need to be addressed, things that come into our lives to be allowed, observed and released.

I looked at this red flag to see why did the act of someone attacking me offended me so much. What came up was that my personal history was one of physical and psychological abuse and threat within the home, as well as nationally, from before I was born to well into my 30s. So, yes, being attacked was a NO NO to me. It meant, stay away from this person, this person is bad news. This was very revealing to me, as it gave me strong boundaries for my personal protection. Now I no longer feel offended, I now simply know who to allow into my life and who not to.

But if we take it a step further, it also means the person is acting in a repelling way. A person can do this to blatantly keep others away, or to find someone who loves them when they are at their most unloving. The person is under the illusion that if the other person can love them at their most offensive state, it means they love them for themselves. Nothing could be further from the truth, the core of the person is never offensive, their true self is not offensive to others.. The other person has issues too, which is why they attracted, or stay, with an offensive person, and his or her reality includes being attacked and offended as something normal or something they deserve.

And a step further than that is, that if that person offends you, you have the opportunity to observe that feeling inside of yourself without judgment, and find the stuck negative energy that is coming up to be released easily and effortlessly. Then you can walk away from the offending person, or attack them back, or hug them, or whatever you choose, from a place of wisdom. And most of all, you can thank that person for giving you the opportunity to have a free ascension session in your day.

So, when someone, or something, comes into your life smelling of skunk, keep him, her or it around long enough to see what this is all about. After you have your information, have released the stuck energy and can move on, release the offense and the person or thing and either keep them around or put up boundaries as you see fit.

Feeling Sick After Eating - More Ascension Symptoms?

After we make an ascension jump, this means moving our core self to a higher, or finer, vibration, all of our bodies move too, including our physical body. When this happens, toxins which the physical body was able to digest without much bother, are now too thick for the physical body to process and we get nauseated, get headaches and basically feel bad.

The most prominent of these toxins are battery grown animals products, including meats, as well as refined sugar, alcohol, onions and garlic. Well, onions and garlic are not so much toxins, as medicines which are toxic in high doses, and interfere with the connections while in meditation.

At times it may seem that everything we eat and drink makes us unwell.

This is simply a time of adjustment. The physical aspects of the being are getting used to the new vibrations. What you can do is simply energize and cleanse food items and drinks, including water, before consumption.

Another ascension symptom you can deal with easily is the feeling of being spaced out, or dizzy, after you have done ascension work, or ascension meditations. This is your Spiritual, or Energy, body feeling the adjustment of new vibrations and increased finer energy coming in. The best thing you can do for this symptom is increase your consumption of protein and water, as well as taking potassium, magnesium, manganese, and zinc supplements. This is because the energy body, on a physical level, works like a battery and these items help replenish that battery so that it can process the new levels of vibration.

Check with your doctor, chemist or nutritionist before making dietary changes, including the taking of supplements and vitamins.

The Fear of Ascension

The fear of ascension has many layers.

To begin with, a person doesn't know what ascension is all about, they might think it is just about 2012, and this bring in a whole load of fear.

Then there is the fear of the person who has been working on their personal growth for years and then they are confronted with the choice of Ascension into Oneness. A huge fear then can be the feeling that they will stop being themselves. That they will cease to be an individual. That they will lose passion, feelings, emotions, importance, self.

These fears take a while to play out. Sometimes the person might undertake their ascension process, and will come to a grinding halt due to their fear.

And it doesn't stop there.

Even after the person has cleansed and integrated the ego, experienced Oneness, has learned how to channel Universal Love Light Oneness into our reality, he or she might one day stop and think, what if this energy is not a positive thing for the Earth? What if I am being used by other beings for their benefit and not the benefit of Earth and all her creatures?

This fear is paralyzing. The person then starts to analyze the energy as it flows in, and of course realize that it is in fact "neutral". That it is "uncomfortable" to the physical body. That it is not something he or she can "use" for anything, such as manifestation, healing, or anything like that except switching on the capacity of others to channel this energy. Initiating others to "Oneness" and the channeling of this extremely powerful energy. In a way "contaminating" them with Oneness.

And what for?

What's in it for us?

Can we really be sure that it is for the benefit of Earth and all her creatures?

And we go full circle. Because these fears are those of the human collective ego. The human collective has the same bodies as we do individually. A physical body, made up of billions of human being bodies, an energy body, chakras and aura, a mental body, the collective consciousness and subconscious, and a collective ego. The survival of the species is its main objective.

The only way to overcome this last fear, if we choose to do so, is to ask ourselves:

How is my life better now compared to before my personal Ascension?

Is life on Earth more precious than life in other realms or dimensions?

When we look into these questions, we realize that we would never go back to a lower vibrational existence. We also realize that in Oneness, all creatures are integrated, all creatures are ONE being. That it doesn't matter if the "I" in another realm or dimension is taking advantage of the "I" here on Earth, as there is benefit, all ONENESS benefits through the experience.

As we move on the Earth in this state of Flow of Oneness Energy, we notice that others lives are changed. That they too go through their "programmed" ascension just through us being near them. Whatever form their ascension path takes, it is one that is real to them. So it is deeply meaningful to them. Some have to reach the ashes before they can rise as the phoenix, others will see Jesus in our presence, others will feel enormous compassion and love flowing to them from us. Others will be overwhelmed with the presence of Mother.

It is not us though. It is what they recognize as their personal contact with the Divine. And all we are is a neutral "catalyst." In chemistry a catalyst is an element, or substance, that initiates or accelerates a chemical reaction without itself being affected. The catalyst stays intact, neutral, but the chemicals around it react and move into another form much faster than they would do without the catalyst. Sometimes no change or reaction will happen without the catalyst.

Is what we are doing negative or positive? Neither really, and both. There are no polarities in Oneness. Only integration.

Yet, just like the fear of the individual ego was unfounded, after all we are still here after experiencing and integrating Oneness in our daily existence, we still have a physical body, emotional body, mental body, spiritual or energy body and ego body. So will Earth and all her creatures still be here after our collective ascension, which is what this energy channeling is all about. Yes. We are but cells in a body, pawns in a game, and that body is Humanity, and that game is Ascension.

Using Dreams for Ascension

Ascension work is all about moving from a lower vibrational level to a higher, more empowered and much more pleasant one. The ultimate aim is to live in a state of Oneness, and experience our Masterhood while in this physical body and this individual identity.

We do this with very simple steps.

One of the steps is to cleanse our spiritual, or energy, body, physical body, mental body, emotional body and ego body, of negative energy. The negative energy that is stuck in these bodies is in the form of memories, programming, patterns (or karma), emotions, thoughts and memories.

Our life gives us situations, event and people that will bring the negativity to the surface, at which point we can release it. But this is really very hard on us.

This is the hard road.

An easier path is to work with our dreams. Our higher self has a great way to give us the opportunity to release old stuck energy by giving us dreams that will bring up the emotions and other expressions of negative energy to be released. We call them nightmares. A recurring nightmare will be something we need to release as soon as possible.

In order to release it, and not have it express in our daily life, simply realize, when the dream becomes upsetting and we wake up, instead of becoming engaged in the negativity, we simply say "this is coming up to be released" and we let the negative thought, emotion, feeling or physical body manifestation, flow, grow and allow it to leave our field. Use the fear processing exercise in your dream, or when you wake.

There is no need to analyze the dream. The content is not important. It is the feelings, emotions, thoughts and even physical effects that need to be allowed to express energetically inside of us and released. We don't engage or wallow in the negativity, we simply let it express energetically.

If you don't remember your dreams you can still work with this. You will wake up feeling a certain way, if it is in any way negative, do the same exercise.

And on a positive note, when we dream a new state of positive existence, when we wake up, we wallow in it, bask in it and remember how it feels. Make it part of our present vibrational signature. Write it down so we can recall how it feels as often as we can.

2012 and Earth Ascension

The North American gulf oil spill is prominent on the news at the moment. The devastating effects of offshore drilling is in the world's eye. This is very significant. Not that the oil is spilling, or that the "world is bleeding" as some sensationalists have put it. The world is not bleeding, as oil is not the lifeblood of the Earth. And, this is not a new problem.

Sometime in the 80s, my family and I, with a few friends, took a road trip to the Lake District in England. After visiting the stunning and energy filled lakes, we continued west toward the coast.

We arrived at the coast at night time, so it was morning before we could go to the beach. Well, to say it was a disappointing waste of traveling time is putting it mildly. What met us that morning were miles upon miles of devastated coastline. The entire place was covered with crude oil. There was no wildlife, the stench of oil was horrible. There were no tv cameras, no cleaning crews, no wild-life workers cleaning up birds, nothing.

After talking to the locals, who were very amused at our need to see their coastline, it appeared that this problem had been a chronic, and ongoing situation since offshore drilling had began years earlier.

So, yeah, not news at all. Offshore drilling, the "lack" of oil resources and unsuitable technology being used for pumping out a substance that is not life supporting in and of itself, but actually kills everything it comes into contact with, is not new.

However, the worldwide awareness of this is new.

And this is what this World Ascension process is all about. A lifting of World Wide Awareness.

Selfish and underhanded acts are in the open for everyone to see. Tyrannic governments, and their acts of violent oppression, are being broadcast around the world. Underhanded financial control is open to scrutiny. Pharmaceutical company exploits and death tolls are slowly coming to the fore.

And, on the other side of the coin, Ascension information and tools are also broadly available to the masses through websites like this one and many, many more.

Like it or not, we are all becoming more aware. And with this awareness comes the ability to respond, the ability to act, the ability to choose what we want and what we don't want.

The human collective consciousness is not only something we can now tap into consciously, but also something we can influence. Now, THAT IS NEWS WORTHY INDEED.

The **2012 World Ascension** is all about our collective existence, collective choices, collective decisions and collective raising of core energy signature.

And just like we cleanse and raise our energy levels individually, so are we doing with the collective consciousness, and so is the Earth in this process by also doing it her own way. Is she bleeding or in danger? No. She is more powerful than ever. It up to us to catch up with her. The many movements for collective prayer, visualizations and command for change are the way forward. And these will cause changes in our collective human life on Earth. As soon as these changes are felt, more people will join these collective movements, and this will have a chain effect on the overall experience of everyone on Earth.

As individuals we can stop indulging in negativity and start letting express, release and replace it with light and universal love energy (suppressing it doesn't work). It is time to stop taking part in the destruction, victim-hood and passive acceptance of life on Earth. Every time we indulge in negative vibration, we are adding to the suffering around the globe. The higher the vibration, the more joyful it "feels", it is not about suffering at all. Personal suffering simply amplifies suffering round the world. The 2012 Earth Ascension might not seem significant when in the middle of a temper outburst or feeling sorry for ourselves, but it is. Every time/space second/inch counts.

Embracing our Seniority

In England, old people are officially called Senior Citizens.

Senior, according to the Princeton online dictionary, means: older; higher in rank; longer in length of tenure or service; "senior officer".

My friend and sister-in-law, Loreto Alonso Alegre Arana recently linked a video of Mayan Grandmother Margarita on facebook for our benefit. This is the first time I have hear of this amazing Grandmother and her teachings.

It is so wonderful to see that here is a woman, Abuela Margarita, who has paved the path of Ascension all of her life. Her message is simple, easy to understand and direct.

There is a point in the interview where Grandma Margarita, mentions that we arrive at a point in life when we have closed the circle. According to her teachings, this is age 52, at which point we go back to birth and begin our work of mothering Humanity. We then have children all over the world. Children that we teach what we have learned and also LOVE.

Although my teachings are mostly agnostic in nature, and from personal experience, I have also had great teachers. Seniors who have taken the time to put down their learned teachings down on paper, taken the time to go out in the world to impart their wisdom and share what they have brought with them. As well as one unwilling Machi, who was placed in my path to share generations of wisdom and knowledge she carried within her.

It is up to us to discern what is right and what is wrong for us, unburdened by the thought that our intuitive knowings and channeled information will be polluted. Not all flavors of teaching will be to our taste, and our inner guidance can let us know if we are barking up the wrong tree.

We must trust our ability to discern what is coming from source and what are ego ramblings.

It is also up to us to recognize the moment we ourselves reach Seniority and embrace it with our love filled hearts. Due to the speeding up of evolutionary process, this moment arrives much, much earlier in life than 52. It is a moment of, "oh, I am a grownup", combined with a sense of single minded embracing of one's life's work, and a sense of freedom never before felt.

Grandma Margarita mentions that some people, when they reach that point of completeness, get stuck there. Women in particular will start looking after grandchildren, or get stuck in "controlling" things. I would add another layer here, particularly for the West, and say some men and women get stuck here trying to hold on to their youth and sexual desirability.

Before she died, I asked my mother what it felt like to go through menopause, one of the things she said was, "with sexual desire out of the way, I can now see and think straight. I feel much saner." It is saddening to think that most women automatically begin hormone treatment or go on the pill to stop menopause and this natural state of saneness.

What seniority has meant to me is a huge sense of release and freedom to speak, unburdened by ego restraints. I can call a spade a spade when it serves another person's evolution, I can then watch as either they defend their rightness and prove me wrong, or step back and have a "wow" moment as their awareness expands.

I can also start websites like this one and put down on "paper" everything I have learned, and am still learning, for the benefit of anyone with an internet connection without having to "color" it to please editors, book publishers, or anyone who stands between an author and a reader, including friends and relatives. Thus delivering the messages with their full unaltered flavor, to be absorbed or spat out by anyone who cares to try it out.

As for my personal work, I am an Ascension worker, this means that whomever is open to ascension and has any length of contact with me, or my work, will go through a personal level of transformation and ascension. Does the contact change me? No. The reason is that

I am not involved in the process. The "I" who is here on Earth is simply a vessel for Oneness to come through, and for the work of Planetary Ascension to be completed. And that is another thing that comes with age, surrendering our "identity" by stepping away and letting our Oneness take over in order to accomplish the work uncolored by ego or personal constraints.

A bit of wisdom I recently learned from another Senior, Denise Linn:

Don't let your judgment of me, get in the way of you learning what you came here to learn.

And I would like to add:

Don't let judgment of yourself get in the way of you teaching what you came here to teach.

With all my love,

Abuela Inelia, title earned and embraced with humble gratitude.

Reign of Terror - How to counteract it?

A very well known modus operandi of tyrannical regimes is to capture civilians, "enemies", people who are against the rulers, torture them, then release them back into the populace injured, broken, and vulnerable. The person will often also be witness to executions and other terrors, which he or she will then relate to those around him or her.

The purpose of this action is to instill terror in the masses. Anyone who speaks against the ruler will be afraid to speak out, act or do anything to bring the terror onto themselves.

Another method of terror, this one at a global scale, is to release "secret" data and pictures of possible "terrible" outcomes or happenings during a massive natural, or man made, catastrophe, with the words "terrifying scenario", "secret", "ignored by the media" plastered all over the articles, which then start circulating among the masses. This terrifying scenario might very well come to pass. At the moment the scenario being used this way is the Oil Spill.

However, the aim here, is to instill terror, hopelessness, anger and frustration. Unfortunately, most well meaning people spread these news without adding a solution.

The only solution against terror, is not to indulge in it, but to counteract it with LOVE, COMPASSION AND POSITIVE VIBRATIONS.

Yes, you can also go and volunteer your time and money to fix the actual problem. But most likely, your time spent in meditative and active channeling of positive energy will be more effective. You see, dealing with a disaster at ground zero is something a person does actively, if they survive. Worrying about it beforehand serves no purpose, EXCEPT THAT OF KEEPING THE PERSON IN A STATE OF ENSLAVEMENT TO FEAR.

And this is because there is a war going on at the moment. The Earth is Shifting into a higher vibrational level as we speak, but there are those who do not want to lose power over the sleeping masses. Therefore, they instill terror. Terror will ensure that those souls will stay enslaved. Terror stops the Ascension process on its tracks.

At the end of the day, it is each individual who will shift either to a higher vibrational and more powerful existence with the Earth, or ... move elsewhere into the terrible scenario they are fearing so much.

You are here, reading this, because you are no longer asleep. You are here because you are actively working on your Ascension, whether using the tools in this site, or learned elsewhere. You are reading this and it is YOU who can shift the tide the other way. Your basking in positive vibration will have a huge effect over hundreds of people because you do it CONSCIOUSLY, while they get taken in unconsciously.

I urge you to join collective movements who are actively shifting the vibration to a positive one through conscious effort, or to start your own! Even if you are a lone wolf, you can do this by tapping directly to source and allowing that Oneness energy to flow through you at various times during the day. And also, to consciously stop indulging in fear, frustration, anger and terror. Yes, do divulge information about what is happening in these situations, but also add what people can do to turn the tide of negativity into one of higher vibration.

Debt - A Link in the Chain of Enslavement

With dual realities, or dimensions, in other words, any dimension that has a sense of existence as "I" that is separate from the environment or other "I"s, there is a very strict law of Energy Exchange.

This energy exchange is basically that when someone gives something that is part of themselves, such as time, a service, product or space, to someone else, the other person has to return the energy in a form which is useful to the first person and in an equal amount of what was originally given.

So what happens if this energy exchange does not take place?

DEBT happens. Karmic debt is a chain that links two people in a negative, "otherness" configuration.

The financial system, as it is designed presently, is debt ridden. This energetically enslaves people to the financial institution they are indebted to.

When a "lightworker" decides that he or she will dedicate his or her life to the good of humanity, giving all of their time, energy, willingness and space for free, "knowing" that the universe will respond in like kind and supply them with groceries, a place to live in, clothes and anything else they need and want, what he or she is doing is actually creating a web of debt that enslaves everyone they help as well as themselves in a negative "otherness" configuration.

There are some individuals who get a lot of satisfaction and fulfillment helping other individuals without asking for anything in return. This often creates co-dependent relationships (Karmic chains), between the two individuals.

Energy exchange doesn't necessarily have to be money. But it absolutely must be something each person needs. So, for example, if a psychic gets offered a reiki session as exchange for a psychic reading, but he doesn't need a reiki session, or it simply vibrates wrong for him but accepts it anyway, the debt is still created.

So, what can you give for free that doesn't create debt? INFORMATION. Information came in to you from elsewhere, it is public domain in a universal kind of way, it belongs to no one. So you can give it away for free if you so please or charge for it if it takes money and effort to get it published or placed in a public place. Once you start using your time, skills, energy or space to assist another person, for that other person's personal benefit, it is imperative that you charge them money or a product or service that you NEED.

If you are involved in a charity that helps society in some way, this does not create debt. The reason is that you too are part of that society, so any improvement to it, also benefits you directly.

It used to be that the tribe would take care of the tribe healer/shaman/educator, she/he would wake up to food, clothes and clean living quarters. The patriarchal system has done away with that cultural energy exchange, often making their work illegal. By no longer having this method of energy exchange toward our spiritual teachers, we are left with barter or monetary payment as ways of keeping karmic relationships clean.

If you feel triggered by the thought of paying for your personal spiritual growth, you are probably being affected by the patriarchal "vow of poverty". A system which was enacted a while back to create co-dependency between certain religious organizations or individuals and their "followers".

The new paradigm no longer has "followers". Only audiences. A member of an audience is, and must remain, FREE to leave whenever he or she wants.

How do you undo the debts, both monetary and energetic, that you are in right now? You pay it to the institution or person to whom you are indebted to. You can also process a "clean slate", where any attachment to debt is released.

How do you stop creating a chain of debt? You always ask for an energy exchange when providing services or products, and you always give payment to the person you take services or products from. If they don't want to accept payment, then go elsewhere.

If you are having money problems, or are triggered by "having to pay" for "what should be free", do this exercise: Reconnecting with Money Exercise http://ascension101.com/en/reconnecting-with-the-spirit-of-money.html

The 5th Dimension and its Role in the 2012 Shift

It has come to my attention that the 5th Dimension is taking a huge part in this Global 2012 Ascension process. After further investigation, it appears that they, the beings and energy from the 5th Dimension, are coming into the 3rd dimension in great numbers and volume at this moment in time. The reason is very simple.

The 5th Dimension is the most stable, perfect and balanced of the dual dimensions. (http://ascension101.com/ascension-information/29-july-2010/90-duality-and-its-role-in-ascension.html) By bringing beings into the 3rd dimension, they create a base of balance and stability that will help bring the 3rd Dimensional Earth back to its natural alignment. When this natural alignment locks in, the "chains" that have kept beings trapped in separateness and conflict will dissolve.

The reason that it was felt to be necessary for them to come in, in their natural form and in huge numbers, is because there are beings, both on our dimension and others, that do not want the Earth to go back to its natural alignment. These beings are creating an artificial duality of conflict and misalignment, creating "otherness" and entrapment.

5th Dimensional beings have taken incarnation in human bodies for decades now, but in small numbers. This presence is no longer enough.

How can you benefit from this? Well, they are here, waiting and ready to serve. All you need to do is to call upon them to assist you in your personal alignment and ascension.

How can you help their entry into our dimension? Ask them to enter your environment and welcome them.

Duality and its Role in Ascension

Duality is a dirty word in the circles of Enlightenment and Oneness. We strive to move past duality and into Oneness, integrating all without judgment.

However, the thought of integrating light and dark, "good" and "bad", male and female, is rather hard to conceive. They are so different, so "opposite" to each other. We tend to take sides.

Often when I speak to people about integrating "dark" into Oneness, they see it as an "absorption" of the darkness into the light. But the reality of it is that this is not so. Oneness doesn't have sides. It is not "light". It is complete. It doesn't have either light or dark, it is not non-duality.

A person or place that is only "light" is in as much dissonance to Oneness as one who, or which, is only "dark".

When "light" is integrated into Oneness, it too vanishes, it cannot exist as light.

So, what is the role of duality and how can we use it for ascension?

Duality exists within the 3rd, 4th, 5th and slightly in the 6th dimensions. In this system there are 12 dimensions which are reachable through conscious awareness. There are however an infinite number of dimensions. The 13th, for example, is out of our awareness, as it exists outside the parameters of conscious observation of the universe, we therefore conceive it as simply a void. Without consciousness, matter and energy do not exist.

In these dimensions, 3rd, 4th, 5th and slightly in the 6th dimensions, there is also the "law" of energy exchange, and the experience of existence within a physical reality, albeit less solid the higher the number. The 3rd dimension is presently upside down with regard to polarities, which causes separation and destruction. Once it moves back to it's proper polarity (which is not about the Magnetic Poles, but rather one of energy configuration within the feminine and masculine energies), it will become balanced and ... well, more pleasant.

It appears that the 6th is the dimension where beings can start to experience existence within Oneness. It is the transitional dimension.

Duality is an extremely powerful and dynamic construct. Putting the opposite polarities of two magnets together binds them as one, creating a larger energy field around them. By turning the polarities around, the magnets repel each other, causing separation and "otherness", as well as stream of energy, which is where our 3rd dimension is at the moment and the shift is about it going back to it's proper configuration, where the ends lock together and create a larger, and stable, field.

In order to understand it more easily, visualizing it as an onion with twelve layers is helpful. However, these dimension all exist within one point. They are not separate from each other, they don't even "co-exist" with each other. They are in fact all One. On Earth there are people, animals, geographical areas and places which do exist in, and hold the consciousness of, each of the other 11 dimensions within our own 3rd dimension.

As the Earth ascends to it's next step, which for some is the 4th dimension, and for others the 5th, all the dimensions will take a leap to their next level. And consciousness will enter the 13th dimension, making it accessible to all beings. At the same time, a new 1st dimension will come into existence.

My thoughts are that Duality is in fact the fuel that powers the evolution of all the dimensions, and thus is necessary, but having it as our primary existence, especially at a time that it is not properly configured, is not a good idea. Try to tap into each of the other dimension and explore them, they are available now, within your self.

The "system" of 12 dimensions is just one way to look at it, a way to dissect reality in a way we can comprehend it. However, we could just as well dissect it into 24 or 30 or whatever, taking smaller and smaller chunks to explore and ascend through. The number of dimensions are infinite and not readily classifiable as they are all integrated in Oneness.

Man - The Structure of Ascension

I was working with Lucia Rene, a leader of our time and author of Unplugging the Patriarchy, a book which, if you have not read it yet, I strongly suggest you get immediately. If I were to set a study course for this year, this book would certainly be an essential component of the curriculum.

In this book she explains the nature of the change which is happening right now and will anchor in 2012, including how roles have been reversed for the last 5000 years and how this has meant a huge shutting down of the Heart Chakra, which is where men are naturally centered.

She also explained to me that Men are Structure. This information put together a lot of pieces for me.

I have been speaking for months (and some people for years) about becoming heart centered and opening the Heart Center.

The Heart Center is a space from between and just above the shoulder blades to just behind the breastbone and below the throat chakra, encompassing the heart chakra. This is where the "form" or structure is contained that links all the different bodies, self, soul and spirit. Command Central as it were. When fully functioning, energy flows undisturbed and healthily, experienced as unconditional love, or simply enormous divine energy.

As you know, men and women both have masculine and feminine energies within themselves, and partly depending on what body one has incarnated into, either feminine or masculine energy is predominant for that lifetime.

The reason we have been healing, opening and changing our viewpoint to the Heart Center is because this is where structure resides. And without structure, power cannot be channeled and embodied in a healthy way.

The natural state is for women to be Power and for men to be Structure. Structure includes defense, nurturing, love, service, and making sure everything is running smoothly so that nothing is clogging up the flow of Power.

This natural paradigm is what we are moving back into on a worldwide scale. It is still dual based, as this is a dual reality (http://ascension101.com/ascension-information/29-july-2010/90-duality-and-its-role-in-ascension.html), but everything is in its proper place. For example, crude oil is not an evil substance. It is part of Mother Earth and serves many roles and purposes. However, when it is in the "wrong" place, it kills and pollutes and creates much suffering.

Duality, as far as I can see, is an integral part of the 3rd, 4th, 5th and, to some extent, the 6th dimensions. When duality is healthy, it is like two magnets which are standing in a way that attract each other and lock together, making a larger energy field. At the moment the magnets are in reverse in the 3rd dimension. They cannot meet. Therefore duality means separation and resistance.

Now that the heart center is activated in a critical mass of people, Power, which is female in nature, is able to flow in. Women and Men around the world will take their place and resonate in a healthy and natural way. They will provide a template which will allow others to align energetically to this new/old paradigm.

There is not one side which is superior to the other. Both are equally important and serve a very specific role.

What men can do is continue to work on their Heart Center, place energy structures that will facilitate the flow of Power in women and defend them from those who are not too happy about the magnets turning to their natural position.

Not all "men" and not all "women" will have the male/female roles so defined. But again, we only need a critical mass to do it in order to fully turn the magnets and anchor the new shift in place.

Once this shift is anchored, people who incarnate in this world will have no limits as to the level of ascension they can achieve in one lifetime.

Woman, The Power of Ascension

Last week, I found myself in a rather painful place. For the previous month, I had been getting very acute pain in my lower back, at the level of the Sacral Chakra. Waking up like this, I would lie down, meditate, allow the pain to grow and engulf me, express to me, and the pain would pass, or sometimes be bearable. At times it would disappear. Almost like nothing ever happened.

Then, a few days later, I woke up with the same pain. I tried my way of processing it, and instead of it disappearing, I got the letters ER across my inner sight.

Now, me and hospitals don't get along. Like any sane person on Earth, I do not want to go near one. However, the message kept appearing over and over. I tried to ignore it, but this time the pain did not disappear. In fact, it got worse.

It got so bad, that I had to go to the ER, my body already in shock from the acuteness of the pain, I was put on a drip, given liquids, covered in blankets and pumped full of many painkillers, muscle relaxants and things like morphine and it's more powerful cousins.

I've never had pain killers like these. I've taken aspirin, paracetamol, those types of things, but nothing like this. Of course those drugs eventually did their magic and took the pain away. They also made me very, very sick for 3 days.

The pain left and did not return. The test results came back with nothing to write home about. A big question mark hangs in the air. Before leaving for the hospital I said to my husband, "they are not going to find anything, this is energetic."

Negativity hits us where we are most vulnerable. But it is also a process in and of itself.

The reason I am telling you all this in an article called Woman, the Power of Ascension, is because for those three days after the event, and during it, I received an enormous amount of direct information from source.

Since this happened I see things that I had not been privy to beforehand.

One of those things was that the pain, where the hips join, was about the power of Women.

I received the information that many thousands of years ago, we, Women, orchestrated a passing of our power to men. For this to happen, we had to program a whole generation of women, and men, differently, shutting off their true natures and allowing the programming to take hold. This programming was that women were dysfunctional and worthless without a man. That only by being in love with a man, or owned by him, would she be happy. That he would protect her and provide for her and take care of everything and all she needed to do was birth children, nurture everyone and take it lying down.

Why on Earth would we do that? I wondered. The response came a few days later.

Then more information arrived, this time that it is time to take the power back from men. That we are the true holder of power, ability to do, ability to be, ability to create.

The "why" came in the form of an interview by CMN of Lucia René. She explained, in this interview, that the reason the power was given over was for men to learn to have power, and for women to learn about men having power. And, I think, about women not having power.

As it often happens, my information was not only validated in others but it was expanded.

Another thing that happened was that I received a vision of many women, elders, around me, and they were lying what looked like white sheets on me, all around my body. As they held their hands out and I stood up and walked with them, I clearly saw a diamond like shape between the crown and brow chakra. It was the point of connection to the female matrix, they said. Many women, and some men, on Earth will have this point activated in this manner, and when the time comes it will be fully "switched on".

I was to switch it on daily, for as long as possible.

Of course, I then googled this imagery and lo and behold, it is a point of energy, not one of the chakras, known in some Hindu traditions to be the point of connection with the Divine.

I still walk with the Elders, the Women. She is Mother, she is Earth, she is US. She is the UNIverse

If you are man and have read up to this point, fair play to you. I love you.

When I do a session, I often tell the person that I do nothing, I am simply their midwife. Often the person has been having a bridged birth for many months or years, I tell them when to breathe and when to push, and out pops another Ascended being.

This pain, it was like a contraction, much more painful, much more localized, but it was like asking for a push.

Will I get it again, not sure, more than probably. For now, it is gone and I am still documenting what I am receiving, the above of which is but a tiny fragment.

AUGUST - *Month for Latin America*

Call to action

For August, the energy otherwise known as the Divine, has asked to concentrate our healing/loving/integrating energy onto Latin America.

This can be done with any modality we already use. We can also tap in and ask the Divine how we can be of service during this month of August to bring back into balance the continents of South and Central America.

There are energy lines of dysfunctional duality (creating separation, otherness, conflict and suffering) mainly from Spain, Germany and Portugal, which go directly into Latin America.

This is not about "destroying" or "eliminating" these lines. It is about integrating, at a personal level, what these lines mean.

We can do this work by our self, either sending modalities of healing and integration to these European countries and/or the Americas, the lines themselves or by processing what this information and the form that the oppression has taken in the Americas, within our own body. Bring up the emotion, and process the emotion.

If you have a network of friends, then perhaps organizing an hour a week of joint meditation, or simply asking people to spend a few minutes a day to focus their attention on South and Central America will be extremely effective.

Our support of this work is key to its success.

Not Sleeping? - It has been rough.

I have had a lot of emails and reports of lightworkers/warriors not sleeping. It started about a week before September in 2010, and it continues.

The overall patterns are the following:

- Weird dreams
- Feeling of giving up
- Leaving the "fight"
- Depression
- Very agitated energy
- Waking up over and over all night, or inability to go back to sleep.

Some of the dream patterns:

- You cannot protect anyone
- Your leaders are useless
- Mother not helpful, or asks you to stop fighting, or leave the planet.
- Fearful images, like "devils"

From my investigation, it could be one of two things:

1. The elite are "test running" some sort of vibrational technology, after all fear and love are simply wavelengths. The technology does exist, as to how they are implementing it on a worldwide scale, that is open to discussion.

2. We have entered what some call the "photon belt" which is purging all negative energies from our bodies. However, from my research it appears that this photon belt would also bring down the electric grid, satellite transmission, and stuff like that, so it is not likely to be this, but I know very little about it, so do your own research on this one.

It could, of course, be a combination of the two above. See which one resonates strongest to you.

If you are at all trained in mystical or shamanic methods, trace the energy back to the source. When I do this, I see the first one to be the indicated reason for our lack of sleep. Vibrational torture.

So, what can we do? At the moment, simply knowing it is not us, is a big relief. It is definitely externally created, or it would not be so widespread.

If you are in an area that is being targeted, there are a few things you can try:

- One of them, stop drinking tap water. Get spring water to drink and cook with. Or if you can, put filters in your drinking water, showers, tubs and wash basins. Use the reverse osmosis filters, as these remove fluoride as well as chlorine and lots of other poisons.
- Another thing is to "focus" your attention on the source of the energy rather than the effects it is having on you. Release anger, fear (http://ascension101.com/en/ascension-tools/ascension-tools/33/105.html) and frustration, simply look at it, look at the source and overwhelm yourself with light and love.
- Meditation also helps. If you are finding it difficult to meditate right now, you can try the five min advanced meditation that you can download free from the Audio tab in http://ascension101.com/ascension-tools.html.
- Any activity that puts you "in the zone", such as sports, tai chi, playing music, dancing, painting, running, brisk walks and such.
- Sungazing. Remember to start a few seconds at a time and ONLY within one hour after sunrise and within one hour before sunset. This is the time when the harmful rays are not there. The sun is our greatest ally during this transition period.
- Smile. Smiling activates certain chemicals in our bodies that counteract negative feelings. It is hard to argue with a goofy smile on one's face :D

I am presently investigating other tools we can use and will keep you posted.

We are stronger than this.

It was DONE to ME - Why we process victim energy.

If you are reading this, the chances are you are either a **lightworker, light warrior, or an ascension worker**. In which case, it is very likely you have had one or more instance of "**psychic attack**".

Now, before we continue, lets look at what a "psychic attack" is. Basically, if you believe that we can send someone healing and love energy, and that the energy we send affects that person positively, then you have a basic understanding of what a "psychic attack" is. It is the opposite. It is the sending someone negative energy. It is also the sucking away of positive energy from someone. Also, these attacks do not necessarily involve "magic" or "esoteric" methods. If you are physically attacked, robbed, or in any way violated, this will bring into your physical, spiritual, mental and emotional bodies, some sticky negative and debilitating energy. So, what can you do with it?

Allocating blame, whether to another person or ourselves, is not going to fix it. Thinking we "attracted it somehow" is not going to fix it. And this is why. You are at the front line of a huge battle. Does a soldier attract the bullet that kills him? Of course not, but he did place himself in the line of fire. And so have you. By taking a stand to support the light in this planet, we place ourselves in the line of fire. Did we attract it, in a way, yes. Was it our fault? In a way yes. No one forced us to get to the front lines. No one said, "hey, you go into that planet that is being invaded by darkness and stay there for as long as you can." **It was a voluntary choice**.

Some people say that the only way to ascend and grow is to suffer. That might be true for them, but it is not true for a lightworker. **The only thing it does to a lightworker is put out that light which the lightworker came here to bring and use.**

So, as a lightworker, light warrior, or ascension worker, what can you do? Process the negativity. And process some more, then some more. And you continue processing until IT IS ALL GONE. The fastest and most effective process I have found is the following: You scan all of your different bodies for the negative energy, for example, "I feel violated", you find it, maybe in your physical body somewhere, or your aura, or your mind as nasty thoughts. And then you say, "[description of what you found] you are welcome here." For example, "tight knot in my tummy, you are welcome here", or "fear in my shoulder, you are welcome here". Then you allow it to be there. You allow it to grow, expand and express to you. You welcome everything it does, any thoughts that come up and you continue focusing on it. It might move to another location, it might bring you memories or thoughts, in which case you say, "memory, you are welcome here", "thought, you are welcome here". Then you embrace it with love.

Here is the Fear Processing Exercise I use myself (http://ascension101.com/ascension-tools/33-ascension-tools/105-fear-processing-exercise.html). You can change it to process any negative energy.

Rinse and repeat.

We don't analyze, try to understand, find the culprit, allocate blame, plan for the future, try to hold the memory, or anything else but processing the negativity. Why? BECAUSE **WE DO NOT HAVE MUCH TIME. The moment when the Earth and this human collective locks into a new paradigm is close at hand**, and we have to remove as much negativity from this planet before that happens as we can. The more negativity we, individually, process, the brighter each and every one of us will become, and the more effective in bringing those positive energies (chi) we will become.

After all, there is no one out there who has not had major "damage" done by living in this planet the past few thousands years. We all have our "sad stories" to tell. But it is time to release them.

Basically, it does not matter what was done to us. Or what is being done to us. **It is irrelevant.** We need to put a stop to it, that is all. And we begin by putting a stop to it in ourselves.

The Global Elite - What can YOU do?

The **Global Elite**, also known as the **Illuminati**, or nowadays as the **Bilderbergs**, are simply a group of people who realized what the true nature of our Universe was, eliminated everyone else who knew this information, and used the information to harness the power (chi, ability to do) of the uninformed masses.

Their methodology is very mechanical in nature. They use sacred geometry, power points on the Earth, as well as mind control via the media and chemicals. Plus a continuing elimination of those individuals as well as native people and cultures who hold the sacred knowledge of creation.

Their bread and butter is FEAR.

Their knowledge has been passed down from generation to generation both by families as well as infiltrated groups, such as the Freemasons.

They, in turn, are controlled by Darkness. Darkness came into this universe several thousand years ago from another universe which is Dark configured.

The difference between a Dark universe and a Light universe (which this one is), is basically that the main "emotional/creative" energy in a Dark universe is FEAR and the basic "emotional/creative" energy in a Light universe is LOVE.

There is plenty of documented and experiential evidence to support the above paragraph. To begin with, most cultures in the world will have an "origin" story where the Earth was a paradise devoid of suffering, fear and death, and then "fell" due to something that humans did. With regard to experiential evidence, ask anyone who has experienced Enlightenment or Oneness and he or she will tell you that it felt like **BLISS, LOVE, ECSTASY**. These higher states of consciousness are a merging with the Essence of this Universe... and guess what... no FEAR or SUFFERING in sight!

123

The Elite are presently working very hard at cultivating FEAR among the masses. They do this by staging, or broadcasting, natural or man made disasters, wars and pestilence around the world at regular intervals. FEAR keeps people ASLEEP. Someone who is ASLEEP has no FREE WILL. They are enslaved. FREE WILL is one of the fundamental laws of this universe. The **Elite have broken that law** by taking away the FREE WILL of billions of living beings in this planet.

They also use music and media to harness the focus of the young toward loveless sex, drugs, and glamorized violence...

They are also creating a FEAR OF LACK by making us believe that "oil and water are running out" and by polluting key very visible areas of the world and broadcasting a belief that the entire world is polluted and overpopulated, when in fact, most of the world is clean, unpolluted, unpopulated and untouched by man. The CO_2 pollution tax is a SCAM to control the fuel sources of the world.

So, now that you know a few of the things these people are doing, what can you do?

Firstly, you can create a FEAR FREE ZONE around you. This means a conscious effort to process any fear as soon as it pops into your body/mind/aura.

Also calling for your guides/angels to create a sanctuary of LOVE vibration in your home and workplace.

Focus on a topic that is close to your heart, could be anything that creates Fear or Despair in the world and send it unconditional love, or beautiful liquid light. If the situation creates a strong negative emotion in you, then process it within yourself first, then do the outer work.

When you see pictures of the Global Elite, you can google Bilderberg members in the news or media, or the internet, focus on them and tell them, "your time is up, all your darkness leaves this universe now", with love and compassion.

RETAKE power points in your area. Visit groves, parks, rocks, cathedrals, and known energy points in your area, and simply call upon the Divine Mother to retake that point. Call upon angels and fifth dimensional light beings to guard it and keep it free, clean and secure. Your intent is all that is needed to do this. It does not matter whether you believe in the Divine Mother with that particular name, or in Angels or other dimensional beings. What matters is your intent to retake the point of energy back for the Earth and Humanity.

The Nature of DARKNESS in Duality

Since I was very young, when others would tell me that there could be no light without dark, and that if we did not suffer we could not enjoy the good times... this belief felt.... WRONG.

During the past month I have been working closely with three extra-ordinary lightworkers, and one non-dual person in order to get the planet and our species ready for 2012. The work involved the retaking of key energy centers from Darkness. Yup, from "Darkness". There is no other word for it. We could call it the elite, the grays, religion, the Illuminati, or whatever label we want to, but the truth is, it was a group of beings working through Darkness. After retaking these power centers, we handed it back to Earth. This work was also facilitated and supported by hundreds of lightworkers around the Earth.

One of the things that puzzled me, as we did this work, was that as I looked at Earth, it was pure light. The centers, after being retaken, were pure light. And the energy that flowed was pure light.

And, as I explored and tried to understand, various bits of information came my way which showed the nature, and the reason, for this work.

Since June, I have understood that we are in an unbalanced and "wrong" structure of duality. One where the polarities are in the wrong ends and causes separation, suffering and otherness. But that if duality was to be in the right configuration, there would be no suffering or sense of separation... and the question is, where does Darkness go when we achieve this balanced configuration?

The information then was that this "wrongness" of polarity in this world was purposely designed and implemented by humans in order to experience an abuse of power, otherness and much more.

It then became apparent that this "wrong" structure should have gone back to the right configuration a very, very, long time ago.

Unfortunately the beings who were able to see the power generated, used it to keep the structure in the wrong polarity for way longer than they were meant to.

Thus most lightworkers began feeling that this has been going on way too long, that they are tired and homesick. A feeling of anger at the length of time this has been going on, has also been expressed. And pure battle-weariness.

When a Dark being attacks someone, or some place, my first feeling is to annihilate it. To destroy it. But I am stopped by my "higher self". Instead, I am instructed to focus on it, as when I focus on it, it can be integrated back into Oneness.

This method of integration is often interpreted by lightworkers as the Dark being having been taken back to the light. But it is not so.

And this is a key clue. There is a Oneness of a balanced and correctly aligned Dual reality, where both polarities are correctly configured and attach to each other, like two magnets, making a large, unified and stable field. And then there is Oneness which is the Source of all realities and all universes. These are two different things.

It is the latter where Darkness goes once it is integrated.

In order to further understand what was going on, I was sent the instructions to study "the return of Horus". When I say I was sent these instructions I mean that I literally saw the words written in my inner vision.

I diligently Googled the following words: "the return of Horus". One of the pages that came up was "THE RETURN OF LIGHT, Revelations from The Creator God Horus, With Elora Gabriel and Karen Kirschbaum". It is a channeled work (albeit not all correct - and allegedly fake) which basically describes the shifting into misaligned duality through the viewpoint of Lightworkers. If you are not familiar with this work, I strongly suggest you read it. However, please keep in mind that it is from ONE viewpoint only, that of Light and also one individual. Also, keep in mind that this

127

work talks about many universes, when my experience has been that this shift concerns two universes only.

In this work, it shows what happened at a universal level, but it also shows how Darkness is being "destroyed" and a battle is raging throughout this universe and many more. A light-being, will certainly perceive what is happening to dark-beings as "being destroyed". Certainly, those dark-beings who are in this universe are being integrated back into Oneness, or Source, **but they are not being destroyed**. Once in Source, they cease to be an individual and also cease to have a "side", whether Dark or Light. This Darkness includes all negative energy structures, including our negative emotions, feelings, thoughts and situations, but at this personal level, it is US who have to do the integrating. However, the book does have value if read as a novel. The parts that resonate will be the ones to take notice of.

Back to topic: one of the mistakes which has been done over and over throughout thousands of years, has been that lightworkers have tried to "fight" the Dark. As soon as the attempt to fight and destroy the Dark is made, the lightworker automatically becomes a pawn in the game of Dark.

But before the "fight" began, whole armies of lightworkers were sent to this Universe in order to "fix" and "save" those Dark beings, as well as fallen beings, and bring the Universe back to a balanced Duality of Light. However, this was a complete disaster. Not only did they not succeed, but a huge number of lightworkers were lost, and those that survived, were contaminated.

By contamination, I mean they started experiencing suffering, negativity, oppression and separation from Source.

You might wonder why, knowing they would be contaminated, the waves kept coming. The reason is simple. These beings knew that for as long as they could hold the light in this sector, within their being, the sectors would not be lost completely. It was a matter of holding the light for as long as possible, giving the rest of the universe time to find out how to retake the contaminated areas.

A first wave of Light-Warriors was sent, but unfortunately, this wave did not succeed. The reason was that they were made of the same stuff as this Universe, and therefore had the same experience as the lightworkers.

That is when an army of beings was recruited which could come into this Universe and put things back into their right configuration. These beings could not be corrupted because they were not dual in nature, and were not made from the same stuff as the Dark and Light universes.

In the book I mentioned earlier, this step was not mentioned. This is because, to Light Beings, the army that was recruited would have looked like Light to those sensitive enough to see them, but in most cases would not have been seen at all.

This "army" is made up of a type of being which is designed to simply put things back to their rightful place. They are not Light or Dark, in fact, their Universe is not Dual in nature at all. There is no "otherness" there. However, in order to enter a Light Duality, or a Dark Duality", this being creates artificial duality configured "soul beings" which then enter the dual reality and go to work.

These non-dual beings are often perceived by people as Pure Light, or Pure Darkness, depending on what end of the spectrum the dual based person is at. This then creates a sense of pure unconditional love, or absolute fear, on the person who sees them.

The non-dual being has no real experience of what is Light and what is Dark, but sees both as existing. Due to the work the non-dual being has been given in this Universe, their focus is to support the light-being and re-integrate the dark-being into Source. They do this without judgment. However, it is important to remember, that these beings will do the opposite in Dark Universes which have been invaded by Light.

The Fall, the moment in which the misalignment of polarities happened, is recorded in many cultures as the moment in which, usually a woman, opened a can of worms. Our culture's examples are Eve ate from the Tree of Knowledge and Pandora opened the

129

box. Previous to this, there are stories of the Devil, having been an angel, getting jealous, fighting God, and falling to Earth.

As I was growing up, I had a recurring dream. In this dream there were two universes, one Light and one Dark. In the Light universe, everything was beautiful, happy and harmonious. On the Dark universe there was great suffering, slavery, pollution and more.

The "Creator" decided that these two universes could learn from one another. That, somehow, if they joined, their evolution would be tremendous. Or something in those lines, in my dream I simply felt it was a "good idea".

There was no way to join these two universes because, due to their absolute nature, they could not see each other.

The "Creator" decided to make a being which was both Light and Dark. This being was a construct that had one purpose only, that of entering each universe and "infecting it" with the opposite "color".

The being entered the Light Universe first. It was welcomed there with trust and love. But every one he/she touched, then became sick. Sickness was unknown and the beings began to die, suffer and question their existence. After a few thousand planets were infected, the being went to the Dark Universe. However, as now there was darkness in the Light universe, it had become visible to the Dark universe and Dark beings were already preparing an assault on the Light universe.

The being of "Light and Dark" entered the Dark universe and was met with distrust and quickly enslaved. However, everyone who came into contact with the being was infected with Light. These beings began to suffer from compassion, love and other unspeakable things. Soon, the being was helped to escape.

The beings in the Dark universe that were infected with Light, also had a deep understanding of the strengths and weaknesses of the Light universe.

Meanwhile, in the Light universe, an attempt was made to "help" and "fix" those beings who now possessed Darkness. Planets throughout the Light universe began to help, but were instead infected. It was realized that these "infected" planets had to be quarantined and beings within them started experiencing the first sense of "disconnection" from source. Unlike the book "The Return of Light", which states that it was the Dark beings who created a wall; in my dream it was the Light which made the barrier around the infected planets.

The Dark universe rulers, eager to expand their territory, began a complete assault on the Light Universe. Because the Light Universe had separated the infected galaxies off from the rest, the forces of Darkness were only able to have access to infected planets in those galaxies, and not the rest of that Light universe.

This is where my childhood dream ends.

As an adult, I had another dream. In this dream I was a being so large and powerful that I could travel through Universes, and my interest was the exploration of those Universes. As I traveled through a beautiful Light universe, which is like swimming through a symphony of song and color, suddenly there is a big cry, like trillions of souls crying at the same time, then, as my attention tries to locate those cries... silence.

There was a section of the universe which was completely and utterly silent. This silence was so intense it was like a dull ache in the fabric of reality.

Myself, and many other beings, curious as to what had happened, travel to that place. We see, behind a wall, whirls of pain, suffering and destruction.

We watch, unable to do anything, unable to understand what is happening.

More beings gather, and there is a call for help. Many volunteer, and they work to first understand, and then reclaim that sector begins.

If the information I have since gathered is correct, then it appears that this planet belongs to a Light universe.

It explains many things.

131

The "battle" is ongoing and, at least for this planet, has already been won by Light. There really is no other result possible. The planet is now pure Light.

There have been many waves of beings entering this planet both before, and after, the completion of the quarantine wall. The first wave to enter after the wall was in place, were the "balance makers", the beings that put things in the right place. They also opened many channels for information and light to come in. The second wave came in to simply channel huge amounts of light, so that the lightworkers who were already here could survive, and also the vibration of this planet would become light enough for a wave of lightwarriors to come in. And after these, another wave of lightworkers entered. The first few waves had many casualties.

What we are doing now, is to integrate all Darkness within individuals and the human collective, so that as many people can go back to their original configuration as possible. Those that are not able to, or do not want to, will be integrated back into Source. There is no gray area. No "special planet" for Dark beings or fallen beings. This universe, and its creator, have decided not to partake in Darkness in any way or form. All portals created by Darkness to enter this universe have been closed. The wall that separated this sector to the rest of this universe is such that only light can come in, but no darkness can pass.

The beings which are designed to put things back in their place, are now facilitating the "ascension" of the entire human race. This "ascension" basically means the lifting of the veil of forgetfulness, the reconfiguration to a healthy duality and the return of the natural connection to source.

With these beings work, lightworkers and lightwarriors are now able to do their job more effectively, healing, educating and saving fallen beings who choose to ascend.

Many more beings have been entering the earth in the past few decades, some to educate, some to channel information, some to bring light, some to heal the planet or the people, or both.

132

The work has meant that we are no longer limited as individuals, or as a species or planet, to what we can achieve. **Darkness is putting up a big fight to keep control of the planet**, and it is up to us to stop it. We can do this at this time by processing and integrating our personal FEAR and SUFFERING.

I would be very interested in hearing what wave of being you most identify with.

See, also :

2. Duality in Light
3. Light Warriors
4. The Fall
5. Light Universe

133

Ascension and DNA - Can we accelerate the process?

Growing up, and up to recently actually, I thought that DNA was static. That whatever we came in with was it, like a solid structure that could not be changed. After all, we can't really change our physical shape right? Become taller, shorter, change the color of our hair or eyes? So, DNA is fixed, I thought.

Then I heard of certain people who had become sick because a certain virus had changed their DNA. WHAT?? I thought, our DNA can be altered in one lifetime?? Because you see, I thought that DNA change, or mutations, happened only from one generation to the next. Not so! And... if a virus can change our DNA, what other things can change it?

As I researched this topic, I found all the information about DNA activation, "garbage" DNA being of alien origin, and lots more stuff. One of the things that really got my attention was "spontaneous mutation", something very common in other species on Earth. And that, actually, generational mutation is really not the main form of mutation.

Then I remembered the work done by Hira Ratan Manek on Solargazing. He had managed to change his physical essence to absorb all he needs nutritionally through gazing at the sunrise or sunset while standing barefooted on the earth. Now, he no longer needs to eat in order to have the energy needed to live. Awesome.

So, my main concern is Ascension of the Species. Sungazing would certainly move us closer to this goal, as the "side effects" that Hiran Ratan Manek had were of bliss, enlightenment and sanity. We all know that the Sun is not the only source of energy flowing through Earth. And I do believe that the Solar System is moving through a very high frequency energy "area" of the universe. Whether this area has come to us, or is a constant and we cross it every few thousand years, I have no idea. But we are in it.

I also know that this particular energy field is a huge opportunity for us to evolve enormously as individuals as well as a species. That was when it occurred to me that if we were able to consciously accelerate our DNA change (like it's done through Sungazing), to resonate more purely with this new field of energy, or to be able to absorb it, or use it, more effectively, then we could really take off.

This is not an original idea at all of course, DNA activation is very well known in the ascension circles. And also, many cultures talk about a "light body" which will be the one we transform into at the moment of ascension.

And here is what I am proposing. That, like sungazing, we accelerate that change of DNA to live in that higher plane, or from that higher vibration, now. Why wait, right?

So, if we follow the sungazing model, all we need to do, is open ourselves to, and look at, the center of the galaxy, or our "higher self", "God/ess". Traditionally we know that this energy comes in via the crown chakra. So we open ourselves up to it. We "look" at it via our 3rd eye and allow it to filter down into our energy body (all the chakras and auras). It helps to visualize it as a bright light coming in and lighting us up like a light bulb. We don't really need a "picture" of what we want the DNA to look like, because we can't presently conceive of its full potential. So the best thing is, if your mind is really active, to imagine the light settling into the space between thoughts, space between molecules and space between atoms. Go as deep as you can. Fill all those spaces with that beautiful bright light.

Anger - why it is important to process it.

Many of us are reluctant to process, or release, anger. This is because it is such a powerful source of defensive energy that we think that if we lose it, we will no longer be able to defend ourselves or others. And it has been used successfully to get people out of depression or abusive relationships, so it must be good, right?

Anger really is one step above fear. It is an overtone of the fear energy, which is what darkness is built on. It is, in fact, very destructive both for us and those around us.

So there are two things we have to come to terms with, one is that if we remove anger we will not become vulnerable, and the second one is that we do not need anger to act on our convictions.

Many times it is anger that will propel us to do something to stop a war, for example. And often it is only anger which those who try to bully us or step on our toes really hear and understand, and thus stop what they are doing. And this is a good thing. But once we are empowered, we don't need anger to do these things, as we have better tools.

Anger can lead us to lose our temper. And when we lose our temper we can hurt others in emotional, psychological and physical ways.

"The verb *temper* was borrowed into Old English from Latin *temper? re* 'mix, blend'. This seems originally to have meant 'mix in due proportion'" (word-origins.com)

We lose our due proportion, our balance.

From a young age we are taught to control our temper. To subdue and suppress our anger. This is also negative. Part of becoming free, is to recognize and express our anger at our life, lot, situation and people who have harmed us or rejected us.

But the emotion, like fear, is destructive. If it is oppressed, it has ahold of us and can burst out at a any moment.

In Ascension, it keeps us firmly in a lower vibration.

And this is a very interesting point. Many people have asked me how to increase their perception of their guides, higher self, angels, or how to communicate with other dimensional light beings, or aliens. We have so many ways to explain this phenomenon. But the question is the same. How do we increase our perception of them, how do we make it easier for them to contact us. Well, there are two fundamental blocks that stops these beings from coming near us, one is FEAR, and the second is ANGER.

Yup, it takes more than psychic ability to contact these beings. They still do get through of course, through dreams, synchronicity and other methods, but it is difficult for them and for us. A highly psychic person can indeed contact these beings easily, but just imagine what he or she could do without any of these blocks on the way? For one, they would not be pestered, fooled, or made ill by negative beings.

I have dedicated a huge portion of this website to disseminating the importance of processing fear. And it still is the most important mission here on Earth, to get as many people as possible to start and successfully process their fear.

And now comes the second phase, that of processing anger.

So, if you are game, please do an anger processing method. The one I use is very simple and identical to that for processing fear:

Breathe deeply three times

Close your eyes

Scan your body for anger

Once you find it in your body, observe it.

Do not analyze, give it reasons, validations or memories, simply observer it.

Now, let it grow, let it get huge, bigger than the house you are in, the world, lets see if can get as big as the universe.

Allow any memories, words, situations or pictures to express and release, if one sticks, making you emotional, simply say, "thank you memory/vision/word/emotion"

Then, fill the anger with love and light.

Rinse and repeat.

It might take a while, days, weeks, or even months, but no worries, continue doing this for as long as it takes. Every session counts not just for you, but for the entire human collective.

Sometimes the anger will turn to fear, sometimes to pain, but continue, simply welcome the new manifestation and finish the process.

UFOs are all over the place! - Alien or government?

There are **UFO** reports all over the media at the moment, and hundreds of posts on youtube with footage of unidentified flying objects. A lot are different from the "usual" footage as they show "fleets" of objects in the sky. So, are they new flying machines that our governments have been hiding from us and now are showing us to get us used to the idea (whether true or false) that there are aliens about to contact us? Or are they extra terrestrial entities showing themselves to us? And why is this relevant to Ascension?

The photo on the right was taken by me September 2010, while chatting with my daughter in our backyard. The object flew at a "normal" speed, then slowed down above us, changed direction, then stood still for about an hour, after which it sped away at a tremendous speed, much faster than any plane I have ever seen.

One thing is for certain, there are objects flying in the sky that we can't identify. At the moment there are movies about alien species trying to take something from us, either water, life, or even the planet. But we've had these movies for decades, what's different this time is that there are a LOT of them coming up, as well as a continuous feed of tv shows depicting the same subject.

There is a very interesting theory going around the internet called "Blue Beam". This theory says that the powers that be are planning on fooling us all with mass landings of craft, which are of human origin, plus perhaps some from not so friendly (to the masses) aliens who made deals with our governments, to create a huge emotional and religious experience which they will use to keep the human collective enslaved. This is a summary of the theory, if you want to know more, and how it is supposed to happen, google the words "blue beam".

Another theory is that there are in fact several alien species flying around our planet at the moment, some terrestrial, some extra terrestrial, and they are slowly getting us used to their presence. The theory is that they are either here to welcome us to the galactic neighborhood association, or simply to witness our planetary ascension.

Yet another theory is that they are here to tell us that we are in fact their petri-dish experiment.

And yet another, is that as the human collective and Earth ascend in awareness and evolution, we are now able to see other dimensions and we can perceive, and record, these crafts more easily.

How does this affect our ascension process? Well, the shift is occurring, whether we like it or not. Where we are when it culminates either next year or the year after depends very much on how much negativity we have processed before then. The main forms of negativity being fear and anger, but also encompassing victim consciousness and wanting to be saved by an external force (giving our power away).

It is blatantly obvious that the powers that be are doing their utmost to keep us in fear mode. How they will use the alien equation to feed fear is open to debate. But they are seeding our minds with gross alien violence in a very open way, by our entertainment industry and news items.

Now, if any spaceship lands in your backyard and beautiful being come out and invite you their mothership in order to save you, make sure you ask for their Light ID. Ask them if they work for the light. If they don't answer the question, but instead give you an ultimatum or warning of things to come, then ask them politely to get off our planet. I can assure you that no light being will offer another to "save them". However, if they are offering to take you for a ride in their latest Model X spaceship, temptation might be too great to say NO, so ask them to come back in January 2013. If they have your best interest at heart, they will. If they tell you this is your only chance, don't forget what your mother told you about getting into stranger's cars, even if they do have alien puppies in there. Any ultimatum is fear based, and not advisable to comply with.

Nothing can stop our ascension if we do the necessary work on ourselves. Nothing. So, aliens or no aliens, it doesn't matter, it is irrelevant. Our collective is ascending and nothing can stop an awakened and fearless person from getting the full benefit of the personal, collective and planetary ascension process that is happening right now.

Manifest Your Dreams Now - how it links to Ascension

A lot of us will link the word "manifest" with the movie "The Secret". This movie was a huge success because it touched upon a basic truth, something we all know to be true but have been denied access to, that we are divine beings who can manifest our own reality.

As we do our Ascension work, one of the side effects is that reality becomes much more pliable. At first we may go a little crazy and go for fabulous material goods, manifest our perfect love partner, or the perfect body.

Then, we move onto more interesting and mind blowing manifestations.

The three wishes that are prominent in most of our lives are, wealth, health, and love. Then we go for things such as psychic abilities, expanded awareness, enlightenment and ascension. But all have an underlying vibration, that of wanting to be happy.

For a lot of people the art of manifestation has not worked. They are still poor, unhealthy, single (and don't want to be), ugly, no psychic abilities, blindness and disconnected from Source.

So, lots of books by self growth gurus came out about the "missing link", or "the secret behind the secret" to make "The Secret" work.

The reason why for one person it works, and for another it doesn't is very simple. One bases their methods of manifestation on fear and need, and the other on light, happiness and love. In other words, they align themselves with their mission on the planet, with their higher self.

It is a simple change of vibration, that's all. So, how does this link to Ascension?

As the person progresses through their Ascension, he or she goes from a low vibration to a higher vibration. Basically they move from fear, anger and suffering, to love, peace and happiness.

But these steps don't all happen at once, so, for example, at some point the person would be much higher than they started, no longer afraid of being poor, but still have an enormous fear of growing old alone. If, at the same time, they are actively working on manifesting their dream life, this can get a bit like driving a Ferrari and not knowing how to use manual gear shift.

As the person progresses in their manifesting exercises, their ability to manifest their dream life increases. And here is the problem, because unless they have dealt with their fears in full, they will also manifest their nightmares.

Again, as we work on our Ascension, our capacity to manifest also increases.

The safest and fastest route to Manifestation is to concentrate all our efforts on Ascension. So, instead of visualizing, feeling and going for wealth, love and health, we start by process our fear, anger and needs big time. And after a daily processing session, we spend a few minutes in the bliss of Divine Love.

A time arrives when we are no longer afraid, angry or needy. When that moment comes, we dive into visualizing and enjoying our perfect life and watch in awe as it materializes around us.

To find out what stage you are in, see if you have any resistance when you read the following sentences:

- I want to grow old alone.
- I am happy with my weight.
- I don't care if my body is healthy or not.
- I don't need to have wealth.

If any of the above made you twinge, then find that twinge in your physical body and trace the energy line to the source. Process the fear, anger or need that you find there. If you find a resistance in that last instruction, it is because you are not ready to let go of your conditions of happiness. Process that too :)

You see, we don't remove our "want". What would the point of a physical experience be without the joy of a magnificent reality? And that's the catch 22. If we need, fear or refuse to drop the "dreams" that we think will make us happy, we can never be truly happy, and our manifesting will be a painful and slow slog. And if we do drop them, we might never get them. But here is the "but", we get things we never even dreamed of, or thought possible. Including a level of happiness unknown to most people alive today.

Firewall to Ascension - the program they don't want you to find.

The majority of individuals in human form have a firewall inserted in their field which stops them from doing self growth, ascension, or any other exercises that will help them achieve their ultimate evolutionary level.

This firewall is an energy construct which "feels" like a metallic implant somewhere in the body. It can, and does, get activated every time we try to meditate, learn OBEs, lucid dreaming, spiritual or psychic development, or any other form of communication with our higher self, guides, the divine, angels or whatever we want to call our entourage of helpers and supporters we have around us. And it appears that its' very specific vibration can be triggered by external forces too.

The way to find if you have one of these firewalls is to complete the following sentence: "I do not meditate / process because_____".

Now, look at the answer, find the energy signature in the answer. Scan your body and find it. Now ask yourself the following:

"Did I put this firewall in my body?" If yes, then why? Was it voluntary or under duress? If not, then who did?

You may or may not get answers to these questions. However, the important things is that you found the firewall. Now, either remove it yourself and send it back to Source, or ask one of your guides or angels to remove it for you. Then fill the space left behind with light and love.

If you find resistance to removing the firewall, focus your attention on the resistance, it could be a backup program to ensure you don't get rid of the firewall. For example: "I need more than this exercise to help myself/my loved one", or, "I can't find it". If you find one, proceed as above, then go back to the firewall. Remember, no analysis, no judgment.

After you are done, go ahead and meditate or process. If the same resistance comes up, do the exercise again. It might take a few goes, but it will eventually all be eliminated and you will be free do the exercises needed to reach your full potential in this lifetime.

Happy hunting :D

Worthlessness - The ticket to enter Earth. Or is it?

Process worthlessness

I have yet to meet a person who does not have some sense of worth, whether lots of worth or lack of worth.

There is a very "sticky darkness" about entering this realm. The earth 3D, human collective, human experience in present day society realm.

It doesn't matter if a person is originally from a light dimension, a starseed, a walk-in, an ascended master reincarnated, or someone who has traveled the full path to enlightenment or beyond. Being human today means that we have a high level of forgetfulness of origin. We also live in an extremely hostile environment (on a world scale). And seeing as our environment reflects us perfectly, and the world is our environment, then that means we have had to, at some point in entering this lifestream, chosen to integrate that sense of "less than what we really are". As we are all eternal and divine beings, this means we have purposely fooled ourselves into believing that we are less than what we really are. With that comes a sense of worthlessness.

This can reflect in our life as not meeting a love partner who is perfect **for us**. But has issues and problems or something that makes him or her worth less than what we really want. It can also be reflected as "not the right job", or the "house that will do for now", or the "country which I'm stuck in", or "family I am forced to live with".

The list can go on an on.

During last night's meditation, I looked into it. I followed the energy of worthlessness back to source. It was something like a black cloud covering a bright star. Lowering, but not stopping it's light and energy.

So here's an idea. How about we look at that bright star which is our true self, and allow that dark cloud to manifest, grow and express, we embrace it with love and light, and release it. The game is changing and that darkness is no longer necessary for our existence here. We can finally let it free to go to its source and without it, we can bring some more light into this planet. The more light we bring, the more others will be able to see too. Deal?

Deal.

The "IF" factor: a curved ball that stops joy in its tracks.

The "IF" factor is that situation which is necessary to make us happy. So, for example, "if I meet the ONE, I'll be complete." The problem is that until we release that "IF", we will never be complete. Then we think, "so I have to give up on my dreams to be happy? I don't want to do that. What's the point of life without dreams?" Or a similar thought. And this is how the "if" factor gets us. You see, it's not the end results that we need to release, it's the dependency of it, it is the "IF" we want to release in order to be complete.

Our resistance is that we refuse to be happy, or complete, UNLESS we get that particular dream. Like we are punishing someone, or something, holding back, until we get our own way. We may as well write, "I refuse to be complete until I meet the ONE." At least this last way of putting it is more honest. What if we change it to, "I am complete, and ready to meet the ONE." That resistance to release the dream, the dream that it is the external "IF" which will make us happy, that refusal to release the condition of our becoming complete and happy, that is the energy we must address.

Most of us will have a long list of "if"s to complete before we are complete. For example:

I'll be happy if I win the lotto.

I'll be complete when my body is _____. (thin, male, female, tall, perfect...)

If I have a baby.

If I get divorced.

If the rain stops.

If I was more psychic.

149

If I meet my soulmate.

The list can go on and on.

Obviously, there are things in our environment, or lacking from our environment, that can make us unhappy. Lack of food, water, shelter, human warmth, can all be said to be basic human necessities. But, the level of comfort we get from them is physical. Some are necessary for our survival and that there is no getting away from that. But others are not necessary. Really. Honestly. Not necessary. They don't need to be present for us to be happy or complete. However, we have stumbled upon a cultural, social, or otherwise learned program that tells us they are absolutely necessary for our happiness. And the refusal to release that program, that dream, what keeps us from achieving completeness.

You see, it's the need of the dream which holds us back, not the dream itself.

The trick is not to look for completeness outside of ourselves. For example, with the soulmate issue, it is best to be happy and complete, and want to share that happiness and completeness with someone who wants to share their completeness and happiness with us, than demand someone else makes us happy, or offer to make them happy. Even if it simply by their presence. Those two last ones NEVER work for very long.

Another curved ball is in the manifestation culture exercises. We think, well, if I release the dream, then I won't manifest it. Or, when I do manifest it, it won't make me as happy as it could have.

That is the perfect example we can use to illustrate how this works. Let's take an "IF". Think of the biggest wish, dream of "IF" in your life today. Now release it. See that resistance? Find it in your body and look at it. Just look at it. It is, in fact, the resistance to release the "IF" which is holding you back from achieving the dream.

Deep down, we do know that no external influence will make us happy or complete, not for very long anyway. So, when we have happiness attached to a result, we will never get that result.

A better exercise is to, for a few minutes a day, close our eyes and jump into completeness and happiness. Not looking at what caused it, simply being in it. We can achieve this state by imagining we achieved our "IF", then as we feel the happiness and joy, we release the "IF" and simply merge with the happiness and joy we are feeling, becoming complete. This leaves our higher self, universe and life to manifest that joy, happiness and completeness in many ways, all ways, always, and in ways which are 100 times better than that "IF" we had dreamed up.

Can you release your dreams in order to receive something so big you had never dreamed you could get? Now is the time :D

The Body Fantastic

I have mentioned a few times that the body is our greatest tool, our greatest ally and our greatest companion.

The body, of course, is part of us. But, like our other subtle bodies, it is also its own energy construct, its own being. It is like the horse that we, the directing being, are riding through life.

If we see the body this way, we tend to treat it much better than when we identify with it as ourselves. If it was a horse, we would love it, give it shelter, suitable food, suitable grooming, rest, play and freedom. We would also, as we ride and also when we interact with it, communicate with it in very subtle and direct ways. A good rider and his or her horse create a close partnership, sharing information on the terrain, and any obstacles and dangers that might cross their path.

The human body, like the directing being in a great majority of the population of the planet, has been kept disempowered, dumbed down and asleep.

There was a time when we, as humans, were able to use the body's abilities to communicate telepathically with each other and other beings, including the planet. We were also able to move huge objects with telekinesis, and travel great distances without effort.

Most people, when they think of these abilities, think that it is the mind that is doing them. It is not. For example, we use our mind to decide to switch off the light, then the body gets up, reaches with our finger and switches the light off. It was the body that did it. It is the body that feels hot and cold, hears music or our loved one's voice, it is our body which perceives the beauty of the planet, and the ugliness too. Our mind interprets all that information and we, the directing being, know what it is and what it means and makes decisions accordingly.

In the same way, it is our physical body which hears other people's thoughts, sees behind the veil of forgetfulness, and can lift heavy things from a distance.

One thing we can begin with, in order to develop a good clear communication with the body, is to start with very simple yes/no questions. So, for example, think of something that you are afraid of that is not logical. It could be dogs, for example, or snakes, and then ask "is my body afraid of [add item here]", it might respond with fear (yes), or not, if not, then ask "am I afraid of [add item here]" and you will know which one is afraid.

If no response is forthcoming from either, then there's something blocking one's communication with self or body. In that case, I would suggest doing the firewall exercise on it.

And now, a few theoretical speculations on how this deadening of abilities came about. This information was given to me by psychic perception, and I have not had time to validate it:

At some point in the past, a species came to the planet who had use of "meat bodies", this planet, and its resources. They implanted various energy structures into the human body. The technology they used is unknown to me at this point. It's possible it was placed directly into the DNA, although its also possible it was implanted into the human collective as well. The result was that, for the great majority of humans, we were no longer able to access various abilities.

One of the abilities was that of telepathic communication. Before this was taken away, all humans on the planet had access to the collective and everyone within it. People were able to communicate across continents, as well as with the animals, plants and Gaia. They were also able to see in various other dimensions.

This event is recorded in stories such as The Tower of Babel.

Another thing that was taken away was our ability to see the alien species, and their buildings and ships, which had done this to us.

153

The reasons they did this are that they are afraid of our power, our ability to do, and they wanted to "breed" us as meat bodies, slaves, to harvest our energy, resources, DNA, and more.

The species that did this to the human race is stuck in a very 3D existence. Their own cultural breeding, indoctrination and beliefs have rendered them unable to evolve past the physical. And, just like the Europeans traveled the planet killing off native people and taking their land, this species have been doing this for thousands, if not millions, of years. But just like the European general population are now much more evolved and aware, and do not murder native peoples to the same rate and extent as they did a few hundred years ago (although it is still happening), the only way for this other species to release slave planets is for them to raise their vibration and level of awareness.

I would ask you, as you ponder these thoughts, and if they resonated with you, to send light and compassion to that species. Our human potential is limitless, it really is. If enough of us focus on them, then we can start liberating them from their chains, and start the seed of evolution to germinate in their people once again.

As to our bodies, give him or her a big acknowledgment, tell him/her that you now understand and will listen to it, helping it to heal and regain all her/his abilities, perceptions and wisdom.

Gaia Speaks - How to hear our Guides.

When we open ourselves to receive messages and guidance from our Higher Self, Source, Gaia, Divine Mother, Divine Father, Guides and Angels - what I call "our entourage", we often become receptive and open to receive what is coming. But then, when it does, we miss it. I get lots of emails asking me how to be able to hear our entourage, how to discern that it is from a positive and benevolent source and how to understand what they mean.

The first thing is to, as we all do, open ourselves up to receiving the guidance and information. Secondly, we learn to discern what is "real" from what is ego or negative entities. We do this by reconnecting with our body, and listening to it very carefully. We listen with our body and the body will tell us. For example, a twinge in the tummy when something doesn't feel quite right after we speak it. Or the openness of heart as we express love and happiness.

Thirdly, we need to establish a language that will be understood by us when we need to receive information. Native people around the world have been doing just this for thousands of years. The language we establish is very culturally based, highly subjective and often not understood by others, unless we explain it. For example, someone might say that a particular person will visit them that day, because a leaf fell from a particular tree, as a red bird started singing at exactly 11:11 that morning. And, sure enough, without calling first, the visitor arrives later that day.

Many years ago, I read a book by Paulo Coelho, one of my favorite writers. In the book, he mentioned that he decided to invent a sign for himself about writing a book. He hadn't written a book yet, but wanted to. So, he went on a pilgrimage (he's a Christian) and said:

""If I see a white feather today, that is a sign that God is giving to me that I have to write a new book." And then I saw this white feather in a window of a shop. And since then, every second year, in

January, I need to see a white feather. And the day that I see I start writing."

When I read those words, I decided that I too would use a white feather as part of my Guidance language. I decided it was to be a positive sign, something that will tell me I was in the right direction, and, or that I needed to take notice of something that was being sent my way.

The way in which I personally get the white feathers is also very significant. One was waiting by my front door one day, another fell onto my lap as I sat down outside. And, one of my favorites was when my 4th child was about 18 months old. I was very, very tired (physically), as any full time parent of a 2 year old will know. Plus, I was receiving the information for a book, and did not know if I should start writing it in my tired state (the energy we have when we write or speak, carries in the words and reaches others), or leave it a couple of years until my boy was a little older.

We went to the park, me in my inner thoughts asking for a white feather if indeed I should go ahead with the book, and my toddler insisting he did not need a stroller, and started wobbling around on the path. All of a sudden he takes off toward a tree. It is hot here in Sacramento, so a tree is always a welcome rest area. I got the stroller onto the grass and followed him. He went faster, falling several times, picking himself up and running, as he reached the tree, he started making all those delightful little voices toddlers make when they find something great.

I parked the stroller, took out a blanket and lay it on the grass. My boy ran back, really delighted, as he got closer, I looked up and saw what he had found. It was the dirtiest, most sorry looking white feather I have ever seen. And it was huge! I gasped with delight and happiness.

It was a sorry looking feather, but brought me great joy. The message was clear, a white feather is a white feather, it doesn't have to be perfect for it to bring inspiration and love.

My little boy saw my delight and happiness, and for the next few months would diligently search around for feathers, because feathers made mummy happy :)

Fast forward a few years. Two weeks ago, I received various emails from different people around the United States, asking me to contact their friend, "Willy Whitefeather", a respected and loved Cherokee Elder.

Whitefeather. A name I could not ignore. I called him right away, and we arranged to meet a few days later.

Willy Whitefeather has been teaching the connection between synchronistic events, words and human thought for years. In fact, that summary does not do justice to his offerings. His language is highly subjective and rarely understood by the western mind. But his message is clear. What we do, what we all do, think and feel, affects Gaia, our Mother Earth. And this is also why we have the ability and power to help her in this transition.

When source sends me a White Feather, I listen.

How to deal with Perpetrators of Darkness - Call to Action

Throughout my life, and at various degrees, I, like other sensitive people, have felt the collective fear, pain and suffering on the planet felt by humans, as well as animals and nature.

All the people, animals, all the plants, all the trees. There's so much pain, so much suffering, so much violence. I feel it all. I hear it all. Every minute of every day. It never stops. I can't stand it. And it's getting louder all the time as the elite use all their tools to increase it.

Those men and women who work in slaughterhouses, the ones cutting down the rain-forests, drilling for oil and destroying our environment, the creators of wars. Those men and women who torture and kill millions of people, animals and trees every day. Those that think animals and trees don't feel pain, fear, and terror, or relish the thought of inflicting these to others. Those who send psychic and physical attacks onto others.

Years ago, I had a German Shepherd, which had caught its paw in a metal gate by the side of the house. The dog was in great pain by the time I got home. He was snapping at anyone who tried to get near as it struggled to free itself.

I walked up to it and held him firmly, but to free his paw, I had to put my arm between his face and the gate. As I did this, he bit deeply into my left arm – I pulled the paw free, which hurt him even more.

After he was free, he was still in a lot of pain, and tried to bite me again. I held his mouth closed, and pushed him to the ground, firmly, thus telling him (in dog language) that this was not OK. He calmed down and I was able to release it, knowing he would no longer bite those around him. The moment he "changed", we both knew it was over. Although still in pain, he became friendly and "sorry" about what had happened.

When someone lashes out, it is because they are in great pain and fear.

I'd like to hold them all in my arms. All of them. I'd like to show them that they are loved, and that they are safe. All the murderers, all the rapists, all the butchers of the seals, whales and dolphins, all the bloodthirsty workers in the abattoirs, the creators of wars, all the beings involved in psychic attacks. And all those individuals who, in their pain and fear, lash out at me personally, on the internet with hate and anger, poisonous words and death threats.

How do we reach those people who have their paws stuck in gates of pain and suffering, fear and distress, who lash out at everyone around them. Who have lived like this so long now that they start taking pleasure out of the suffering of others?

It is not about who's to blame. Yes, we take responsibility in minimizing the pain and suffering of others through our actions. We can go out of our way to eat meat from small farms, organic producers who love their animals. Yes, we can buy furniture from renewable sources of wood, clothes from factories which don't exploit people. But what of the perpetrators of fear and pain? We might hold them in our field of light, and allow Gaia to do her work. As a 'singularity' – I am but one person. But WE are many.

If we dedicate 10 minutes a day to holding these people in our collective light, it can make a huge shift for them and us. After the 10 minutes, let us focus on the compassion and love of the millions of lightworkers and lightwarriors around the planet, our brethren, so that our collective power increases -- making each one of us more able to accomplish our collective work.

I also feel the love, light and compassion of billions of people around the world. All those parents who hold their newborn baby in wonderment and deep love, all those who behold our Mother Earth in awe as they sense Her power and compassion. I also feel millions of lightwokers and lighwarriors diligently doing daily acts of selfless love and compassion to bring light to others and the planet. For every murderer there are 10 healers, for every abuser of animals, there are a thousand who hold animals in respect and equality. For every creator of war, there are millions of us who do not agree with that particular game.

If I didn't feel the LIGHT I would not be alive today. Mother Earth made the call for assistance, and we, all of us, are the answer to that call.

Sickness and Death

Recently I received an email from an individual who has a very serious physical condition, and below is my response:

I am not a healer, and although healings have occurred in my presence, it has simply been a matter of energy transmission from Source. If that is meant to happen with you, then it will, there is no choice or intention involved at my end. You are, however, in my focus.

There are a few things you can do to see if you need to "heal" from this condition.

One of them is to ask yourself: How is this condition serving me?

Ask your body: How is this condition serving you?

Ask both yourself and your body: What is the agreement that allowed this condition into my life/body?

Then remove your agreement from it. One can change one's mind at any time/space.

Process the fear around this condition, the full text for the fear processing exercise I use is on the Tools section of the site. Do it at a general body level, as well as at a molecular level.

And finally, ask your body "are you ready to release this condition?" and ask yourself "am I ready to release this condition?"

If the answer is yes, then free it back to source. If the answer is no, then ask "am I willing to consider releasing this condition?" and continue processing.

Most periods of sickness, of course, do not end in death. But why do some of them do?

We are all going to leave our physical bodies at some point. How this comes about is open to choice and agreement. That's right, we choose when we die and we agree on how we die. When the agreement comes through fear, it is not pleasant and often it is a "trick". A way to remove us from the planet before "our time". But how does this work exactly? If it is our choice, then how come we can be tricked into death before we are ready?

This is one example of how one can be tricked. Since I was a young child, I could "see" the energy around people. This energy would be interpreted by me as qualities of color. I learned that when a person had a quality of color which I interpreted as a kind of dull grey, they would die within a year. Sometimes, the color would appear, the person would have it for a while, then, when the moment or condition came, they would choose to stay and the color would go to a healthy bright transparency. They would then heal or be miraculously saved from something. But most would keep the color and would leave within a year.

A few weeks ago, August 2011, I looked in the mirror and saw that dull grey on my reflection. The first thing that went through my mind was, "Oh, so it's within 12 months". Then I noticed something. There was something "not right" about the energy color. So I looked deeper, and noticed that it was a superimposed image. It wasn't "real".

Fascinated I traced it back to source, and it was a certain group trying to acquire an agreement from me, to die within 12 months. I thought about it for a few seconds, then decided I would stay on track and keep my agreement to work on the mission until 2017. The color lifted and I was back to "normal". The point though, is that even though it was a "trick", I still had a choice. I could have chosen to agree with them and leave within 12 months. This example is not about developing "sight" to see the color change, that was just my personal experience of how others tried to get me to agree. The agreement comes in many forms and whether it is a trick or part of our life path choices, is not the point. We get to choose.

The agreement is necessary whether it involves a sickness, accident, or physical attack. None of these can take us out if we don't agree with them. This is why we hear of "miracles" where a person has an accident that totally destroys their car, but they find themselves standing next to the car wreck after the accident. The state of our bodies are left after "survival" is also our choice. The agreement comes and you will have a choice. Might be in a millisecond, or might take months.

Healing often happens "miraculously" for the same reason, suddenly the person KNOWS they are healed and complete. Most often, this knowing comes from the person giving themselves permission to heal. This can happen in many ways, due to a personal experience, or through guidance from a healer.

Is the point to stay alive at all costs? No, of course not. But, consider this. I am personally booked for this work until 2017, so we don't have that much long to go. After that, we decide if we want to retire and enjoy our results on the planet, join a new mission, or leave. What do you say?

Spaceship Earth - and YOU are the captain.

The shift has reached it's final stage... now it is up to you.

On the week of the 22nd to the 28th of August 2011, I was kindly asked by Source to step outside. This doesn't happen often, it is rare, and normally lasts a few minutes, hours, or at the most a couple of days. This time, it lasted a whole week.

What does this mean? It means that I leave a "placeholder" in this reality matrix, but I, the being, steps outside. The body, subtle bodies, and "awareness" stay, but it is like watching a movie, or a car driving on the highway, which one's body is driving, but one is watching it from afar.

As I observed "reality" from the outside, I could sense big shifts happening, enormous changes, the walls between dimensions becoming thin, my "human" perceptions could detect movement, lights and shadows.

Then, I was asked to return. And the news is big.

At the same time, my friend Lucia Rene, a top ass-kicking mystic, sent her newsletter out. In the newsletter she expressed her feeling of leaving behind the old world, and entering the new. She wrote:

"Have you seen the movie The Lord of the Rings or read Tolkien's wonderful trilogy of that name? If so, perhaps you remember one of the last scenes where the elves, Bilbo, Frodo, and Gandalf get on a pretty wooden boat, sail out of the harbor, and disappear from view. They leave for a new world. "That's it," I thought. "That moment in the film captures the feeling perfectly!"

It's as though I've gotten on a boat and am sailing out toward the unknown. The unknown isn't scary. It's actually quite peaceful. It holds the sense of returning to something long forgotten." Lucia Rene

I knew something was up, big time, but did not understand what had happened, as I was outside, and why had I been taken out of the picture while it was happening?

Lucia and I had discussion about it. And while we talked about what each of us had experienced, I realized the truth.

As she calls it, the Splitting of the Worlds. This event, mentioned by so many, awaited by millions, mentioned in religions and cultures around the world, had happened. That much I knew.

The souls divided between light and dark, awakened and asleep, aware and blind.

What I realized, was the reason I was taken out of the equation was two fold.

One, this is not my game, I am just here to raise the level of vibration of the planet, including the collective. I do not choose the outcome of the collective, or its individual members, the collective does that. Yet, I did not agree with this outcome. I wanted, yes, I really wanted, for all human beings to be lifted in their vibration for them to wake up enough that they make an educated choice. But that did not happen. An agreement was struck roughly a year ago, about what happens with those who did not wake up enough to make a choice. The agreement was that the "dark side" take them into their new reality. The reality where enslavement, pain, suffering and fear reign. Why? Because there is something in the game called "free will". The population was informed, and if an individual decides to ignore that information, it means they do not want to know. It means someone else can make a decision for them.

Secondly, the movement of those billions of souls into darkness would have been too painful for me to "experience" and survive in human form.

My heart ached. And I was surprised... I didn't think I would feel it. It is what the collective wants, after all. But my physical and subtle bodies feel the loss. Is it ego? Perhaps.

This sadness, deep sorrow, I felt it once before. A few weeks back I was in touch with the consciousness of the Lemurian collective. And that was what they expressed. At the time I understood that back in Earth history a splitting had happened and that the sadness the Lemurians felt was from leaving their brethren behind, all those humans that did not awaken. And, what we call the "middle Earth", is that Earth that moved on, into a higher vibration, occupying the same location, but a different space/time vibration.

And it has happened again.

What we are experiencing now, this week, the presence of fear, darkness, war, famine, suffering, and sleepers, is the "shadow" of the previous reality. The only way to remove it is to process fear and inject light and love into the planet, BIG TIME. Big events, such as the hurricane in NY, and the Elenin comet, that were "supposed" to make a mess of certain areas of the planet, have fizzled away to not much at all. The Fear Machine, is failing. The human spirit wins. In the next 3 generations, the sleepers and their masters will leave our planet as they live out their lives, and will not be able to return. What happens during those years, is up to us.

Now for the important information. How do you, as an individual, steer the Ship? Because you can, you see.

Learn the rules. And the first, and most important rule to learn, is that whatever happens on the planet, or in your life, cannot happen if you do not agree with it. And everything that happens, happens because you either agree with it, or do not cast a vote.

It is not up to me to choose whether those billions of sleepers are carried by us, forced to wake up, or left to their choice of wanting to stay asleep, not responsible for their actions, and let the "dark" take responsibility for them as they take them into a denser, darker Earth.

It is not up to me to decide how fast we remove the shadows and step fully into the new, higher vibrational, reality. Why wait 3 generations when we could have it in 3 months? We decide. We decide what we agree with and what we don't agree with.

We all cast our vote.

So here is what we do, here is how we cast our vote:

Choose a person, situation, location, personal topic, or worldwide event, that you do not agree with. Then, draw a red circle around it, and a line across it. Say the words, "I do not agree with this". Next, visualize what you would like to see, what you do agree with, and place a green tick next to it. It is very, very simple, and quick. So much so, that one might think it is not life changing, but it is. Try it. Try it with the big things, and the little things. Use it every day, and watch. What do you have to lose by trying it out? Nothing.

Agreement - our choice.

(handwritten: Each & all)

We don't walk in reality, we agree what reality is, we then have an experience in it.

And since we moved paradigms into the next "level", this fact has to be part of our basic education. At this new paradigm, it can no longer be an unconscious game.

Our agreement is personal, at a singular being level, and also collective at various levels. We, each, belong to different collectives. One is our immediate reality shared by others who live, or are, close to us at a physical level. Another could be ideological agreement, another could be national, and another could be species collective.

Even at a species level, we could form part of various collectives, the ones who added genetic material to our "evolution". Or, the collective where we spent most of our evolutionary path on. Many concentric circles (circles inside circles), which "forms" our reality.

What we experience, from a personal point of view, as well as social point of view, is what we agree with others is "real".

One might say, "well, I don't agree with the war in XYZ, so why is it still happening?" And that is an excellent question, you see, we just moved away from a reality where those who knew how the game worked, worked very hard to make a very specific type of game. One based on fear. And, everyone being born inside that particular game, was sucked into the fear. So, some will experience war, either in their own homes, or hear about it on the telly.

The blind following of the "masses" with regard war, murder, fear, paying for living on the planet, or whatever other ridiculous belief they hold to be necessary, creates the consensus of the human collective.

But there is something else that is happening and not being reported for fear, on the part of the powers that were, that it will annihilate them. And they are right, it will.

168

The awakening, and disagreement of the masses to being led where they don't want to go. There has NEVER in the presently accessible history of humankind, ever been so many awakening teachers, or individuals deeply wanting to advance in their own personal evolution. NEVER. There has never been such free access to information to anyone who wants it in the history of humankind. There has never been so much disagreement with having to pay to live on the planet, having to "accept" war, famine, or pestilence, or natural disasters. There has NEVER been so many individuals and groups actively focusing their attention and intention on natural events, human created disasters and other potentially catastrophic happenings, and STOPPING THEM.

The powers that were are trying harder than ever, trying to create disasters, using the Fear Machine to the max, but it is not working for them. Individuals are saying, "NO", and opening their hearts instead. The tremendous movement to create a society that only cares about personal survival above all else has collapsed. More and more individuals will put themselves on the firing line to give a chance those who are cannot help themselves yet, to give them enough time to wake up. Enough time to see that they are not victims after all, that they are in fact powerful eternal beings who can take charge of their own experience on the planet.

One might think, well, if we are influencing others, by casting our agreement or disagreement vote, are we not dictating what happens to them? And the answer is "no". You see, they are as powerful as you are. And guess what, they will move into a reality where your agreement doesn't win, but theirs does. And you move into one where your agreement rules. Multiple timelines. Compatible vibrations congregate in compatible realities. There are not "right" or "wrong" realities, there are just different ones. Eventually this will mean that we move into a new form of experience, one based on a type of cosmic dance where we are the choreographers. At the moment, of course, there are those who are fighting tooth and nail to stop us from casting our vote. And... from teaching the masses that each person, each man, woman and child is an EXTREMELY POWERFUL INDIVIDUAL. An individual that, when he or she epts this fact, process all his or her fear around it, and others being just as powerful, will be able to move through d space in all directions, and no longer create an scious, or fear reality based on someone else' vision of what the life should be like.

I agree with an empowered collective, where each and every individual has the power to CONSCIOUSLY create his or her reality. It's a big ability which comes with a huge response-ability. Are you ready for it? If that question gave you a twinge of fear, go and process that fear right away :).

Choose a person, situation, location, personal topic, or worldwide event, that you do not agree with. Then, draw a red circle around it, and a line across it. Say the words, "I do not agree with this". Next, visualize what you would like to see, what you do agree with, and place a green tick next to it. It is very, very simple, and quick. So much so, that one might think it is not life changing, but it is. Try it. Try it with the big things, and the little things. Use it every day, and watch. Inelia Benz

The United States of America - Call to Action

I was brought up to "hate" the United State of America. "They" had, after all, paid for the brutal and bloody right wing military coup that destroyed my family and killed many of our friends in Chile when I was 7 years old.

As I grew up in the UK, more "hate" was taught about the USA in the local culture, as well as validated by most of the refugees we got to know from different parts of the world. Yes, the USA had a lot to answer for.

But I was guided to come here, to this land, and in particular to California. I have been given ample opportunity to "run away" from this land, go somewhere safer, more balanced, less chaotic. In my stay, I decided to observe and study the collective energy, the culture and the people in the USA.

The first thing that became clear, was that it was not "Americans" who had destroyed Chile, but a small group of individuals in the "powers that were" category. Most Americans didn't even know where Chile was or that it existed.

Secondly, and this is one of the important points, the American people are among the most oppressed people in the world. They are drugged via drinking water, food, chemtrails, vibrational technology (HARPP - and probably others), "medical drugs", alcohol, duped via television, radio and has one of the worst, most severe programming, educational systems in the world. Their "health system" is designed to make and keep people sick, and is not interested in cures (that would destroy the pharmaceutical industry).

I had to ask myself, why are trillions of dollars being invested in suppressing this nation? What is so important, what is so unique about the USA that all this has to be done to destroy their basic human freedom, their potential, their innate powers?

Well, the USA was the birthing ground of the New Age Movement. Of the Internet. Of personal computers, the "green movement", and much more.

There is something about this land that brings into the 3D things that completely alter the path of the entire world.

It could be that from it's inception, the USA was meant to be where people from around the world could come and be free, be themselves, achieve their dreams. The first place where the shackles of enslavement to monarchy were first seeded into the collective.

Yes, the journey of freedom has been hijacked over and over again, even creating a force of enslavement identified with America to create hate around the world for this land and its people. But something remains. Something always stays.

From October and November 2011 people walk the streets, demand change. Not only in the USA, but all over the world.

In the USA, the government has systematically been taking away the rights of individuals, and it wouldn't surprise me at all if they declare martial law. In effect, make this place a military dictatorship... or at least try.

I have seen individuals around the world laugh at the American spirit of "not going to happen here, I pack a gun". But I feel sure that if "the powers that were" try to destroy this nation, not only Americans, but people from around the world, will stand shoulder to shoulder in order to support what is coming. And what is coming?

Another birth that will spread around the world. The nature of this new wave is one of "mass awakening". Yup, an awakening that will affect even the most sleepy of sleepers. Maybe not awake to the full awareness of our new paradigm, but at least make them compatible to live in it and not get freaked out.

A few months ago I was asked to increase my meditation time (for me personally, this is a time in an altered state where energies can flow into the planet) from half an hour to four hours a day. I am still working on it, my body is not trained in this and it needs time to adjust. It is about anchoring the higher vibrations into our place of residence, and into all the collectives we belong to.

What can we all do to support and help in this birthing process?

Use the tools I have provided to process your personal fear, then move onto your national fear, and world fear; to make your personal vibration higher, to visualize an unpolluted world collective, to finally release the baggage that holds you down. Do the ascension course!

Use all the other tools and modalities you have found in your travels that increase and empower each and every person on the planet. Remember, we are the ones we were waiting for. We are the "angels" and "saviors" so many generations have prayed for... we enlighten and save ourselves. And... send light, pure, unconditional love, to the United States of America (process any charge that comes up when you read that last sentence).

Fear events have been planned in America, and probably other nations too. Lets disagree with these plans and agree with our clean collective and planet instead :D

At this precise moment, I am staying in the US of A, for as long as necessary.

What it means to be HUMAN

What does it mean to be human?

Often individuals will say things such as "I'm only human", or "it's human nature to do that". Mostly about negative actions. There is one adjective which is used positively, and that is "humane".

There is so much conflicting information about where we came from. Some say we were created by a god, others that we evolved from monkeys. Others that we are a mishmash of alien and Earthly DNA material.

And, our nature, what it means to be one of us, a human being, is riddled with cultural, religious and social programming.

I would like to share with you what I understand being human means. Also, give you a viewpoint as an observer which is one that is probably different to most.

First of all, I see a human being as a symbiotic relationship between a "person" and his or her "body". The body has its own intelligence, as well as its own evolutionary path. The body is the most evolved material manifestation of Divine Consciousness.

It is amazing how many feelings, emotions, thoughts, and states of "being" are the body's alone. Including the fear of loss. Or bad moods due to low blood sugar. Or wanting to be with other humans.

One little secret about the human body that "the powers that were" do not want you to know, is that it is the most advanced artifact in existence on the planet (and probably lots of planets). And when we unite with other "bodies" to meditate, or do energy work, we can shift mountains. We were disabled vibrationally and genetically to stop us from knowing and accessing these abilities thousands of years ago and anyone who reactivated them was burned at the stake.

The second little secret, is that all we need to do to activate the abilities and skills of the human body, is to raise the level of its and our vibration. And all we need to do in order to achieve that is to detox both physically and vibrationally. Physically by what we eat and drink, and vibrationally by processing our fear.

The person, or "soul", is the most evolved manifestation of Divine Consciousness as Other.

Of course, when we look around, we see many individuals, including ourselves at times, who do not seem very evolved at all.

This is where the veil of forgetfulness comes in. In order to play a game at the level of a singularity in this planet, we choose to forget our divinity and omnipotence.

All sentient singular consciousness constructs, whether human or other species, have by default forgotten what it is to be Source. There are different levels of forgetfulness as we become a singularity, but there is always some level of it.

The reason for being on the planet also varies to each person here. Many just want to stay alive for the sake of living, no matter what that life brings. Others want to "evolve" into something else. Someone more aware perhaps. Ascend into a state of life which is "higher vibrational" than what we have now.

Personally speaking, none of the above apply. I am here to do a job, which is to raise the vibrational level of the planet, and everything else is irrelevant. As far as I can see, I did not have a "soul" life before this one, nor will I have one after this one is over.

At the same time, I have a 45 year history on the planet. Most of those years were spent in anonymity. I also have four children, two siblings, and many relatives and friends. Basically, I have lived a "human" life.

Most of the time I have spent as a human being has been a complete puzzle to me. A very unpleasant and unwanted experience at an experiential level. However, what I "feel" about existing as a singularity although irrelevant at a "personal" level, has proven to be very helpful in the job I came here to do.

What it means to be human at this particular planetary time/space has never been more exciting. On the one hand we have millions of individuals who have incarnated here from other planets and dimensions, for the past few decades in order to raise the vibrational level of the Human Collective. On the other, we have a whole group of sentient beings who have lived off the energy generated by humans for thousands of years, and as we raise the vibrational level of the planet, the entire planet is becoming toxic to them and they are doing everything they can to keep their "cattle" asleep.

War, starvation, pestilence (and the fear they bring) are completely unnatural to the human species. This is why so many soldiers come back "broken people" from war zones. We are not built to live in low vibrational environments.

Death is only experienced at a "body" level. The body dies and disintegrates. Its "intelligence" moves on and forms another material body.

The "being/soul/person" can move in and out of his or her body, can even switch bodies and can reincarnate into a new body once it loses the last one.

So why do these other "negative" entities want us to stay asleep? Why do they use us as their personal batteries?

The reason is that our bodies are the most amazing artifacts in existence. We can not only create things in the material world, but we can generate enormous amounts of energy/vibration in our physical and subtle bodies. As these negative beings are not native to our "matrix", they need to feed on something in order to exist. And that something is our fear and other low vibrational emotions.

As I walk through the city, I am in awe at what we create. From the smallest thing, a light-bulb for example, to the most amazing buildings and all the technology that is used to keep it functioning. Even something like a car, it is amazing to behold.

We, as a species, have created technology which compensates for all those abilities that were taken from us thousands of years ago. Even though most of us can't easily telepathically communicate with another individual or group at a distance, phones were created to accomplish this. Even though most of us can't tap into the collective databank for information and skills, we created the Internet where we can do just that. Even though most of us can't teleport across the world in an instant, we have managed to create very fast forms of transport.

There is still much to learn, from my perspective, of what it means to be human. However, one thing I do know, we are here at this junction of time/space, all of us to be just that: HUMAN.

Feeling Lonely

December often brings about a sense of loneliness, melancholy, loss and lack to adults, and some children too.

These feelings are perpetuated by the media and by society.

We also get feelings of wanting to share, to give, and we feel compassion for those who are not as "lucky" as we are throughout the "holiday season".

The winter/summer solstice (depending on where in the world you are located), is charged with Gaia's dormant and potential energy in the North, and plentitude in the South.

How to respond?

Throughout my life I have had Decembers filled with joy and sharing, and others where our family did not have food to eat. I too have felt the loss of not being able to share this season with those who have left the body, or who have disappeared into the world, never to be heard of again.

If we were in touch with our local geographical energy, if the season had not been hijacked by the media, commercialism and religion, this would be simply a time to celebrate the season's gifts. Or not.

Feeling lonely is an act of separation. The sadness we feel at not having someone by our side is something that is natural for the human species. Our bodies need human contact, and our being does too.

Our being. Our essence of singular expression of consciousness as a member of the human race, is cut off from other humans, as well as from Source. This is NOT a natural state for us. As we raise our vibrational level, we begin to feel less and less lonely, less cut off, less dependant on those tiny moments of human contact and more able to embrace the entire Human Collective.

One of the tools used to separate us is Language. Verbal and written language is not natural to the human species. These words that you are reading right now, are not our natural form of communication. They separate us, they separate energy and ideas. But, for now, it is the only way to communicate complex ideas through the mediums we have access to.

However, we can move past this form of separation. Twenty minutes a day, minimum, of silent meditation is a very, very powerful tool that moves us past "language" and into the form of communication which is natural to us. Direct connection with source and others of our, and related, species.

"But I can't meditate!" some of us might shout. Not so. If this comes up, do the firewall exercise on the Tools section of the site. And the Fear Processing Exercise too. Most of the time, the inability to silence our minds comes from fear alone.

And, as Yoda from Star Wars said: "No! Try not. Do. Or do not. There is no try."

At the end of the day it is very simple. Do we want to move past this paradigm of separation, or don't we? There is no right or wrong answer, they are both as valuable and honorable paths of evolution as each other. They are simply no longer compatible.

So, when we feel lonely, we look at it. We don't judge. We don't analyze it, we don't try to suppress it or make it go away. We look, and we welcome the emotion, we let it grow, we feel gratitude, we send it love and light and embrace it back into Oneness... we free it.

2012 Here we go!

I have been asked various times what I see for us in 2012. And as we move into this new year, there is a definite charge in the air about what will happen on the planet.

One thing is for certain, the "powers that were" have really stepped up the Fear Machine and we will probably see some drama coming up.

There are two aspects to the New Year. One is the end of the old, and the other is the start of the new. Even though not quite aligned with the solstice, and natural Earth rhythms, the calendar new year is charged simply by being accepted and used by millions of individuals to have closure on certain things, and place intentions of new things to come.

Indeed, this is a perfect opportunity for all of us to ride this energy and enter new cycles. What is your greatest dream? Daydream it as being a reality in 2012.

With regard 2012...

I sat with this famous year for a while now, and I am optimistic. I see our role here on the planet as being successful. That the transition to the new agreed reality (which is what a new paradigm is), be smooth and effective.

We could have the transition overnight, yes. But that would make sure that millions of individuals don't make the jump. By going slowly, and working on our own vibrational level, and working on the collective vibrational level, we can be sure to have many more individuals on board the new reality.

The cycles at a galactic scale are so large, the celestial bodies involved are so huge, that thinking everything will align in one hour of one day of one month in one year, is not logical or possible. Unless, of course, enough human beings are convinced that this is going to happen. Then, the agreed reality manifests for all of us.

But at a galactic and planetary level, the shift has been happening for decades. And during it, the "powers that were" have been busy trying to stop it. They have a huge amount of time and wealth invested in keeping an enslaved reality, and for the majority of their brethren to move to an empowered paradigm fills them with fear.

But that does not concern us. What choice they make is theirs alone. Their path, the path of power over others, of victim/aggressor patterns, the path of learning through suffering, of pain and shock, that path is as honorable as the path we choose to move into. But the two are simply incompatible now. We cannot co-exist in the same planet and have both running side by side. The shift happened earlier this year at an energetic level, now it is manifesting at a physical level.

How do we move out of their reality? All we have to do is say "NO" to their actions and reality, stand in our power, raise our vibrational level and infuse our planet with light and love.

There is a window during this year that might be forced open by the other side. If this is the case, it is really not something I am that concerned about. The window is called "Three days of darkness". During this period the population will be strictly split between those who are still based on fear, and those who are heart centered.

In my viewing, if this window opens, it will indeed provide an opportunity for the shift we experienced in August to manifest at a collective human level in a rather brutal fashion. However, billions of individuals have incarnated on the planet at this time, and for decades now (including you), in order to make the shift a joyful, smooth, and empowering one for as many people as possible.

But at the end of the day, all that happens on the planet, at a global and local level, is a collective decision. The Hundredth Monkey effect. The consensus. And I honor that completely. This includes the manifestation of "the powers that were" and all their wars and atrocities.

I myself am nothing but a manifestation of a collective call for help in raising the vibrational level of the planet. If I was manifested as a human being to carry out this role, then nothing can stop us as a species in manifesting the most amazing and awe inspiring reality where we can continue to play and "experience" life as a species.

I am indeed very, very optimistic. This next year will see an enormous awakening, a growth of individual power and ability, and a return to our native abilities.

We humans are about communication. We are about Divine Unconditional Love, we are Source manifested. What we can do as we unite is unimaginably great. Gaia already made the jump in 2010... now she is simply waiting for each of us to do the same.

Process the fear around 2012. Raise your vibration. Learn about your nature, bodies and power. Infuse your body, surroundings, and the human species with light and love!

Acceleration of Ascension - 2012

The past two years have seen quantum jumps in the collective expansion of awareness (ascension), and the awakening of the masses.

Words such as Karma, chakras, manifestation, and all sorts of other words that are normally the vocabulary of those who are in a path of self discovery, are now used in society at large.

This year it accelerates a thousand fold.

A few days ago, I was chatting with three women I am collaborating with in a journey beyond mysticism, and after the call, I had the "instructions" from Source that it was time to stop walking on the planet with cotton gloves at an energy level, and to "let it all out", become unlimited. I looked at the instructions and decided to go ahead and apply them. Of course, the instructions are not just for me, but for everyone who is reading this article too.

Yet it was not quite clear to me what it is that we need to do to allow this to happen. How do we allow all of our "Self" to come through? All the energy which makes up our singularity to shine through? How do we shatter all the cotton gloves, all the stoppers and limits and just shine?

If you have had any contact with me, whether through this website, or personally at a meet and greet, or other situation, you will know that I don't "use my own energy" for the work I do here. I step out of the way, and allow source to come through. So, this particular set of instructions was rather puzzling.

I sat with it. And I saw something.

During my life, I would often be visited by a "future me". She would step out of a portal, and into the "past", where I was having some sort of difficulty. There was something extremely pure and light about my future self. She was the type of person I would feel reverence toward. Not in a patriarchal way, but of pure unconditional love and trust. The type of reverence one feels for a sunset, or a huge, beautiful tree.

Her advice and guidance was always spot on. And sometimes, she would simply be there.

Every now and then, I will tap into the future and visit her. I will do a comparison of me now and me in the future, and always felt there was a long ways to go.

And as I started to allow "my energy" to expand, following the instructions from Source, I saw all the "differences" between myself now and that future self.

I realized that there were still "importances" that had built up in this singularity called Inelia. I looked at them very closely. They were resistances to becoming all that I can be in human form. They were solid. They had to do with keeping the physical body solid, and also with keeping reality as solid as I could. It was rather funny for me because I have spent most of my life trying to build up a sense of singular solidity in order to live on the planet. And now... that need is gone. There is no reason to stay small, singular or solid.

And it struck me that in order for our light, our higher self, to come through 100 percent into this singular self (now it can because we are in our new paradigm), we really do have to dissolve every attachment we might have to our solid, singular, important selves.

Fear is the most solid of all energies. And importance is based on the fear of loss. If something is important, it is important because we don't want to lose it.

Simple.

So, to really trigger those things that are holding us back, we can ask: What's important to me?

And then process the fear behind losing that thing/person/situation/dream.

Ah! Then comes the fear of, "I don't want to lose that as an important aspect in my life."

You see, we have been taught that it is the important things that give meaning to life and if we lose all the importance from our lives, then there will be no reason to live.

Yet, it is just those "importances", no matter how important, which are the "attachments" that keep us stuck in a low vibrational level existence.

The illusion of having to "move" to another dimension to have this higher vibrational experience is just that, an illusion. We can exist in this planet, now, as higher vibrational beings. And yes, we will still be seen by those who don't shift gears with us.

Are you ready to step into this newly available level of experienced existence on this planet? I sure am.

I am a victim!! - A link in the Chain of Enslavement

The victim/aggressor cycle is another link in the chain of enslavement.

It is so severe that most individuals are completely unaware that their life is a constant cycle of either being a victim or being an aggressor.

When being a victim they have, of course, someone or something to blame for what happened to them. And when being an aggressor, they too have blame to give or receive.

Attached to the cycle, is the energy of "savior".

From before birth, to my mid 30s, I experienced a lot of physical, emotional and psychological aggression. It was highly orchestrated and persistent. The aim was to either enslave me as an aggressor or victim, or take me out. It didn't work in that I never identified with either role. It was simply experience.

There were a few times when the pain was so excruciating that I decided to die. I learned two things, one was that my higher self was not letting me die, and the other was that all I had to do was to stop the aggressor by either removing myself from the situation, or removing them from my environment. What was not an option, was to engage them in their game by either feeling victimized, allowing the aggression to continue or becoming an aggressor myself.

It is encoded in the victim/aggressor cycle roles to look for and engage others in the victim/aggressor game, either consciously or unconsciously. But it is just that. A game. No judgment.

It is very important, as we move into the new paradigm, to realize that we are in charge of our experience on the planet and beyond. That we decide what we agree or not agree with. And so are the "victims" and "aggressors".

186

Many individuals, when they read that, think, "what about the innocent child who was raped and murdered? He/she did not choose that!"

There are many layers to that thought. One is that if we think that, we are stating that the child is not a complete, divine, infinite entity who chose to come to Earth to have that experience with the perpetrator of killing and raping. We declare ourselves superior to that child's singularity construct.

Another is that by sending the energy of "victim" to that child (alive or dead), we are strengthening the cage of "victim-hood" in that entity's life, making it harder for him or her to get out of the cycle. The same thing applies to the perpetrator.

By thinking of someone as a victim or aggressor we lower their vibration. The chains of enslavement are made of "low vibration".

Yet another layer is that, yes, at a certain level we all chose to come in and forget we were unlimited and divine. And also agreed to enter a planet that had a very powerful victim/aggressor structure in place. Just watch a history show on TV and you will see how established in time, and prevalent, this program is on the planet. This strengthened our point of agreement in "experiencing" these type of situations either as participants or "observers".

Does that mean that if we see people fully engaged in the cycle we do nothing about it? No. They came into our awareness because they want out of the cycle now. They are ready to leave. Both the victim and aggressor are "done".

So, we disagree with this particular cycle. It has no place in the new paradigm. Anyone who wants to continue in that cycle, can go elsewhere.

We process all the strong emotions that come up when we see individuals in this cycle, and, once those emotions are fully integrated back into Oneness, we state our vote:

"victim/aggressor person, you are an infinite, divine being, you can, and are able to, move into a new empowered experience and break free from the victim/aggressor cycle. And if you choose to not move past this cycle, you are not welcome to experience it in my reality as I do not agree with it."

And then, move out of the way, and allow light and love to infuse that person/s.

If it is easier for us to say "you are a divine being" to the victim than the aggressor, and so much easier to say "you are not allowed to have that experience here" to the aggressor than the victim, then we need to process our own "judgment" and attached "savior" energy we might have on the planet.

We can't have saviors if we don't have victims and aggressors :)

Another layer is that this cycle is being used by the "powers that were" to keep the masses enslaved. Making it hard for ordinary folk to move past their own victim self or aggressor self.

The "elite" create conflict, wars, "terrorists", gestapo like violations at airports and other locations, and they are also very much involved in recruiting servants via the use of physical torture to force individuals to commit acts of the ultimate aggression, which is to take a life (either their own or someone else's).

By perpetuating the cycle, and making it "normal", they strengthen an environment filled with drama and fear, which are very tasty to low vibrational entities.

So, we look at the elite as a group, or focus on an individual and say:

"[President Obama] you are an infinite, divine being, you can, and are able to, move into a new empowered experience and break free from the victim/aggressor cycle. And if you choose to not move past this cycle, you are not welcome to experience it in my reality as I do not agree with it."

And then we step out of the way and allow Source to use us to send light and love to that group or person.

Interesting question, when you read the President's name there, did you see him as a victim or an aggressor? When someone is deep in the cycle, it is hard to see where one role ends and the other begins.

Call to Action - Financial Construct

The steps below will have a real effect in our personal lives, as well as on the planet. It is energy work. And when thousands of individuals join in one intention, real, tangible, shifts occur. This article is going to over 12,000 people, many of whom will forward it to their loved ones, friends or mailing lists. The website where it is posted has so far had nearly 2 million page loads and nearly one million unique visitors. I ask you to become part of this healing process, and do the steps, share the article using email or your personal networks, and thus inform others about their innate, divine power of co-creation.

We are presently going through an enormous Human Collective transformation. As each of us raises our personal vibration, we raise the vibrational level of the entire collective. When this happens, people wake up. Lies get exposed, and corrupt systems break.

This presents us an opportunity to transform our systems.

There is no doubt about it. Our financial system is changing.

- Call to Action step One:
  Process your fear around "financial collapse". Use the Fear Processing Exercise. The full text for the exercise is under Tools at the ascension101.com site. Process fear of losing what you have, your job, your home, your wealth, starvation, seeing your loved ones die, war, and any other fears that might come up when you think that the financial system will cease to exist in the near future. Process "helplessness".

We tend to externalize the reasons why our present financial system is corrupt, and basically designed to enslave. After all, we had nothing to do with its creation. We were born into it. And that was true up until a few years ago, when we started to wake up as a species and now, we can do something about it.

Now, we can transform it.

Money is nothing but the objectifying of a natural and free flowing energy of support and abundance that has been in the planet since time begun. We originally created money in a way that would allow for energy exchange in a precise and helpful manner. By creating energy exchange, we stay out of energy debt. Energy debt is not a good thing when we have it while living in a physical reality. You can inform yourself about energy exchange, and debt by reading the article Debt - A Link in the Chain of Enslavement.

By reconnecting with the true energy behind money, and healing our relationship with it, we can not only transform our personal support systems, but as awakened individuals we can also transform the planetary financial system to something which is pure, clear, clean, impeccable, and supportive of every sentient, and non sentient, being on the planet. This second part of it, the fact that as we heal our own relationship with money, we also heal and transform our system, has not been picked up by many. Which is why I feel it necessary to underline again here. And that is why I am asking you to take the second, and most important, step in this collective intention project.

- Call to Action step Two:
  Carry out the Reconnecting with the Spirit of Money Exercise for the next seven days. If you can, and feel inspired to, for the whole month of March. But, even if you do it once, that will help. You can find it under the Tools menu tab at ascension101.com.

Two simple steps. Let's do them! :D

Thank you for your support and your continuing work to co-create an empowered human reality!

WE ARE ALL GOING TO DIE!! - Not.

Whenever individuals would ask me about December 2012, that was my favorite response. I would say, "we are all going to die. Every person on the planet is going to die. But not at the same time. Some die today, now, as we speak, some in an hour, some tomorrow, some in a week, some in a year, some in 90 years... and so on. But every person on the planet is going to die. Just not at the same time."

And that was not quite accurate, because it was really our physical bodies that were dying at various times from the present time to decades in the future. Not ourselves.

However, when I say that sentence now, the "we are all going to die" sentence, it no longer resonates. It appears that our physical bodies are the ones making the shift in physical existence from the 3D, where in the past it needed to die in order to be recreated, or shift awareness to a more subtle dimension, to a reality where we can help it become more subtle without dying.

A lot of people talk about moving into the 4th or 5th dimension during this transition. What that means is basically that our physical experience is presently transitioning from a seemingly very solid, "unchangeable", stuck physical experience, to a more fluid, pliable, empowered experience. As our physical bodies are reflective of our personal experience here, the "soul's" or "spirit's" experience, and our physical reality becomes more fluid, so are our physical bodies becoming more fluid.

What does this mean? It means that we have the chance to see if indeed we will be able to keep our physical bodies in a more fluid and pliable form. Allowing the body to transition between dimensions without having to disintegrate and reform itself via birth and death.

So, basically "we" never die. Ever. Our bodies have been dying in linear time since linear time began. And, it appears that soon that will no longer be necessary either. We will be able to make our bodies as subtle or solid as we want, while experiencing a physical reality existence.

How do we do it? We raise our personal vibrational level, the higher it is, the more subtle, empowered and pliable our physical bodies, and environment, becomes. Do the Fear Processing Exercise and the other Tools in the vibrational Tools section of the site, do the Ascension101 Course, read the articles, listen to the interviews, watch the videos. All these are here to provide forms, ways, and information that will facilitate your personal transition into empowerment. If they don't resonate with you, keep searching! There are thousands of pages out there, and books, that have tools that raise your personal vibrational level. Or create your own. But don't wait! Start raising your vibration today.

Having SEX in the 5th Dimension - whoa!

When I released the WE ARE ALL GOING TO DIE -Not. article, someone asked, "what about doing sex in fifth density ? ... we would be immortals ?"

An absolutely fantastic question.

Sex is not necessary to start a new physical body. Cloning involves the cell of only one animal, not two. At a physical level, what sex does is create a more genetically varied body than we can achieve by cloning. Life in this planet doesn't all begin through sex. There are various forms of physical reproduction methods, many of which only involves one being, not two.

But there is much more to sex than producing bodies.

Yes, for Humans sex is used at a physical level to create new physical bodies. Creating new physical bodies is not redundant in more subtle dimensions. Although we will be able to make our physical bodies more subtle, and also be able to keep them forever if that is our choice, there is also a choice for new bodies that can be "housed" by beings who have not had an experience in that reality yet, or want a new body for other reasons.

However, there is more to sex than just making physical bodies. At least as far as Human Beings are concerned. The energy used and gathered during intercourse has been used as a tool for enlightenment in various cultures. India being the best known to us, via the use of Tantric Sex.

The energy released during orgasm has also been used in various cultures to manifest and create particular outcomes in our environment. The best known method in the West is that used by Magik. This is the method where the person, or two people, release their creative intention at the moment of orgasm through thought and emotion.

Both Tantric Sex and Sex Magik can be practiced with another person or by oneself.

Joining with another

Anyone who has had an active sex life will know that not all sexual sessions, nor orgasms, were created equal.

First of all, sometimes our physical bodies will be attracted to another "body", even though the person inside that body might be repulsive to us. This is often due to the other body being biologically very compatible. And the reverse also happens. Our "soul", or "spirit" is totally in love with, and wants to be with the other person, but our bodies will be repulsed by their body.

And this is more like what sex in subtler dimensions is like. It is about energy compatibility and "joining" than physical compatibility for reproduction purposes.

Even now, think of your partner, if you have one, or a partner that you are considering. Now look into that "joining" and ask yourself, "do I really want to merge all my energy and being with this person? Or do I just want to join my body with theirs?"

You will get surprising results.

One of the main aspects of sex is physical, mental, energetic, and emotional pleasure. Pleasure, or bliss, is also the energy of enlightenment, which ultimately is about become One with Universal Divine Consciousness.

For more about sexual energy, read this article:

Carnal Pleasures and the Ascension Process - Sex and Enlightenment

For a deep exploration of this important subject, and manifesting exercises get:

Sex, Love and Soulmates in the New Paradigm

So, will we be "doing sex in fifth density?" If we want to, yes.

We are leaving POO behind!

My friend and colleague Mary MacNab, with whom we are presenting Beyond Mysticism together, recently bought our fundraiser Talks Rules of Engagement - Entering the New Paradigm, and wrote me back with the funniest observation which I just had to share with you, simply because it is so funny and true!!

She mentioned this particular section of the talks:

"Power", even the word "power" has a lot of emotional and ego charge in it, the word as well as the concept.

The entire paradigm we are moving out of is based on Power Over Others. The society we carved out is based on power over others and power over environment. Concepts which were seen as advanced and necessary for the good of humanity. Which is why so many individuals react in fear or negativity when they hear the word "power". The concept is that power has a hierarchical format, that there are people out there who are either less, or more, powerful than we are. Although we might think this structure is only used by "dark workers", it is not. It is also used by "light workers". For example, in order to be of service to others, a person needs individuals, or situations, around them that either have sleeping individuals (who they can help awaken), or victims (who they can help out). The lightworker, is then in a position of having power over others who are not powerful enough to help themselves. When someone is in the path of Bodhisattva, they need people and environments that are suffering, so they can go in and help out. It is a good path to eventually leave the cycle of power over others, but it is the path, not the destination.

And she wrote to me saying...

"The reality we are leaving is based on **P**ower **O**ver **O**thers....

it's based on POO!"

I found the whole thing extremely funny. And particularly because there is so much truth in it!

196

It is so cool. Sometimes in the seriousness of it all, we forget to laugh, yeah out loud!

And that's it. If it makes you laugh, it was worth sharing :)

Hugs

Inelia

P.S. I can't wait to see how our volunteer translators manage to translate this article!

Your Greatest Manifestation Tool

Manifestation happens all the time. It is not something that we "start to do" when we become conscious of it, or our awareness expands. We literally do it all the time. Even "time" is an act of manifestation.

Now, in the paradigm we are leaving behind, we decided to have set, solid, agreed parameters manifested and locked into place, so we could have a very particular type of experience.

The new paradigm we are partly into has us consciously manifesting what we want to experience.

We do this by first deciding what it is that we want to manifest in our lives, and then using various tools to consciously do it.

The biggest and most essential of these tools is DAYDREAMING.

Everything that you see on the planet was once daydreamed. It then became "reality". And I am not just talking about technology, art, buildings, religions, ideologies, countries... and other "human" constructed objects and ideas. Even the "physical" ground you walk on, the trees, flowers, animals, the planet, the entire universe, was once (and still is) but a dream dreamed in conscious awareness.

So, what exactly is a daydream? Wikipedia has a lovely sentence to describe it:

"Daydreaming is a short-term detachment from one's immediate surroundings, during which a person's contact with reality is blurred and partially substituted by a visionary fantasy, especially one of happy, pleasant thoughts, hopes or ambitions, imagined as coming to pass, and experienced while awake."

I fully suggest you read the rest of that wiki daydreaming article, it will amaze you as to the effort extended to eliminating this particular skill from our world.

Daydreaming is often categorized as "fantasizing". The main difference between the two words is that a daydream has the "possibility" of becoming real, while the word "fantasy" has been designated the energy of "not real".

As a manifestation tool, this is how we use it:

1. Decide one thing you would like to manifest. It could be a better connection with your guides, a new "something" in your life, a creative project, a trip, meeting ETs, your shopping list, or even sitting in front of something blank and "creating" it in the daydream... anything at all. But only one thing for now.

2. Sit somewhere comfortable. Lying down is not a good idea, or you will likely fall asleep.

3. Your eyes can stay open or closed. This is a personal preference. If open, you will find your eyes moving toward the top right or top left of your vision field. And moving the eyes there, whether open or closed, can help start you daydreaming.

4. Now, "imagine" the scene, like you are watching a "memory" of something which has already happened. You are the director, so allow yourself to create whatever you like.

5. If you have the problem of not being able to "visualize", then use a pen and paper, and write it down, or a recorder and speak it out loud. Looking at a picture, like the rose in this article, and imagine touching it, smelling it, and looking at it in "real life", also helps. So, get a picture of what you want to manifest and use it in your daydream.

6. Any fears, or "this will never happen" type thoughts, are welcomed and embraced in light and love. The reason is that it is just a daydream, no need to get overly worried about it.

7. The next stage is to "feel" it. Feel what it is to be there, do that, create that, experience that. A millisecond of "feeling" energy will do. But sustain it for as long as possible.

8. Now release the daydream as something that has been lived already.

Enjoy!!

P.S. for guided daydream exercises for your personal ascension do the Ascension101 Course.

Call to Action - IT'S TIME!

For the past two weeks every time I sit down to meditate, daydream, doing, or not doing, a strong message comes through. The words are:

IT'S TIME

Just that.

I have sat with it, and followed the energy. I find a wealth of information when I do that. One of them is that the major conjunction and physical expression of the shift starts this June Solstice. The energetic shift occurred last summer (2011). If you are in any way sensitive, you will have felt time and vibration accelerating to incredible velocity the past month. It will continue to escalate, peaking during this June Solstice, and manifesting for the next two months at a physical level, and finally settling throughout the rest of the year.

This might manifest in our lives as a huge acceleration of personal awareness. Our experience of moving out of Linear Time. I also get that more and more "extra terrestrial" contact will happen both at a personal level as well as "media events" level. We are simply graduating as a species. But I have the sneaky suspicion that each person will get slightly different information that corresponds to their particular mission on the planet. So, tap into it and follow the energy of the message to Source.

What can we do to facilitate this transition in our own lives? Four things:

1) Meditate - spend at least 60 minutes per day in silent meditation. Ideally at once, but if not then spread it out during the day.

2) Daydream - again, at least 60 minutes per day daydreaming. This can be done while busy in other activities, make sure not to be using heavy machines at the time though!

3) Doing Nothing - This is a state of silent contemplation, just BEING for one hour. And it is the most important as we come up to the June Solstice. Do nothing, and Be for an hour.

4) Process your Fear - Key aspect of raising your personal, and our global, vibrational level and awareness.

Before you think this is too much time, remember that it takes at least 2 hours to watch a movie. However, if you manage a few minutes per day of each, that's better than not doing them at all :)

Following the Solstice, continue these exercises as much as you can, even if one per day, until next January.

As our Global Action, I will be facilitating a day long silent meditation on **July 2nd from 9am to 6pm Pacific Standard Time** with many other individuals who are traveling to join us in person. The intention is for hundreds of thousands of other individuals from around the world to join us in Silence that day. Ideally for the full day, but if you can only manage one hour then that's cool too!

Take the day off work, or book a hotel, hang out at a mountain or forest, or simply let your loved ones know that you are partaking in a global event of silence that day.

If you are a seasoned meditator, then spending the day meditating would be awesome. If not, simply staying silent will be fantastic. Of course we will be taking short breaks to eat, go to the bathroom and drink pure water :)

So, for your calendar: *** JULY 2ND 2012 SILENT MEDITATION VERY IMPORTANT ***

Contracts - How to make sure they don't hold you back...

Have you made any contracts lately? In this lifetime? In previous lifetimes?

By "contract" I mean any piece of paper, notebook page, or electronic note where you have written what you want out of life. Where you make an agreement on what you want to manifest.

It could also come in the form of many manifestation exercises, such as collages, photo collections or drawings.

When we make contracts, they might feel very expansive. After all, we make them to improve our lives. Indeed they do work, most of what is in those contracts comes to pass.

Some contracts are contracts we have made with others, such as marriages, mortgages, work contracts, rent contracts, lease contracts, loans, and more.

However, if we take a step back, and look for limiting language, situations, and beliefs within these contracts, and process them, we can really expand our lives.

Even if they are contracts that are with third parties and we feel they are "not fair", or no longer suitable, or we were forced to take the best we could, or we are unhappy with them now, we can really shift things in real life simply by sitting with these third party contracts and allowing all our negative emotions to exist, expand, and be infused with light and love, thus liberating them back into Oneness.

If you haven't already, do take a look at how to cleanse negative energies in this youtube video:

http://www.youtube.com/watch?v=2GozVABN1xI

Now, the contracts we have made ourselves, we can go back and either wipe clean, or review and rewrite, and sign again.

This is a list with possible limitations:

1) A love relationship manifestation contract that **has a named partner**, whether a spouse, boy/girlfriend or the person of our dreams. This is a biggie. Energetically speaking this is one of the worst contracts we can write. Even if we really, really want our relationship with one particular person to manifest, or improve, by naming them, we limit the Universe from helping us manifest our greatest possible outcome. So, if you have one of these, erase the person's name, remove the photo, throw away their personal possession (in case of using magik), and replace their name, or object, with a description of the ideal partner. Even if you describe them, make sure that you do not emotionally "wish" it was them, but simply concentrate on the happy and satisfied feeling you get when imagining yourself with that perfect person.

2) Any contract that specifies **things you will do in order to get something else**. Especially if those things are difficult to do, or involve other individuals to help you accomplish it. For example, an environmental contract that specifies you will, renew, decorate, declutter or make your home beautiful in order for it to be supportive of your life, but you live with one or more other people who do not cooperate or refuse to make the place the way you want it. Or you don't have the income to renew or decorate it. Change it to making a contract with yourself to live in a 100 per cent supportive and nurturing, beautiful, safe, home.

3) A contract that specifies **how you will receive wealth and abundance in your life**. For example, you want to become rich, or successful in your chosen career. A popular artist, professional, well known, etc., and that is the only way you will become wealthy and abundant. Make sure that the two are not tied in together. So, in this case, you can make two contracts, one specifying that you will have multiple extremely effective income sources. And the other that you will be extremely happy, satisfied, and successful with your chosen profession.

These are just examples, but they delineate some examples of how we can limit ourselves.

Take a look at your contracts, manifestation exercises and art and documents, to make sure you clear up any limiting energies and vocabulary from them, then watch your life expand.

One way to make sure that a certain manifestation exercise, or wish, is not limiting, is to do the goals exercise which you can find in the Ascension101 Course. The exercise teaches you how to "test" different outcomes, giving you very clear and precise information on how to achieve what you are aiming for without limiting factors.

Breaking Barriers - Your choice to be free.

Extract from Processing Barriers MP3 Transcript, available for download for free from our Newsletter Subscriber Only area of the site.

Processing Barriers by Inelia Benz

"The reason I wanted to talk about barriers is because these are coming up big time for all of us at the moment. We are moving slowly but surely into an area in Time/Space where this is really - I don't know if to call it a test or a hurdle or simply a point of choice for us, all of us individually, of whether to move on to the new Paradigm or to stay in the duality Dark/Light paradigm.

And there's really no judgement on either of those, there really isn't.

Some of the ways in which this hurdle or resistance, barriers have come up are in a very huge desire to retire. Whether it is from work, from our relationships, from our mission, or from life. We simply feel a very powerful sense that it's time to retire.

It is our interpretation at an energetic level of a big, really thick type of wall that we're going through in Time/Space. It's like a door you know, and we need to push the door open, basically.

Now, if you're really ready to retire and you're thinking 'you know what? That's all very well but what if I retire? Does that mean I'm choosing the old paradigm?' No, no it isn't, it doesn't actually mean that. It simply means that something within your own timeline, within your own life has to shift big time and that's why this barrier has come up. One of the things that happens is - and we go back to the same old exercise, the Fear Processing Exercise (which you can find under the Tools menu tab in the site) - is that most resistance or most barriers that don't allow us to move forth as quickly as we want or reach the manifestations or the life that we really want to have on the planet are based on a very low vibrational kind of energy packet.

And this low vibrational energy packet is invariably Fear. Whether it is our own fear or whether it is an injected fear, or whether it's artificial, somebody else's fear, whether it's the Collective's fear. It's really quite irrelevant because if this fear or this package or this vibration or program wasn't in our own lives, then we wouldn't be feeling it. So it doesn't matter where it came from, or who put it there. The fact is that it's there now, and because it's there now in our own field, we can shift it.

One might think 'well, why bother shifting it if it's not going to, you know... affect anything or it doesn't really make any difference?' And I would say that when we feel that type of resistance or blockage, it means that whatever is on the other side must be really worth getting, really interesting. That's why the resistance and barrier has come up.

It feels very much - from my conversations with other workers, ascension workers around the planet - that this is quite a common problem right now. A lot of people are feeling, or have felt in the past few months that they want to retire, they want to move on or they want to give up. So it is something that we can really look at and explore and see where we want to go from here.

For me personally, if anything comes up like this, something that's resisting, whether in myself or from outside but resonating within my own field, I see as a challenge. I see as: you know what? My decision, I like to take my own personal decisions from my own choices, from my own desires and my own moving forward as it were.

I don't like decisions to be imposed upon me. Whether through my own programming, or barriers that were placed there by myself or others. I want the choice to stop to come from a place of joy. And that's the key..."

Awakened Western Woman - You are the Key.

Awakened Western Women are the Key. This is a sentence I have heard over and over again in the past few months, although different words and descriptions have been used. Many male spiritual leaders have spoken it, as well as many female spiritual leaders.

But what does it mean?

If you are reading this article you are either an Awakened Western woman, know one, or are a man who knows at least one woman.

The concept that spiritual and social change is brought about by women is not a new one. It is well established.

When one, just one, woman learns a method to raise her personal vibration, in other words she starts ascending in evolution, she will share it with her friends, she will teach it to her kids, and will also share with her family and partner. Or try to.

This is why women have been the target of religious and social programming for as long as we can remember. Because it is through women, that belief systems, teachings, social rules, and reality, is spread into our human collective.

Let's think of children and who forms them. Most teachers are female. All mothers are female. And yes, what you do in your pregnancy does affect the fetus. So even if a child is being raised by men, he or she had a big programming session for nine months inside the biological mother's womb. Most religious followers are women. Women who then take those teachings home and teach them to their kids. Or to school, where they teach it to their students. And most of this is done unconsciously, unthinking, just through actions, and emotions, and the sharing of interest.

I have been working for two years now with Lucia Rene, who is fully dedicated in teaching women to stand in their own power. Her mission, and journey, has been met with horrendous resistance. She was even killed once for it. But she came back. For most of these two years of working with Lucia, I did not understand her passion, her unwavering stubbornness in her mission of working only with women. Yes, her teachings are available to men and women alike, but her personal work is only with women. Then I got it! I was able to experience what power a woman has, and what an unstoppable force a group of women can be, at a global scale.

Just like Lucia Rene, there are hundreds of thousands of women out there. A few of them in the public eye, but the great majority working quietly and unanimously. Unwavering in their mission to empower other women, to empower children, and to empower men. Hundreds of thousands of women warriors, teachers, healers, speakers, mothers, sisters, daughters and friends.

Imagine what will happen if we add a few million to the list!

This is what we can do: we teach at least one more woman how to easily and quickly raise her personal vibration. There is no mystery, no gurus, no religion, and no qualifying characteristics on how to do raise one's vibration. Learn how to do it yourself, and teach at least one woman how to do it.

CALL TO ACTION - Let's reach 10 Million individuals who are willing to change the course of history.

Share, forward, email, copy/paste, post and DO the Fear Processing Exercise. If we get 10 million individuals around the planet to do this just for 5 minutes out of their entire life, we will shift the planet into a higher vibrational reality:

The original exercise is here: https://ascension101.com/en/fear-processing-excercise.html

Fear Processing Exercise, by Inelia Benz

You can do this exercise at any time, whenever you feel fear.

For best results, it is best to do it in a quiet and private space and working through a list of fears you have written beforehand.

Sit or lie down comfortably with your back straight and close your eyes.

Breathe in deeply and slowly into your abdomen, then breathe out as fast as you can.

Repeat, breathe in slowly, then out as fast as you can.

And once more, breathe in slowly and slowly, then out fast.

Now continue breathing at your own pace.

Scan your physical body from head to toe, to find the energy of fear.

Look for fear. If you cannot find it, read one of your fear items in your list and scan your body again.

Once you find fear in your body, simply look at it.

Don't analyze it, just look at it.

Allow it to be there.

Allow it to exist.

Allow it to grow and to be.

It could be a physical discomfort, such as a knot, a pain, a location of energy, or through a thought or memory, or it could be just the emotion of fear.

Just look at it.

Observe it.

Feel it.

Allow it to be here.

And say, "fear, you are welcome here."

Welcome here.

Welcome fear and allow it to grow.

Let it get bigger and bigger.

Allow it to grow, and grow... as big as it can go

Let it be as big as it can possibly get.

Allow it to express itself to you.

But don't analyze.

Simply allow whatever comes.

Whether words,

thoughts,

memories,

Follow it if it changes into another emotion,

or changes locations in your body.

Whatever it does, welcome the new expression. "you are welcome here, thought... you are welcome here emotion, words, memories, you are welcome here fear."

You are welcome here.

Watch it. Observe it.

Now, allow yourself to get closer and embrace fear in whatever expression it has chosen.

give it light and love, and allow it to exist.

Thank it for whatever job it had for you, for being with you for so long.

Now, release it into Oneness. Allow it to go free back into Source.

Breathe deeply now.

As you breathe in, breathe in light and love. And as you breathe out, allow that light and love to go to and fill the space where fear used to be.

Now, simply breathe deeply and slowly.

Breathing in light and love, and as you breathe out, allow that light and love to expand throughout your body and out into your environment.

Now, scan your body from your toes to your head and see if there is any of that fear left. If so, repeat the exercise straight away. If not, you can use your list to repeat the exercise, or end now by opening your eyes and having a good stretch.

Repeat this exercise every day until there is no more fear in your life.

Did You Hear? We can do it today!

The information in this article is highly empowering, and reveals deeply known, yet forgotten, facts about our true natures. Feel free to share it, email it, and post it to anyone you feel it will empower. Although simple, it goes to the core of how the Light/Dark Paradigm has been able to function for so long and how we can consciously move back to our true natures of Light/Love, bringing in the New Paradigm with us into what we know as a "physical reality". Most of us have heard of the "Tower of Babel". If you haven't, the biblical story goes like this (copied from wikipedia at http://en.wikipedia.org/wiki/Tower_of_Babel):

"According to the biblical account, a united humanity of the generations following the Great Flood, speaking a single language and migrating from the east, came to the land of Shinar, where they resolved to build a city with a tower "with its top in the heavens...lest we be scattered abroad upon the face of the Earth". God came down to see what they did and said: "They are one people and have one language, and nothing will be withholden from them which they purpose to do." So God said, "Come, let us go down and confound their speech." And so God scattered them upon the face of the Earth, and confused their languages, and they left off building the city, which was called Babel "because God there confounded the language of all the Earth" (Genesis 11:5–8)."

What does the story of the Tower of Babel have to do with our Ascension into a new vibrational level? This story illustrates what happened thousands of years ago, when we were still **connected as One as a species**. And it goes to the core of reconnecting with Gaia's true energy field, the expansion of our personal awareness, and also the movement of the human species into a higher vibrational reality.

Somewhere in the past, a technologically advanced species removed the ability for human beings to communicate naturally with themselves and the planet. They programmed in, or disconnected, our ability to become one with anyone on the planet at any time. To trace any person's vibration, and locate them. To merge and share experiences with any species or human being at will. They cut us off from each other. And we were programmed to believe we were singular beings unable to connect with others except with voice, touch or pictures. But as the planet rises in vibration, it is naturally removing all those programs and broken links. We are evolving back to our natural, connected state.

Human communication, as we know it today, is about a communicator projecting a message that is received by a recipient. For the communication to work, the projecting person has to have the intention to be received not only by the recipient's physical senses, but also his or her's conscious, or unconscious, awareness. This is a direct relationship between the Tower of Babel story, and the way in which we communicate. Basically, this type of communication comes from the illusion that we are separate from each other, and that the only way in which we can reach others, is by projecting ourselves out there strongly enough that we impinge into the other person's awareness field..

However, our true form of communication is different. When we understand the difference, we can understand the saying, "divide and conquer" at a global scale. Our true form of communication is not to project and to be received by another, but to **open ourselves up and allow the other to exist in our field**. To become ONE. This is easiest when we are talking about a beautiful flower, someone we love, our pets, or a beautiful sunset.

That is why I often mention to individuals that if they want to communicate with nature, with an animal, tree, plant, or Gaia, to start feeling that what they are trying to communicate with is beautiful. To feel how beautiful it is, really feel their beauty inside of us. It is because when we feel something, or someone, is beautiful, we open ourselves up to let them enter our field.

But when it comes to the darker, or criminal aspects of our society, we cringe and pull our fields closed. The reason is that we fear that those dark entities and energies will take us over. That they will "pollute" us. That we will lose our minds and souls to them. That we may be influenced by them. And, if we open ourselves up to them in a state of fear, that is exactly what will happen. If this paragraph made you cringe, or have reservations about dark beings, or fear, use the Fear Processing Exercise on the fear before you open yourself up to any being out there.

So, why is it so important to learn our true form of communication? Because it is the way in which we can move away from the hive mentality of the Old Paradigm (boss at the top dictating what happens to all the divided minions below), to a healthy collective New Paradigm mentality (all beings are equal and have equal say in what happens as a species, are full owners of their own singular reality).

And this is exactly how we can reach Gaia in her new vibrational location today. Take a few minutes to breathe deeply, and then visualize, imagine, or give yourself the instruction to open up wide and allow Gaia's new vibrational reality to enter your field, your aura, your mind, your senses, and every cell in your body. By using our natural communication form to be ONE with Gaia in her new paradigm, we also shift the human collective that bit closer to becoming an awakened species.

Here is a recording that might help you:

https://www.youtube.com/watch?v=RkYQnVFjEyQ

Of course, if you feel inspired, you can also try it out with other people and learn what true telepathy is all about :)

CALL TO ACTION - Change of Human Collective Operating System

I am presently in Spain, where I will be attending two events. One event is in Barcelona, on the 13th of October 2012, and the second event is in Madrid on the 20th of October.

And, the information I will be sharing at these times, are that we now have the capacity, power, and ability to change the Operating System (OS) of the Human Collective, to the New Paradigm version.

The OS is carried within human verbal language, and our DNA.

And Source, Gaia and the Planetary Council needs volunteers to become conduits for the new OS to enter our Human Collective. We need volunteers who speak every modern language on the planet. Spanish, English, German, Italian, Chinese, Japanese, Indian, Korean, Portuguese... in short, YOUR MOTHER TONGUE. If you are reading this article, it means you are personally being asked to partake in this download.

This is crucially important. This informational article needs to be translated into every language on the planet. Please send your mother tongue translation to info @ ascension101.com, and we will link it to this article, so you can then forward it to everyone you know who speaks that language.

Here are the instructions:

On Saturday 13th at 4pm Spain Time Zone - I will be sharing this information in Barcelona Spain.

On Saturday 20th at 10am Spain Time Zone - I will be sharing this information in Madrid Spain.

On the next Saturday AFTER you read this message.

If you don't know what the new OS is, ask your higher self to show you first.

Please, if your timezone and calendar allows, at one or all the allocated times above, go to a public place where it is normal for a person to sit, such as a cafe, park, beach, or meet with people you know at an assigned place such as your home or public area, and sit with your eyes closed and IN SILENCE, with the intention to BECOME A CONDUIT FOR SOURCE TO UPLOAD THE NEW PARADIGM OPERATING SYSTEM into human collective language (your mother tongue and DNA) throughout time/space. If your timezone or calendar doesn't allow to join in the above allocated times, then do it as soon as you can after reading this informational article.

I will be joining you for one hour every Saturday from today to the end of 2012.

Share, send, copy/paste to your blog, list, FB page, talk to your local radio stations, TV stations, groups and friends, and everywhere you can think of, let them know what you are doing, and ask them to join you in intention.

New Human Operating System Followup

Firstly, I would like to thank you for participating, and forwarding, the information on last Saturday's Call to Action: https://ascension101.com/en/home/free-articles/67-october-2012/277-call-to-action-change-of-human-collective-operating-sytem.html

The response was extraordinary. The page itself has already been shared on FB over 3000 times. And people from just about every country in the planet joined in to partake in the download, and translations to many languages have been received and published.

This is huge! We, as human beings, act as ONE. Even though it is sometimes hard to imagine, everything that happens on the planet, has been decided by our human collective. The nature of our experience is colored by our "programs". These "programs" come from our own species, they come from the wishes of the collective, Gaia, and the Planetary Council, as well as from our culture, religion, society, education, family and our own and our body's "karmic" leftovers.

All these programs function within a type of Operating System. A base range of programs of a certain vibration and nature, that allow certain things to be carried out, and others not to be carried out.

The New Operating System is basically a higher vibrational base for having a physical human experience on the planet. It, for example, supports full awareness, as opposed to the veil of forgetfulness. It also supports self empowerment of the individual, as opposed to giving one's power and authority away to another being or organization. These are but two of the new range of experience we can have in the New Paradigm.

This new OS is embedded in our DNA, which is directly affected by our verbal and written language.

How we use language, what words we use, and the act of becoming conscious of the vibration and meaning behind words, is all part of the new OS coming online.

Practical ways in which we can support the new OS for ourselves and those around us, is to, for example, stop complaining. If a person cannot help you with a certain something that happened, don't complain to them about it. Also, and very importantly, is the act of responding instead of reacting to situations, vibrations, and individuals. This last one is amazingly empowering for both ourselves and the other individuals involved.

And, of course, simply sitting in silence, while basking in the new vibration which we have made more readily available to the rest of the planet, is also very important. Take time every day to simply enjoy the new vibration!

As a followup to last Saturday's event, tomorrow, I will be talking about this collective act and choice to several hundred people in Madrid, Spain, beginning at around 9:45 am Spanish time. If you are able and circumstances allow, do sit and bask in the new OS for that hour. We act as ONE. If, due to timezone restrictions, you are unable to join us at that specific time, do take an hour during Saturday to join us.

Spread the word, the action, and decision, to move into the New Paradigm, embodying this new OS in our own DNA, our own lives, and thus making it available to everyone on the planet. We, by sheer numbers, have a huge effect on what happens on the planet at every moment of our lives.

It's HERE - You can Choose your Paradigm

As the collective geared up big time to the "date" of December 2012, a window of opportunity opened up for all of us to shift vibrational gears since then. Why? Because it is our Human Collective that decides what happens to us as a Species. And it is up to us individually to decide what happens to us personally.

There are two main choices:

One = Stay in the old paradigm of Light/Dark, and continue on a journey of experience of POO (Power Over Others). We make this decision by staying disconnected from each other, our bodies and our environment. By giving away our power and authority to others, and identifying with victim or aggressor. By expecting someone, or something, to save us, or doing our best to save others. The energy of the martyr is also here.

Two = We move into the New Paradigm of Light/Love. This sets off a journey of new experience where manifestation, synchronicity, authentic self, connection to body, self, others and environment is realized as being ONE with all. We take back our power and authority of self, and identify with Divine Spirit Universal Consciousness. By taking full responsibility (ability to respond) for our own expansion of awareness, development and raising your vibration and that of our environment.

Two clear choices that have been with us since August 2011, when the split happened at an energetic and intentional level on the planet.

There is a self imposed race by our Shadow Self, manifested by us in what many call the Illuminati, or Cabal, to get as many people to consciously, or unconsciously, choose Option One. Stay in the Old Paradigm and continue the games there. There are many ways they are carrying out their plan. Polluting the planet, our bodies, emotional bodies, and minds with noise, fear, and chemicals, distracting us from doing the necessary choices and work to raise our vibration. If you want to find out the mechanics behind it, read "Interview with an Alien", a novel specifically written to bring this information to the forefront of consciousness.

What can we do to not only make sure we are making the New Paradigm choice every single day, but also helping those around us do the same?

Well, there are various tools we can use. Check out the tools section of the ascension101.com site. And, with regard others around us, these are some of the things you can do to assist the planet:

- Acknowledge that the other person's higher self knows better than us on what paradigm to move to.
- Allow the other person to exist without judgment from our part.
- Allow our self to exist and energetically express without barriers or stops. Accept our present existence in the Now and release any resistance to it.
- **Detox** our physical body and our mind. Drink distilled water, eat chemical free foods and switch off the TV.
- Detox our emotional body using the Fear Processing Exercise.
- **Be fully aware** of our intention and energy behind words, whether written or spoken, expressed to ourselves or others.
- Spend time to join thousands of people around the planet every Friday 11pm or Saturday 11am (PST) for an hour of silence with the intention to amplify the new Operating System.
- Join thousands of people around the planet every Wednesday at 8:30am PST for a silent hour with the intention to join Oneness.
- And KNOW that we are unlimited, divine beings that have the power to create whatever reality we want.
- KNOW that we are NOT ALONE. We are ONE.

- Share this list with everyone we know.

This is Inelia Benz, and I am here to raise the vibrational level of the planet. Wanna do it together?

The 5th Dimension is not a location, it's a Creation.

We create our own reality. This is something that has been taught for thousands of years, and also a well kept secret in Western society for as many years. It is also the one biggest piece of information that the "powers that were" are trying to stop from reaching the sleeping masses.

The reason that this knowledge is being kept secret is that when a person is asleep (spiritually unawakened), they can be lead to create someone else's reality by the use of fear, persuasion, and created illusions of reality that are sold so hard, it's hard to think they are not real.

But when we think about the 5th Dimension, or any other higher dimension, we often forget that the same applies. We still create our own reality.

In more subtle dimensions, the core material there is more subtle physically, and what happens there, what we experience, even merely entering that less dense reality, is our own creation. In order to enter a more subtle and pliable dimension, we need the awareness and capacity to allow ourselves to be and create that less dense reality. We do that by becoming less "dense" ourselves (no pun intended).

Due to the less solidity of the 5th Dimension (or 4th, or 12th and everything in between), those who make it part of their environment are more aware of their own nature, and the nature of their reality. We are "able to to" much better than on the 3D solidity.

In the more subtle dimensions, in order to "use" another person's power, we need their conscious agreement. The reason is that in those dimensions there is very little unconsciousness left. And what is left is not easily used by others.

223

We create the 5th Dimension.

Yes, all physical reality is multidimensional and an illusion, and we create them to have an experience of singular individuality. They all exist in the same "location", which is infinite. But at the same time, we choose to be aware of only a tiny little spectrum of that all encompassing "reality". That tiny spectrum dictates what we experience as "real".

The difference between the 3rd, 4th and 5th dimensions are ones of empowerment, the subtlety of solid matter, and capacity to do.

Therefore, what we experience in the subtler dimensions is what we choose to experience there. They don't "exist" until we create and move our awareness into that space.

There are no dimensions in Oneness, because there is no singular construct of individuality with "other", whether "other person" or "environment.

From a standpoint of Oneness, the difference between the 3rd and the 5th dimensions are infinitely small and insignificant. But from our standpoint, and awareness, there could not be two more different experiences of physical existence.

And, the most important point, these are not dimensions we move into, but actively create moment by moment by our raising of our personal vibration, raising the vibration of the planet, and being fully aware of our intention and energy behind all our communications with other and self. It's a personal process of creation.

How do we get to that point of conscious creation? We raise our personal vibration, we raise our environmental vibration, we embody the new Paradigm. How do we do it? Find the tools that resonate with us. There are thousands of them out there. If what I am saying resonates with you, see what you can use at the Ascension101.com Tools section. There are tools for you, the planet, the human collective and the entire matrix. At the writing of this article, the free content at our website has been accessed by over

1,600,000 individuals, who have accessed the pages 3,362,410 times. These individuals will often learn the tools, then teach them to others.

Word of mouth is the number one path with which these individuals have found the ascension101 website. A person will share what works for him or her.

Also, if you are interested in your personal growth, the Ascension101 Course was specifically brought forth to create an energy exchange line that will not only **benefit you** in your personal expansion of awareness, consciousness and ascension, but also supports the Ascension101.com staff and website so that millions more can access the information, inspiration, and knowledge available here. The income from the Ascension101 Course allows us to have the time, tools and skills to create the World empowering free content you see here every week. The site will be around until 2017, at which point it will no longer be necessary (if we do this right) because we will have reached a critical mass of empowered individuals, shifting the entire species into knowing all these tools and capacities without having to do a course, using a tools, listening to an interview, or reading an article whether in ascension101 or other location.

What is left to do after we raise our own vibration, the planet's vibration and create the 5th dimension?

Well, that is up to you. My role is not that of creator, it is of inspiring you to be self empowered, taking back your own authority, being the sovereign of your personal reality, showing you that you have the tools, capacity and abilities at your disposal, so that no one else can ever take away your power without your conscious consent again. **It is your role to create the new Paradigm**, the 5th Dimension, or whatever other name you might know that experience in subtle physical reality as. When do you start it? I say, **start NOW!**

YOU are the creator. Start creating that new reality right now. It is not a location to arrive at, it is something **YOU** create today by raising your own vibration and deciding what you want to create.

My name is Inelia Benz, and I am here to raise the vibrational level of the planet. What are you here for?

Clearing Your Wealth Lines

Excerpt from the Clearing Your Wealthlines MP3+PDF Download:

"... I've managed to really create a supportive environment for myself so that I can do this full-time, I don't have to have a part-time job anymore to support myself while I'm giving out the message and being a voice for this message. And one of the things that I had to work through and I'm still working through, in fact, is another teaching that came from my parents where my sister and I when we were small, **we were able to tap into the collective and find out, for example in a race, what horse was going to win.** Things like that. And we were very good at it. I'll tell you a little story about that - and this is part of that program, right, one of the programs that I'm still actually working on, there's a little bit of it left so I have to really fine-tune it, I have to go in and see. Where is that energy and allow it to exist, it's hiding, moving around, as they do, they hide, they move, they morph, they change, they become a physical thing, then they move back. Some of them are quite hard to find but we can do it, we can do it if we keep at it and then we infuse it. You know, if all else fails, just infuse it with light and love, yeah?

Anyway this story, what happened was, I was about let me think, I must have been 12 years old. Yeah I was about 12 years old and I lived in England, I lived in Nottingham with my mom and my brother.

We lived in a really, really tough neighborhood but funnily enough I never saw anything bad happen there. Nothing bad ever happened to me there either. Apart from a dog that bit me once, haha. But that was because I was projecting hate to that dog, thinking 'you're horrible, go away'. you know? But anyway, what happened about the teaching of the money thing was that we had a friend who had been my teacher in Scotland. When we lived in Scotland before we moved to Nottingham, this woman, she was an English teacher and I was taken from school and I was put into her class in Stirling, from Falkirk to Stirling. And she would supposedly teach myself and other foreign kids English. But she actually used to disappear for a whole morning and let us play with lego and other stuff, it was really boring. I used to wander off, it was a beautiful castle in Stirling that was part of the university there, I think. It had a beautiful cemetery next to it. The energy was really interesting. But this woman had a really interesting character. And when we moved to Nottingham, she actually moved down as well. She followed us down there. I don't know why but she did, and I used to spend a lot of time with her. She was really really great. She was a really fun woman. And she used to bet on horses with her boyfriend.

One day she had promised to -because I love horses- she promised to take me to this racing track. So I went with them and they were like really heavy-duty gamblers, they were really heavy-duty. So I went with her and she said to me 'okay I'm going to give you like £1' -a Pound, which is the money over there- for a horse, so pick a horse and then we'll put the Pound on it for you. So I went around, I literally walked around all the, where the horses were standing and I asked them 'are you going to win today?' and one of them said 'no, no, go and check over there' and eventually I reached one of them and I said 'are you going to win?' and he said 'yeah, I'm gonna win today!' So I said 'oh cool' and I went back to her and I said 'I want that one', and she said 'oh but the odds are such and such on that one and it's probably, bla' and she explained all sorts of things to me and I said 'no no, no I want that one anyway' and she said 'are you sure? And you want the whole Pound on that one?' And I said 'yeah, just that one, that one's gonna win'. So she put the Pound in, and sure enough the horse won and she said 'how did you know that?' And I said 'well, the horse told me' and she went 'really?!', I said 'yeah'. So, of course, the next race she says 'can you go and ask the horses which one's gonna win'? So I did, and of course the horse won and the third horse, of course, they put all of their money onto this third horse. And so yeah, it won, and they got a ton of money, it was a huge amount at the time -I have no idea how much it was- and she said that because they'd won so much money she gave me a tenner, she said 'this is for you', it was really funny, I was really happy, you know I'd never had so much money. And we went home, and they bought a new car and they moved to a nice place, and all sorts of things. And my mom, when she found out, she said 'Inelia, that was VERY, VERY wrong, you're not to do that again' and I said 'why?' She said 'because that's cheating, gambling is all about people not knowing who's going to win, and then everybody has the same chance, but what you did wasn't right because you knew who was gonna win so that wasn't gambling so you took away everybody else's chance'. Which was, thinking back, really illogical because everybody could've bet on the same horse. It didn't really affect what other people were betting on. And, well that program went in really deeply, you know? It's like 'oh my gosh, you have to be really fair' and I can't win any more lottery tickets and I can't win the horses, and I can't win anything because that's cheating, you know. So that program went in really deep, and even today, whenever I'm going to bet or something, I still have that energy come up going 'wow' you know? It's like 'you're being a bad girl, type thing'. So yeah, I'm still working on that one myself, and I'll let you know how I do -or maybe you'll find out!

But yeah, so we work on those very specific personal programs and belief systems and emotional packets of energy that will prevent the energy field, the elemental of money from entering our own field. So just work at it, allow it to exist there and even if you can't let it all the way in, just allow it to be like, I don't know, 10 feet away or something 'alright I'll let you in 10 feet from me and there you are, I can look at you and explore you'. And do that. See how close to your field you can allow the elemental of money as it exists today on this planet, right now, with all the stuff that's attached to it. How close can you allow that into your own field, can you allow that fully into your field? Because if you do, it's going to be cleansed, it's gonna be infused with Light and Love and it's gonna be morphing into its natural energy. It's natural composition. It's going to free all of the chains and pollutants that has been added to it. And the more of us that do this, the healthier as a collective we'll have with the elemental of money. The elemental of energy exchange.

So, just as it exists today, how close can you let it? And allow it to push your boundaries a little bit, to push your comfort level a little bit, just pull it in a little bit closer. And just walk around it, energetically or in your mind, walk around it, look at it, allow it to sit, sit with it, just sit and look at it. Just look. You might get information from it, you might get visions or flashes like movies playing in your mind. And allow those to happen. Just look at everything like you were looking at a movie. Look at any emotions you may have. And bit by bit, move a little bit closer, allow it to move a little bit closer to you, you know.

Do that for the next few days as well. I'm giving you loads of homework and I want to hear back from you, saying what's been happening with your homework on the forum.

That's the first part of the: 'how to look at our constructs and things'.

The other part, the second part of this same topic of the energy or the elemental, are money lines..."

The above is an excerpt from the Clearing Your Wealthlines MP3+PDF Download.

Power - Rules of Engagement

Abstract from Rules Of Engagement - Entering the New Paradigm

"Power", even the word "power" has a lot of emotional and ego charge in it, the word as well as the concept.

The entire paradigm we are moving out of is based on Power Over Others. The society we carved out is based on power over others and power over environment. Concepts which were seen as advanced and necessary for the good of humanity. Which is why so many individuals react in fear or negativity when they hear the word "power".

The concept is that power has a hierarchical format, that there are people out there who are either less, or more, powerful than we are. Although we might think this structure is only used by "dark workers", it is not. It is also used by "light workers". For example, in order to be of service to others, a person needs individuals, or situations, around them that either have sleeping individuals (who they can help awaken), or victims (who they can help out). The lightworker, is then in a position of having power over others who are not powerful enough to help themselves. When someone is in the path of Bodhisattva, they need people and environments that are suffering, so they can go in and help out. It is a good path to eventually leave the cycle of power over others, but it is the path, not the destination.

Let's take a look and see if we have some charge on the word "power". The easiest way to do this is to use the word in a few sentences and see if we react emotionally to it. So, here goes:

"I have power"

"I am all powerful"

"She has power"

"She is all powerful"

"He has power"

"He is all powerful"

"You have power"

"You are all powerful"

"They have power"

"They are all powerful"

Interesting stuff, yes?

Of course, if any programs, or charge, triggered while you heard those sentences, go and process them right away, or after you finish listening to this section.

Let's take a look at the definition of "power". Power is the "ability to do", a "capacity of action", and it is also "energy" as in, "Chi". And also "prana", which is the Sanskrit word for "vital life" or the concept of "filling up".

If you are familiar with my work, you would have heard me say that women are power, and men are structure. And, it is up to us individually, to have a good healthy male and female balance in our singular construct. That way we have infinite power, and the structure to be able to use it in a healthy, and "empowering" way both for ourselves and others.

A quick summary of how to go about balancing our power and structure is to move out of the way and allow pure Universal Divine Consciousness to come through us, this is power. And moving our main focus or viewpoint from our head to our heart center. This is structure.

Put your focus in your heart center. That's the middle of your chest and expands out toward your collar bone, esophagus, shoulder blades and front rib cage. Put your focus there now.

Power is important to understand, and own. Power is the main aspect of human beings which is behind the interests of rulers and other parties. And the reason for so much battle and effort going on to keep humans asleep.

Each individual person on the planet is a source of, and a potential tool for, infinite power.

Really infinite, unlimited and uncolored power.

Abstract from Rules Of Engagement - Entering the New Paradigm

What? 2013? Whatever next...

My position on December 2012 was never popular, and I got a lot flack for it.

"I'm going to buy popcorn and watch the proceedings"

"I'll be Christmas shopping"

"Nothing is going to happen"

"We still have a possibility of dramatic change, but Gaia doesn't want it, nor does the collective"

To tell you the truth, and as I stated before, this seeing **was not popular with me either**. I really, really wanted to wake up on the first day of 2013 to find that all wars had been cancelled, poverty eliminated, the pharmaceuticals removed from the business world, chemtrails gone... and on and on.

This seeing is not new, since I answered the call from Source to become public in 2010, I set up my page to read "Personal and Global Ascension 2012-2017".

These years are the ones that we, as a human collective, are set to raise our own and the species vibration enough to reach critical mass, the hundredth monkey effect. In 2017, it will no longer be necessary to "spread the word", because everyone on the planet will have it accessible in a moment's thought. After that, it will take about 2 and a half generations to fully integrate the New Paradigm.

Yeah, 2 1/2 generations is also not a popular seeing by me either.

There are many, many people around the planet who have had an enormous boost and expansion of awareness this past December, and this is good! Now they are ready to start the work of becoming custodians of the planet.

Many felt absolutely nothing. And of these, many are now disappointed, feel conned and wonder how come there are wars still happening on the planet.

This is a sign that that person has not left, and never had left, the victim/aggressor/savior/martyr cycle. They expected something external, and also for the species to get on with it.

The media is going crazy spreading this feeling of disappointment, spreading fear, and trying to force dis-empowering laws to pass as quickly as possible.

So, what can we do? What is next? How can we move things along?

First of all, realize that the New Paradigm, the 5th Dimension, or whatever we name it, is not a location (either in time or space), but it is a creation that begins inside each of us.

We raise our personal vibration, we process all negativity, we infuse our reality and our bodies with our Essential Energy, Source Light/Love.

NOW is when the work begins. Now that there are no more instant gratification dates for us to be distracted with, we can start creating what we really want to experience on this beautiful planetary being, Planet Earth.

If you are tired, and I am, take a few days off. Just disconnect from the internet, emails, newscasts, and go off for a few days into the wilderness. Breathe, reconnect with the good stuff, Gaia. Everything else is just an illusion of confusion. And then connect with five people who you consider to have a very high vibration. Whether you connect with them via their books, blogs, retreats, or know them personally, make them your five top relationships on the planet.

The five people we connect most with in daily life, are the ones we shape our reality with.

For a more in depth presentation see: Rules of Engagement in the new paradigm.

Inelia Benz

Letter from my Brother - Darkness Released

I received this letter from my brother Alex this morning. It is very personal, and at the same time, very relevant to us all. It is a real life example of how we stop creating Light/Dark Duality and move to creating a Light/Love duality.

He said I could share it with you, even though he doesn't know how the story ends.

After reading it, have a look at your own field, your own self, and see if you too are holding onto your Dark Side.

"A Personal Story"

"As with you when I was little, I would have conversations in my head with this person that would sometimes tell me things. I never saw this person and suspected that it was really me.

When little, sometimes I would have long conversations with him because the world was a weird and not a very pleasant place to be, and I had big doubts about being here... or not.

Once, when I was about 7 or 8, I seriously considered suicide. But talking with this voice about the pros and cons of suicide, we came to the conclusion that even though life seemed like a very unpleasant place, with short burst of niceness ever so often, which my younger logical self thought it was not worth living, it was only so if you looked at it from the perspective that in a short-ish amount of time everyone dear to me would get over my death, and that the planet was full of life anyway.

So one less life would not make much of a difference really. But if you looked at the bigger picture, where our planet was a very lonely island of life in a huge big universe, a universe so big and with so little intelligent life, then my life was worth a lot. So for the sake of the universe I continued living. (this being a side effect of reading about astronomy from a very young age).

The conversations carried on for years and when I was a teenager in Argentina I was sure I was simply talking to myself. The weird thing was that a lot of the time "myself" knew things which I didn't and after some weeks or months turned out to be true.

During one of these conversations me and "myself" came to the conclusion that we were living in a pretty much rough and violent world, which of course we did at the time, and that the energy we used should be one that should be able to handle everything we faced. I used to be into martial arts so I liked to read about it. Through this, I had discovered the concept of Ying and Yang. So with "myself" we decided it was a cool thing to be a "balanced" person. This meant that from then on we had to walk the fine line of keeping in balance our bad (dark) side and our good (light) side. I have to say this worked quite well for a very long time.

About 15 years ago I started doing Tai-Chi, then moved over to Tai-Chi with Zen meditation, and about 11 years ago I started spiritual meditation. It was during these sessions that I discovered there was something different about me.

During group meditations people would describe meeting beings of light. They described them as guarding angels, higher self's, etc. In my case I describe them as higher self's and sometimes I had three and sometimes four but the strange thing was that one of them was always from the dark side. A situation no one else seemed to have. After realizing that this being was always with me, I reached for it and saw that it represented violence, aggressiveness, selfishness, etc, etc. but that to me it was a very friendly and loving being. It was there because I called it, so that I could be a balanced person.

Now we come to the end of our time according to the Mayans. I only mention that because around the middle of December 2012 I was going through some very hard times. I had closed my software business and there was no clear professional path in front of me. This carried a lot of financial uncertainty and I was very stressed out about it.

This whole situation started in September and during my meditations I constantly asked for guidance and help. Then in December, during a meditation, I was upset that no help came to me and as I saw my higher selves and guides at an equal level to myself I told them off for not doing their part.

The answer I received was that they could not help as long as I had a hold of the dark side. I thought about this answer for a few days and I realized that I had to let go of my old friend the Dark higher self. So one day I meditated and connected with him to do just that. First I asked him what he thought about my releasing him, and he told me that he didn't think it was a good idea, considering the times we are living in, but that it was up to me. So I told him that, because of exactly that reason, that I had to become a being of light as it's during dark time that light is needed and I asked him to go and he left.

I have to say that it felt just like when a dear old friend leaves and we know that we won't see him for a long time. Even now I feel an emptiness where that side of "me" used to be and I do miss my old friend but I knew that the path was the right one as when he left I recognized in myself a person I hadn't seen since I was very young.

As for the last few months I can now do lightning fast meditations anywhere, I decided to meditate while having my afternoon cigarette and straight away my three other higher selves appeared and we all connected to Gaia and the stars. Which is something I do in most meditations.

This time though when I was visualizing my life energy connected to the planet via a stream of energy to the stars, these four beings of light that most definitely were not my higher selves, came down this stream of energy from the stars and surrounded me. They felt more experienced, more "real" or more external to me than my higher selves who by the way where very interested in the whole process. Well these beings surrounded me and told me that they where here to help and protect me. That I should trust in me and in life and that they would make sure everything was OK. And I did.

Right now they are still with me and little by little, day by day it feels like they are becoming a part of me. They don't talk much but I can feel their presence all the time. Also and just as they said things are getting better in many forms. Unexpected help from family and friends and at work lots of "lucky" situations and moments are happening. Now when I meditate the words "I am light" pops up all the time. And during one of the group meditations we did during winter solstice when I connected to Gaia and the stars, which usually is a little stream of energy flowing, a huge unstoppable torrent of energy burst through me from Gaia to the stars and then back from the stars to Gaia. This also happened a second time during another meditation but this time I wasn't so surprised. Not sure what it means though, but I'm not looking for explanations. It's simply the way it should be.

Un abarzo,

Alex."

Impeccable Intention and our Capacity to Manifest

Manifestation of our "wishes" is becoming more and more instant. The choreography of Universal support to our desired outcomes is more powerful every day.

Younger children, teenagers, and young adults, seem to be able to manifest much faster than we did at their age, or, in many cases, us now.

That's because they don't have the same programs we were injected with, they are growing up in a higher vibrational environment, and "manifestation" is in their everyday vocabulary.

Impeccability rocket fuels our manifestation capacities. But how do we achieve a state of impeccability? What does impeccability even mean?

According to Merriam-Webster (dictionary), impeccability means, "not capable of sinning or liable to sin", and "free from fault or blame; flawless". The origin of the word is "Latin *impeccabilis*, from *in-* + *peccare* to sin".

To sin, in most languages, means "missing the target", or a "separation from the law of God."

Translated into non religious language, this basically means veering away from our Higher Self. Veering away from our core essence energy, which is Light/Love.

How do we know if we are being impeccable? Well, if we are thinking of something we want in our lives, but it has any lower vibrational thoughts, emotions, or physical reactions, it is the emotion that will be manifested.

Anything that doesn't quite resonate "right" in our physical and emotional bodies, is "separate from our higher self".

Therefore, if we want a large, beautiful, house because we want to "show them how we really are better than them," whomever "them" are, we manifest poverty. Or we want to find our "soul mate" because we are extremely lonely and can't stand the thought of another visit to the movie theater alone. We manifest "lonely". Some of the loneliest people I have met are living with a significant other.

And sometimes we want to manifest things because we are taught that those are the right things to have in order to be "happy".

Most lower vibrational "reasons" attached to our goals and wishes, are based on fear or need. And many times, the hidden reasons for us not to manifest are also fear, or need.

Sometimes we can be afraid to manifest things, especially money or healthy relationships, because we are afraid we will "abuse power", and sometimes it is because we are afraid we will "lose it" afterward. And sometimes it is because "we are not ready to commit" to the response-ability of it. I recently experienced this last one myself!

What can we do?

1. Make a list of three things you want to manifest very quickly. It could be something physical, part of our environment, a type of human relationship to end or start, an emotional change, anything at all.

2. Decide on which one is the most important to you.

3. Ask yourself if this is "your own" desire. If you get a "no", ask your body if it is "her/his desire". (If you are having difficulty communicating with your body, get the Ascension101 Course and do the "Reconnecting with the Physical Body Exercise" for the next 21 days.)

4. Ask yourself "why" you/your body want it. Take a look at the answer, is it fear based? Is it "need" based? Process it.

5. Ask yourself "why" you/your body want it, again, and see what the core energy is of that response. If it is a

lower vibration, process it. And repeat until there are no more answers.

6. Once there are no more answers, the final answer is usually, "because I want to be happy".

7. Manifest a state of joy in your physical, mental and emotional bodies right now. Gratitude for something wonderful in your life is a great way to go into a state of joy.

8. Once you are in complete joy, you are free. Once you are free, you can revisit the thing you want to manifest and see if you "need it" now, or not.

9. Once you no longer "need it", or have any negative vibrations attached to it, you are home free.

Basically what we are doing here is removing the manifestation item from our lower vibration (separation from Source), and putting it squarely inside Source (love/light).

We manifest with our physical, emotional and mental bodies. If they are in "need", "fear", "anger", or any other type of energy that is not joy, light, love, they will manifest the emotions and situations we "believe" are possible.

We create the fifth dimension, we create the physical world, we create what happens in our lives. We have been doing so since we were born, but unconsciously. We do it based social rules, and programs such as fears, needs, and the illusion of lack. What we accomplish with the exercises above, is that we start creating our world **consciously**. That is the only difference! We become **aware** of the process, and we consciously manifest.

The higher our vibration, and the more in touch we are with our body, emotions and mind, the faster we can manifest a fantastic reality, not just for ourselves, but for the entire human collective.

The Power of Sex

During my preparatory work for the Sex, Love and SoulMates in the New Paradigm Talks which start March 21st 2013, I remembered something that happened in the early 1990s.

While I was in college, at Dublin City University, I was at a lecture being given by a world leader in sociolinguistics.

From Wikipedia, the free encyclopedia:

Sociolinguistics is the descriptive study of the effect of any and all aspects of society, including cultural norms, expectations, and context, on the way language is used, and the effects of language use on society

During this lecture, he was talking about how rape had nothing to do with sex, sexuality, or even sexual desire, but all about power. How one person was basically physically bullying another and forcing the other person to submit physically, so that the perpetrator could feel powerful). As this lecturer was a world respected leader in his field, extremely intelligent, and a formal government "expert" who was a key decision maker on laws and guidelines for the country, his view was more than just a personal opinion.

Half way through this lecture, I put up my hand, something unheard of during his lectures. When he saw that my hand was up, he immediately asked me what it was I wanted to ask or say. My response was very short and in the nature of:

"Of course it's about sex, sexual desire, sexual energy, sexual power, and sexual dominance. Otherwise their genitals would not be in the equation. To say it has nothing to do with sex, when it is the sexual organs that are being violated, or used to violate in many cases, is ignoring the elephant in the room, it's a way to make it 'comfortable', as we don't talk about sex in Ireland. I would have to disagree with you, and say that although rape is about power, it is also all about sex."

The lecturer went into a huge defensive monologue for the rest of the lecture. To which I did not respond in any way or form, except by staying wide open to what he was saying, without judgment, to see if he was indeed right.

On his next lecture, he began by reminding everyone about the statement I had made the previous week, and how he had defended his own position on the matter. He then said words in the nature of, "I was wrong. Rape is completely related to sex. Yes, it is about power, but to separate sex from rape is not possible."

By the end of the year, this change in view had been reflected in Irish governmental documents and formal policy reviews.

Of course, the entire rape thing is a core victim/aggressor/tyrant/martyr/savior paradigm program. And what we can do about it, if it triggers an emotional charge in us, is to process that particular paradigm.

The reason I am sharing this story at a public level, is to express something, an awareness, a view, that was in fact missing from both of our viewpoints at the time, and it is so obvious, and so talked about, that most of us take is as a norm, but often don't even see it.

Sex is Power.

When we think of power, in the western world, we immediately think of power over others.

When we think Sex is Power, we often think of a woman holding this power to further her own agendas, for others to use the sexual power of women to sell cars, clothes, and everything else that can be sold.

We might think of a history lesson where we learned that women stopped a war by withholding sex from their men. There is more than one example of this.

Throughout the few thousands years we have lived through, women's power has been equated with their Sex. Not gender, but their sexual organs.

So, why is Sex so Powerful?

The answer is very much related to the energy centers (at a chi level) of the physical body. It is related to the bringing forth of a new soul into the 3D, and also the creation of a physical body for that soul to incarnate into.

However, before concluding that they are powerful because they are there solely to bring forth new souls and bodies, think that perhaps the organs were placed in the powerful location to facilitate the bringing in of new souls and bodies. That the power center was there to begin with, and something else was placed there to take advantage of it.

Basically, the aim of this article is to start you looking at the construct behind Sex. To see its Power as independent from Sex. And also look at the possibility that EVERYTHING we think and "know" about Sex is simply an external program designed to have a particular response in us.

Imagine, for a minute, if all those programs were gone, and the Power (chi) was free from any programs or roles, or predesignated jobs. What would happen?

Some of these programs, which really are not related to sex, but we think they are, have to do with:

Procreation

Being loved

Perversion

Being touched

Soul Mates

Power over others

Distraction

Self worth

.... the list goes on and on... and on.

245

As we move into the New Paradigm, by creating the 5D, our awareness of this source of Power (chi) and all it's constructs, programs, belief systems, uses, abuses and capacities, needs to expand. We can do that when we feel "safe" to do so. We begin by processing all our fears around Sex, Power, and the Power of Sex. Make a list today, and start that processing!

Another thing we can do, is simply to have the intention to "look" at this topic within our own lives.

Note: If you are interested in exploring these topics more there is an in depth discussion and course on Love, Sex and SoulMates in the New Paradigm at ascension101.com

The Lemurian Connection

I have been contacted by different people, groups and collectives throughout my life. Some of them are human, some are not. One thing to remember is that we all have a right to CHOOSE the nature of communication we have with others. Whether others are other humans, organizations, or other species. We choose whether to engage with the other person or species or not, and how we engage. I choose to engage with all beings at the essence of our human basic building block, the level of joy/light/love. If others don't like it, then they can move their engagement and communication elsewhere.

This article is aimed at showing a timeline of the contact and information I have had with one particular species, the Lemurians. Whether we believe that the Lemurians exist or not, an exercise of looking at their culturally allocated existence in our subconscious mind, will be of benefit to our own personal evolution. So I invite you to look with me. I am only 99% certain they exist, because I have not experienced them at a physical level. Yet, they appear to be very, very real in every other sentient sense. No one has ownership of Lemurian "real" information. This has to come from YOU. If you are interested, it is you who needs to engage at a personal level, not through someone else.

I have chosen to share this with you now, because it is an evolving process, a growing awareness and connection that is happening at a global scale. The reason, from what I can gather, is that we (the human species) were, and will be, Lemurians to a large degree. They are not Gods, or saviors, they don't consider themselves above us, below us, or better or worse than us. They are here, and always have been here, and are our brothers and sisters. They want to collaborate. Why? Because we are Gaia, and they are Gaia. Because we are of the same essence, and live as the same planet.

There is a lot of mystery, mysticism, legends, and data regarding the Lemurians on the internet today. Most of this has been colored and interpreted by the person receiving the communication, having the personal contact, or the culture coloring what and who the Lemurian's are through religious or social beliefs. It is important to realize that my own experience, delineated below, will also contain my personal filters and "stuff", and as it is a developing communication, it is lacking in many areas.

Timeline

In 2011, between March and August, I had the first conscious "contact" that was telepathic in nature. The name Lemuria(or people of Mu?) came in (I feel the name Lemurian is not quite accurate?). I did a small amount of research and found lots of things about them that did not resonate on the internet. But there was an energetic "line" that was consistent. Something that said, "group of higher vibration, more aware, more able, clean living, equal society, no dark/light duality".

The telepathic contact I received in 2011 was that they wanted to share something. When I went into it, I felt a great sadness at a split on the plane that had happened many thousand years ago. The sadness and pain and having to "allow it to happen" due to free will of those who wanted to stay in a dark/light duality, was overwhelming.

Families were split, many chose to die and be reborn in the lower vibrational Earth so that they could carry the energy and light forth through the ages, as human beings. Others simply wanted to experience dark/light. The separation of the "collective mind/soul/spirit" was extremely painful.

At the time of the telepathic contact, the early part of 2011, I did not understand why they were showing me this. It seemed irrelevant.

In August 2011, I was basically taken out of the matrix and while I was away, a split happened in the human collective between those who wanted to stay asleep and those who want a more empowered and awakened reality. You can read more about it in the article "Spaceship Earth and You are the Captain". When I returned into the matrix, I felt the pain of the split, and it was many times worse than what had been shown to me by the Lemurians. The intensity was because I experience life, for all intents and purposes, as the human collective. So, when this collective split into two, it felt like my "body" had been ripped apart into two pieces. It took me a few weeks to recover. And I understood that their sharing was to prepare me for what was about to happen.

The Lemurians continued to contact me telepathically, they wanted to meet, they wanted to collaborate. But I could not understand exactly why, how, or what they wanted. I knew that they could materialize if they so chose, and suggested they manifest at my front door and come in for a cup of tea. They did not, and I think it might be because they are being monitored by the human military. But I could be wrong. It also could be a tool of empowerment. If we are able to go to them, then we have broken through any filters that were placed in our awareness and capacities in order for us to have a limited physical experience. Almost like "we are here, and it is you who choose not to see us, so choose to see us" type of thing.

Soon after that, a person who had been a total stranger came up to me and gave me a crystal she had been carrying in her purse for reasons she did not know. She'd had it for many years and that day placed it in her purse, and when we met, she knew the crystal was meant for me.

As I was not able to get much information from the Lemurians directly, and could not understand how to meet them in the physical plane, I put them out of my mind.

A while after that, another random person gave me a Lemurian crystal that they had been carrying for years. These crystals were given by people to whom I had not mentioned Lemuria before our meeting.

I could feel the Lemurians trying to communicate several times, but I was unable to get clarification on their purpose or agenda, or plan, or form of collaboration.

On a trip to Mount Shasta, I scanned for their vibrational signature (they are very distinct), and was not able to detect it.

On a trip to Oregon, a friend of mine "coincidentally" had an old friend of hers staying at her place and she told me that this friend had an experience which I had to hear.

Her friend went on to tell me all about a first hand encounter with Lemurians in Mount Shasta a couple of decades earlier or so. She was totally genuine. She had met them physically, at Mt Shasta, had been in their land, come out, and not been able to find the entrance again. It was years later she learned that they were known in the area, and what people called them.

I will often feel the Lemurians in my field of attention, they have a very distinct energy signature, but I have not been able to connect with them fully or physically.

On the 13th of October 2012, I was in Barcelona Spain, giving a public talk to several hundred individuals.

After the day talk, I met and greeted everyone who wanted to hug. Among these individuals was a woman who told me she was a dimensional caretaker of Montserrat, a mountain nearby. I cannot recall if she mentioned Lemurians or whether she called them by another name, or at all. I told her that I would meet her there the next day as I was going to go visit the place before my flight back.

My trip to the mountain did not happen the next day, I had gotten confused and it was actually scheduled for the day after, the 15th. So the chances of meeting her were minimal.

As soon as I arrived, I felt the distinct energy signature of Lemurians. My daughter was cold, so we went into a cafe to get some hot drinks, and this caretaker was "coincidentally" standing inside the cafe.

I grabbed her by the arm, and the entire group climbed the mountain to do a connection exercise with the Lemurians. It was very energetically clear, but not much information came through apart from validating the caretakers position and gratitude for her life's work.

We rushed to the airport.

This weekend, I was at an event in Southern California, and just before arriving, I kept trying to remember the name "Lemurians", as I felt they needed to be mentioned.

There was a gifted channeler there, Nora Herold, and she channeled them for a few minutes.

As I sat there, I felt the room for their presence, and it was very strong. It felt "home" like, warm, familiar, caring and loving. They also had some urgency in our collaboration, conversation, communication.

Again, I felt that we needed to make physical contact somehow, but did not know how.

A few days ago I decided to sit down and do some research. I had a skype meeting with a collaborator who is highly intuitive and as we started talking about Lemurians. After our meeting was over, I opened my email box, and saw that there were several emails from a couple who have written a book, in which they mention me in several places. The book has no relation to Lemurians, but as I had not heard from this couple for a long time, and the emails had come in at the same time as I had been talking about the Lemurians to my friend and collaborator, I decided to go out on a limb and ask them if they knew anything about Lemurians. As it happens, both of them have an amazing connection to the Lemurians. A connection that is quite unique on the planet. They have since sent me various articles, and resources, and have also sent me a book, with a huge amount of information.

Some of the information gave me further clues on the Lemurian timeline in my life, which is not so new apparently.

- When I was a teenager, I was guided to search for and study Saint Germain, I was not able to find anything of significance and dropped it. But he did come up again and again throughout my life. There appears to be a big connection, and mention, between Saint Germain and Lermurians.

- In my twenties, I was guided to learn about Madame Blavatsky, again, I looked into her, and loved her energy, but did not see the connection. In my 30s she popped up again, but I did not see what it was that I was meant to get from her body of work. She covers Lemuria quite extensively apparently.

- I was also guided to look into the work of Edgar Cayce, but again, nothing "relevant" was found. Again, he mentions them in a couple of recorded readings for people.

The common thread on all these individuals are their mention of Lemuria. And the thread was seen for the first time when reading through the material I received this month.

The connection is something I am actively working on at the moment. It almost feels like they are reeling us, the human collective, in. Pulling us "back" to them. But not in a patriarchal, savior way. Instead in a way in which a friend smiles enthusiastically and waves hello from across the street.

There is a sense of urgency on their wanting to communicate, and there is a resistance in my part. The nature of the energy that I am resisting, is the "belonging", or "ownership" to any particular species, race or collective being on, or off planet. It is important not to "align" myself to any one group or species, because if that was to happen, then "otherness" gets activated. Yet, when I process this resistance (which is ultimately "fear"), I drop into BEING a larger collective than just the Human collective.

And I can't help thinking to myself. Perhaps it is part of our expansion of awareness, when we become more than just Human beings.

In the meantime, I have been spending time every day, more than once, simply sitting in a location and daydreaming of sitting with and being in that free connection and communication space. The past two days it has been raining there a lot. In the daydream. So, I sit in the rain. The area is green, beautiful, dark clouds and rain covering everything. It is warm and pleasant. When the rain subsides for a little while, I can see the shiny droplets hanging on the petals and leaves around me. I will simply sit there for now, and I will keep you posted as to what happens next.

Coming up in May, I will be leading a open teleconference call to connect with the Lemurians. Subscribe to the Newsletter to receive the date, time and location of the call.

The Divine Masculine - Call to Action

As we create the new paradigm, we hear and use the words "Divine Feminine", "Goddess Within", "Mother Earth", "Pachamama", "Solar Feminine", a lot.

They represent what is best about the feminine energies in our selves and our planet.

But what of the "Divine Masculine", "Pachapapa", "God Within", "Father Earth", "Solar Masculine"?

The Divine Masculine energy has been hijacked by our collective choices the past few thousand years to be the "bad guy" in the story. Not the accused "bad guy", which was the feminine, but the "actual" bad guy.

We have projected onto the Divine Masculine, as a society, the Tyrant, the Aggressor, the Rescuer, the Martyr, the Savior, Teacher, God All Powerful. In other words, all the "doers" in the victim/aggressor cycle.

During the past few thousands years, to experience the Patriarchy, we have used culture, religion, and genetics to establish power onto men in a configuration which is corruptible. A power configuration of hierarchy of power over others.

Hierarchy is not of itself corruptible, nor is power corruptible. There are hierarchies of responsibility, for example, which are anything but corruptible. But, power over others is indeed corruptible. And, as a species, we used the Divine Masculine to experience and promote "power over others".

So where does that leave us today?

We have, as individuals and as a society, an enormous amount of programs, beliefs, religious doctrine, and cultural patterns, that color, filter and interpret the "Divine Masculine", into the energies of Tyrant, Aggressor, Rescuer, Martyr, Savior, Teacher, God All

Powerful. All mighty, scary and cruel, gentle teacher, suffering martyr. Does it sound familiar?

Men, who are working on their ascension, find it difficult and often overcompensate one way or the other in order to make amends to society, the women in their lives, their kids, and their own lives.

They try to be the rescuer, savior, teacher, guide so that they balance the tyrant, aggressor out.

But these configurations are still giving power to the victim/aggressor cycle.

As a species, most of us, don't KNOW how to reconnect with the healthy, pure, crystalline energy of the Divine Masculine, without projecting something for it to do for us. Whether to save us, protect us, love us, rescue us... the list goes on.

Yet, just like we ARE the Divine Feminine, just like Gaia IS the Divine Mother, just like the sun IS the Solar Feminine, so are WE the Divine Masculine, Gaia IS the Divine Father, and the sun IS the Solar Masculine.

Power, chi, energy, that has been polarized into feminine and masculine, but are in ESSENCE the same. The only separation, and the programs, roles and beliefs attached to each, come from us. We have physical sexual organs and identity genders that puts us firmly into being able to filter and tap into this CHI essence as either Feminine or Masculine, and use it accordingly. We can also tap into the other one, the one that does not correspond to our sexual organs or gender. But there's often resistance.

CALL TO ACTION - If you are willing, as men and women, let's INTEND to become ONE with and experience the Divine Masculine in its pure, unpolluted, unprogrammed, healthy, whole, complete, unchained form. Let us SEE the Divine Masculine in pure, unpolluted, unprogrammed, healthy, whole, complete, unchained form in the men and women around us.

For now, the INTENT is enough. As we progress with the intent in the next few days and weeks, and process any issues that come up,

255

we can then start moving toward BEING the Divine Masculine incarnate. Let's take back the Divine Masculine, clean him from programs, projections and chains, and see what happens.

Write down all the resistances that come up when you read that. Also any programs that get triggered. And simply observe them, allow them to express, don't judge them or push them away. Simply allow them to exist in your field, while you watch and acknowledge them.

If they are stuck programs, or heavy triggers, use the fear processing exercise on them, or find another useful processing and deprogramming tool to use on them.

What say you?

Have You felt Afraid, Angry or Stressed recently?

On Friday the 5th of April 2013, I felt a rumbling ANGER in the collective vibration. The anger built up quite dramatically and drastically, bringing chaos and fights to many sensitive people around the planet, and peaked on Tuesday the 9th of April.

Looking into it with other intuitives and seers, we saw that it was a powerful energy of "doing" and "achieving" that had been somehow artificially piggybacked by our shadow selves to turn it into anger and a "I've had enough of this" energy <read "I've had enough of this", with your right fist punching the sky, a deep frown, and frothing at the mouth>.

The artificial waves were huge and hit the collective very badly. They were further amplified by the media with anger generating stories coverage.

But it was not over. The rumblings continued after Tuesday, and built up into a different "flavor".

On Friday the 12th of April 2013 we were artificially hit again, but this time it was FEAR. It has been building ever since, and peaked on Tuesday the 16th of April. Again, they were amplified by the media with fear generating stories coverage. It is manifesting as stress, irritability, watchfulness, feeling like someone is about to hit you over head, or stab you in the back, kill you, torture you, or an energy of "something terrible is about to happen".

As I allowed the fear energy to exist, while processing it, I noticed something very, very interesting. Again, the vibration of fear was artificial, like the anger vibration of the previous week. But this time I realized that the energy, the chi that it was riding, was independent from it. This energy of chi was powerful, strong, very "hot", filled with light, it was pure and unflavored. And it was in **every cell of my physical body**. In every genetic strand, and even molecule.

I realized what has been happening is simply the intent we had last year, and the intent we have this year. Last year, to download the new operating system (joy/light/love), incarnate our higher selves on these bodies, and this year to BE joy/light/love, be our higher self at a physical level.

It's happening! The **power, the chi, is pure**. The piggy back artificial vibrations are resonating on our own physical body as "terror of the change" in it's molecular and genetic structure. Our physical bodies are FED UP of the pollution and physical hardship on the planet and now are AFRAID of the change they are undergoing. They are like beautiful racing horses who experience something they have never experienced before, they get confused, fearful, they kick and try to bolt.

What can we do?

First of all, we allow our bodies to express to us that anger and fear. We allow the high vibrational "chi" to exist in our physical bodies. And simply observe it. Soon, it starts separating, the chi becomes a buzzy energy, and the fear or anger, simply that emotion. The emotion, as we allow it to exist, dissolves. The buzzy energy we allow to grow, all the time letting our bodies know that we are here for him/her, and that she/he is safe. Any thoughts of being conned, fooled, trapped, used, enslaved, and taken for a ride we allow to exist and we observe them. We thank them. We process them.

Look see where the chi is "coming from". If it appears to be external, then process the projection of your own power to a "higher being". If you externalize your own power, that externalization can be used against you. If it's coming from your own body, then you have tuned in. It might appear to be coming from every cell, every molecule. Or from your heart center. It's not external.

Remember, power is not corrupted in and of itself. It is only we who can either use that power ourselves, out of our own free will, or can hand it over to something or someone else to do with it what they want.

And that's the core of that shadow self fear. Our physical bodies are simply afraid of unlimited Chi because we have let others use it for our detriment. And also used it ourselves for our own detriment. And any time in the past when our body elementals have incarnated this purity of chi, they have been burned at the stake, tortured, drowned and murdered in many other painful ways.

We can either choose to BE that chi, without flavors, or shadows selves dictating it, or we can say we are not ready to go there, and demand that chi to stop existing, staying physically as we have been up to now.

For the time being let's not "use" that chi, but simple BE it. Allow our physical body molecules to exist as pure, unflavored, free, CHI. Breathe in, breathe out. Breathe in, breathe out. **Exist as high vibrational, unflavored, undefined chi.**

If you have forgotten how to communicate or connect with your physical body, use the Reconnecting with the Physical Body Exercise, in the Ascension 101 Course so you can make that reconnection with the body and work with it freely through this transition. You can also use any other tools you have that reconnects you with your physical body, or look for new ones on the internet. Make sure, if you do look around, that what you choose is a stand alone tool that is not dependent on a guru, master, teacher, or belief system and doesn't claim to be "the only solution"!

I can't wait to see what flavor piggybacks next Friday! Whatever it is, remember that by sitting with it, and allowing it to exist so you can observe it, it will disentangle from your true energy/power.

Share this information with others too, as many people think they are the only ones going through these waves of powerful negative emotions. Let them know they are not alone, and not helpless. As we become aware of what is happening, and how our bodies are reacting, we take our power back and no artificial or media generated negative emotional wave on the human collective can stop us from physically becoming who we truly are. Empowered, eternal, divine beings.

May 2013 Update and Inelia's Schedule

Wow! Was April long or what?

Not sure if you experienced it too, or it was just me, but April seemed to go on forever, which is weird because time seemed to have sped up so much before April. But here we are May has arrived, the flowers are in full bloom, and we are moving ahead no matter what the world governing individuals are up to.

And, yes, they are up to a lot of stuff. We can easily fall into the victim/aggressor cycle here and feel all the rage that deservedly is felt when we look at what humans are doing to each other all over the planet.

HOWEVER, let me also remind you that NEVER in recorded history have there been so many awake and awakening individuals taking action, raising their vibration, and creating or sharing tools so others can raise their personal vibration too. The time for saving or serving others, or be saved by or be serviced by others is over, and the time to teach ourselves as equals, and co-create a fantastic physical life together as One is here.

There are organizations, groups, and individuals organizing themselves all over the planet right now, to live, work, play and exchange in new and different manners. And just because all these millions of people and organizations don't appear in our daily dose of media drama, doesn't mean they don't exist!

There is so little "natural" violence in the world, among humans, that governments are going out of their way to organize big media coverage of staged events, as well as pushing unstable individuals over the edge with fear to get them to "go nuts". They are so few, and far between in comparison with the millions of people who are each day acting from light/joy/love, that it's silly to even consider or contemplate that the planet is going downhill.

I feel, and have been feeling, a huge shift happening this year. And I think it's coming July/August. And it is GOOD.

There is more and more evidence now that we are not physically alone on this planet, that we have cousins and brother and sisters in humanoid species that we have known and talked about throughout time in our mythology and legends. Now there is a race that is afoot, between those individuals who are desperately looking for a new war enemy and have "aliens" as their new target, and those who know that these other humanoid species come in all sorts of levels of vibrations and intentions, and it is UP TO EACH ONE OF US to decide at what level we want to engage.

And that's the crux of the matter. It is up to us. We have the choice. We are waking up to the fact that we have always created reality, but have done it unconsciously. The change now is that we do it consciously. Our biggest stumbling block is simply FEAR. Once we process fear, we allow it to exist, reintegrate it into our field and move into that joy/light/love mode of existence, which is our true essence, we can move ahead in our lives filled with excitement, inspiration, and creative power.

You will be receiving a lot of Doomsday information coming in from all sorts of locations until around 2015 The dates will keep moving, the end is near! Everything is about to collapse! And it is getting EXHAUSTING. And that's the point.

But once we step out of the drama, really step out of it, and simply shift our focus on what we have in our lives, what we want for our lives, and how we want our lives to be different, and how that difference will affect others on the planet. Once we realize that it is our own individual actions and responses (not reactions), that do dictate what happens on the planet, that's when we can start breathing deeply and moving forward as a species.

In that spirit, there are, so far, two actions and four events I would like you to join me for the moth of May 2013:

- Action One: If you are highly inspired by one person or organization, send them 10% of your income for the week. Review each week who inspired you most and DO IT. Remember, its not who deserves it most, but who gave you the most via inspiration. Inspiration is that energy and enthusiasm, that realization that we are joy/light/love, and energy that moves you to change your life, or act on your knowing.

- Action Two: Go out of your way every day this month to inspire someone else. Or at least, have the intention to do it and do it as often as you can. Tell them your story, show them a picture, inspire :)
- May 3rd 2013: Journey into Manifestation - Let's get the ball rolling at a personal and global level here.
- May 7th 2013: The Nature of Realty and Its Rules of Engagement - remembering the key aspects of how our paradigm and physical reality work, and how we can consciously move to a higher level of existence **right now**.
- May 17th 2013: Brainstorm QnA session. Bring all your questions and let's explore together for the answers.
- May 25th 2013: The Lemurian Connection - A free call hosted by AWAKEN Academy, that will cover my personal time line with our Lemurian cousins, and a daydream journey where we will visit with them. Each person will get a chance to have their own personal experience of reconnection and remembrance. They want to collaborate with us as they are in the same boat we are: Gaia.

Remember that you can be the still point in the storm. As all chaos ranges around you, the place holder for the new emerging paradigm and the expanded awareness for our human collective. YOU are the second coming. WE are the second coming. What comes? Our stepping into our true essence and power, creating a physical reality that reflects our true nature as human beings. Joy/Light/Love. Everything else are low level games which are are DONE with. Now we can look into each other's eyes and really SEE.

The time of the savior is over, the time of our own sovereignty is here and it's an exciting journey of growth and discovery. I am honored that you have chosen to share it with me.

Being joy/light/love, I greet you.

Inelia Benz

Free Energy

I received this email from my webmaster **Ilie Pandia** today. We have been discussing Free Energy and how to bring Free Energy into the human collective consciousness as something that is real and already happening. Which it is. His passion and drive to make this information and technology available and accessible to the entire human collective, knows no bounds.

Ilie has been co-creating ascension101.com with me since 2010, he is the most gifted programer, web admin and solution finder I have ever met. His energy is clear and his path is paved with impeccability, truth and trust. **It is an absolute honor for me to be able to work with him every day**.

Here is his email message:

Everything runs on Energy

Something that escapes most people is that all the processes in and around us are powered by various forms of Energy.

Most of the Energy we use today on our planet is Solar energy. This solar energy has been captured by the plants in the past and converted over a very long period of time in coal or oil, that we are burning today to power our homes, our cars and our factories. Our own bodies also take up energy in the form of food. This energy is used to grow and repair the body and a lot if it is used up by our brain. To grow this food, to package it, to transport it and store it in places where you can buy it, you also require Energy.

The idea is that everything on the planet right now is an Energy game. How this energy is produced (extracted), how it is exchanged and how it is converted in forms that are useful to the Human Species.

Introducing Free Energy

Ever since we have discovered fire, humans have been on a fast track to harness more and more energy for their use. More energy always meant a higher standard of living. Slavery was made obsolete by more energy. Women's status has improved as soon as more energy was available. Large families stopped making sense, when child labor stopped making sense, and that was due to more energy being available. Life in US is so much better than other parts of the world, because there is more energy available for each person living there. And we are just scratching the surface of what is possible.

At some point along this line, what I will call the Global Controllers had a realization: as soon as any human on the planet has access to abundant, unlimited clean energy their "power over others" games would be over. They would have to leave and play their games elsewhere. At that time, a campaign was started to suppress, by ridicule, the idea of Free Abundant Energy. It has been declared "proven to be impossible" as it "violates the laws of physics". Even so, some scientists (starting most likely with Nikola Tesla) have been able to tap into various forms of Energy that are not powered by fossil fuels or radioactive material. This Energy source has sometimes been called "Zero Point Energy".

The proof of this is beyond this writing, but anyone reading is invited to look this up, and read about it. For a few days just ignore the "laws of physics" and pretend this is actually possible. Have a look a it. If it were possible, how would it work? What would change in our world?

We the creators

The greatest victory of the Global Controllers is that they have made Abundance and Free Energy unimaginable. We are all familiar with "You can't have something for nothing...", "You gotta work for a living.", "There is no such thing a free lunch". And so on.

All the above are bits and pieces of what I call "The Scarcity Program" that is deeply embedded into our subconscious minds.

I don't want us to fall into the "victim/aggressor" paradigm. I acknowledge that the Global Controllers act as a parasite but their actions are made possible by our collective agreement to "not even imagine abundance".

So while I acknowledge the suppression and the vested interests to keep us addicted to fossil fuel, I choose to act as a creator and focus on abundance instead. Let's choose to make the Global Controllers obsolete. If they have no one to control, they have no choice but to either join the party on our terms or pack and leave.

Free Energy, Sentience, Love, Joy and Abundance are linked together. And I will not be surprised if one day we will discover that in essence they are the same thing.

There may be many, many ways to raise our awareness and make manifest Heaven on Earth, but as far as I know, none of them will work faster and help more Humans (and other lifeforms on the planet) as bringing Free Energy out in the open.

There is a bit of a catch 22 here: Free Energy will make it so much easier to raise our awareness and yet it seems that we need to raise our awareness of Free Energy technologies first and how they would change the world, before we are able to manifest it into our reality.

An abundant, Free Energy based world

So let's pretend for a moment that we have Free Energy now. Suspend your beliefs that it is not possible.

Each and every one of us has access to unlimited clean Energy and devices to convert that energy to various useful forms for us: electric, thermal and mechanic.

How would our lives change, now that you will not have to work for a living? What would you do if money or survival will no longer be an issue.

Free Energy would make profit obsolete. And once profit is out of the equation, then quality will take its place. Now every product we make, we make it out of joy, out of a desire to express our creativity, to be of service to us and our fellow humans and non-human life. We no longer work for money and we no longer work in jobs we don't like. Just imagine how would that feel?

With abundant, clean energy the war for resources will stop making sense. Taking it from others so I can have it will no longer be required. Mining the Earth for oil will no longer be required. Free sharing of technology and information will come naturally once you no longer have a "profit margin" to maintain, or a competitor to wipe out. I can easily imagine a joyful coming together to eliminate poverty and hunger from all over the planet. With Free Energy that can be done in matter of days. Just think of the human potential unleashed, of all that creativity waiting to express itself in safe, abundant environment.

Virtually every aspect of our lives would be impacted and greatly improved with the advent of unlimited clean Energy. The way we think about family, relationships, sex, marriage, work, creativity, boundaries, nations, language, health, learning, traveling, food production, relationship with nature and the Planet. Everything would change.

The most important change however, would be within. In an abundant society, you would have to become a "response-able" Creator. There will be no one left to blame, no one to complain about. You will no longer be able to act as a victim (or aggressor for that matter). You will have full freedom and with that comes full responsibility for your life. We will truly be "self determined grown-ups" :).

And this, is just the beginning of the journey.

Let's Pretend - Fear Free Life...

By pretending, we initiate a possible outcome in real life. Children do this naturally, and animals do to when they play. They pretend doing what they will need to do, or want to learn how to do, when they grow up.

By pretending, we put our hands into the field of infinite possibility that is the space between thoughts, and the area between particles in every atom. We bring forth something that did not exist in our minds before. By pretending, we give ourselves permission to bypass "what is real", "what is possible", and "what is doable", and simply allow it to exist in our imagination, in our writing, in our drawings, in our games and in our conversations. Imagine, pretend, write or draw, about a **life without fear. YOUR live**. What would it look like? What would you do?

I was looking at this myself, and the first thing that came to mind was, I would "look more". I love looking, I love observing. Having to be a public voice to raising consciousness, empowerment and awareness on the planet is a busy schedule, and simply looking has moved to the back of the list. But, as I indulged in my pretend game of NO FEAR in the world, my job of raising consciousness and raising the vibration of the planet was done. I was simply left with Observing. Looking. Exploring. And that was a fascinating thing in and of itself.

When in January 2010 I was asked to go public, I had no idea why. Or even why me. It occurred to me that the people that had come in to do that job had been somehow taken out of the game and I was their tenth backup plan. The reason I thought this is because I am an extremely private person, and prefer to see and observe, rather than be seen or observed. Particularly as Inelia Benz is irrelevant and really does not exist. Nothing to see here.

And this week, as I was playing pretend with **NO FEAR in my life,** I saw that that was the whole point for having me become public. It was because not only did I have no attention on being seen because it didn't cause any drive in me, or fulfill any desire or need, and yes it had a dissonant energy in that up to now being public was about the "I, me and myself" paradigm, and I didn't have any of those, but also because **I loved to be the observer.**

As we move away from the Savior/Aggressor/Victim/Martyr paradigm, the need for saviors and guides, or deities as focus of our attention, is no longer necessary. All the information we could ever need, is already available. And if it's not available right away, many people are working to make it available. If someone really wants to find something out, they can. The time of a guru or yogi "giving" enlightenment experience to others is no longer useful. What we are left with, is remembrance and multiple viewpoints. The more viewpoints, different viewpoints, looking at the same subject, the more we can access about that subject.

What the new role of those who in the past may have started groups, religions and followings, is to simply inspire an audience to look at what the speaker is seeing, looking at, exploring, and not themselves - the speaker. The person in the audience can come and go at will, listen to and explore new seeings with different speakers at will, and when all is seen, and he or she can access new seeing, start speaking and expressing those seeings so others can experience that new point of view too. In this new structure the speaker becomes irrelevant.

And from pretending **a world without fear** what resulted was a realization that **WE CAN START NOW.** By two or more people looking in the same direction, pretending the same thing, or intending the same intention, we bring a level of "agreement" into the reality construct we call the physical universe.

One of the "laws" of physical reality, is that it exist through agreement. Agreement comes in packages, programs, cultural beliefs, social media, religions and all sorts of other things. At the moment, our reality is filled with fear. Fear is everywhere, in every aspect of our lives. However, it is just a "point of view". An energetic expression of attachments, survival, and avoidance. Some individuals believe that "fear is necessary for survival". Others think

269

it's ok to feel it but do stuff anyway, and yes, this is a way to start dissolving fear, because we realize that the sky did not fall down when we did what we were afraid to, but this method can be long and arduous, and can backfire. Others try to suppress it, or push it away, or hide from it in a bubble of light. But by pushing it away, we make it stronger. So we process it. And that works really, really well at an individual level. The more fear that is resolved through processing it, the higher our own vibration becomes and the more expansive our awareness becomes.

And now by pretending our life without fear, and then a **world without fear**, we can bring a new paradigm possibility into the human collective consciousness.

So that's how my life looked like, and this is what I have decided to do different: I have decided to **start looking now** and not wait until we are finished with our job on the planet. I want to look, and I invite you to look where I am looking simply because it is fascinating and the more of us that look the more we get to uncover, discover and remember.

For this month, let's spend some time, even if a few seconds, looking at the "reality" of having **fear free** personal life and planet. Get a pen and paper and express what **YOUR life looks like FEAR FREE.**

What say you?

Are You Making Ends Meet?

If you are interested in being fully supported in life, either just because you exist, or through your art, skills and dharma, then you might be interested what has been coming up so far for me with regard the energy exchange models and flows, and how we can start tapping into higher vibrational ones right now, while the planet is still hanging on desperately to 3D life and energy exchange models.

On the one hand, we need to live and be able to function in a 3D world, but we are also aware and able to tap into the New Paradigm. Where we are able to manifest all we need.

Examining energy exchange models

My ultimate question is how do we basically transition from 3D energy exchange models to 5D, or New Paradigm, models. This is an exercise in advanced seeing. We all do advanced seeing when we have a problem, we look for solutions. We send our mind into the future to test out possible outcomes, "if I do this, then would this be the result?", or "this is the result I want, so what do I do to get there". That type of thing.

What I am doing in this instance, and I can't wait to hear your input, is to look at present business models, then look at what it would look like without the "power over others" paradigm structure.

This was my thought process. I have looked at it from a business point of view, because business are something we all know have an energy exchange flow:

1. Every business is created for a purpose. We don't just pop them up for the sake of it existing. Purposes can be:

> **a.** to make money: turn creative energy into material energy so we can then interchange for other material energy or creative energy (from others).

> **b.** satisfy a personal desire to use our skill set or creative power (however, this doesn't need to be a business unless we

271

need energy or materials to carry it out - received from external sources)

c. to fulfill a planetary need.

2. A business needs, by default, more than one person to exist. Most these groups have one or more people in them:

a. Chi - Energy - Materials

b. suppliers of materials or energy (they receive money from the producer to be able to supply materials)

c. producers of item, service, information or skill (they receive money from the "receivers" to pay the suppliers so they can produce)

d. receivers or end product (they receive the end product, and send back money to the producer so the cycle starts again)

Now let's look at it as a flow of Chi. At the moment we have money as the representative of Chi.

If the Chi stops anywhere on that previous cycle, then the natural conclusion is that the cycle stops. If the Chi flow is not equal in all sections, then we get buildups in some parts, and starvation in others (sounds familiar?). A beggar has no way to deliver 2.c, maybe through sickness, or mental capacity, or medical or physical condition. Now he is at the mercy of 2.d, without being able to provide anything tangible, in order to survive (he/she does provide some sort of energetic savior satisfaction to 2.d). At a world scale model there is a huge flow of Chi that go from the masses to the Cabal at 2.a, 2.b and 2.c. and very little comes back in return.

This list came up as I was looking at areas of life which I am looking to find insights into, so I could bring these to the table on our brainstorming session on May 2013. The Brainstorming session covered healing, bringing up children, free energy, quantum physics, dealing with sleepers and more. Including our own physical body cycles of existence. Eating, functioning, working, and communication to our environment and others.

Let's look at this list with a real life example. Let's take Ascension101.com as the model.

1. Ascension101 is created for a purpose: Delivering the message of inspiration and empowerment to the masses. A huge outflow of Chi.

2. Ascension101 needs, by default, more than one person to exist:

> **a.** Chi - Energy - Materials: Money, equipment, staff.

> **b.** suppliers of materials or energy (they receive money from Ascension101 to be able to supply materials): Third party delivering methods (internet, advertising), items needed to survive in the physical, workers.

> **c.** producers of item - Inelia and the Staff at Ascension101 (receives money from the "end receivers" to pay the suppliers so they can produce).

> **d.** end receivers or product or service You. (you receive the end product, and send back money to Ascension101 so the cycle starts again).

When we are going to create something new, say, at a personal level, me writing and publishing this article, I need several things in 2.a and 2.b. and 2.c. I need a computer, a desk, electricity, the internet, software for my computer, an internet service, staff to program and administer and support the website that you are reading it on, a house to hold all the services, the desk and me, food and water in my body to function (I'm not yet a breatherian), an accountant, customer service person, and the list goes on and on. All these items are supplied by other human beings and they get my personal Chi in return so their cycle doesn't stop. I send them my personal Chi in the form of money. I pay for internet, house, food, electricity, staff wages, and all the rest, with money. The end result is this article, which you, the end receiver of the product or service (2.d), get to read.

We have also provided clean and clear methods for you to send Chi back, so that the flow doesn't stop. Including free tools that empower them to open channels and entry points of Chi, so you can have TONS of Chi and can become an empowerer of others. Sending you power, Chi, so you can have number 2.a on your cycle, and the whole global continues and grows. Many individuals organically and naturally feel the energy exchange desire to balance the flow out and send us gifts, donate funds or buy products to send Chi back, and that's why those who don't, can read this article for free.

Most people do not send Chi back to us. Those people have received our time, skills, information and the Chi it took to get this article out there, for free (although it requires huge amounts of Chi to put it out there), which means that if they have acquired any benefit, information, or inspiration, and don't send Chi back in a format we can use, they are in fact stopping the Chi flow and also creating energetic debt to the staff and to those who do send Chi back.

What would this example look like if the flow stopped? If individuals stopped sending back Chi in the form of gifts, donations or buying of products at ascension101, then I would no longer be able to sit at my desk and write this article, the rest of the the staff would have to get different jobs, and there would be no website for you to read it on. And even if, while working as a highly paid communications consultant at some huge company instead, I wanted to sit down and write the article, I would not have the time, nor the staff at ascension101 to put it online. And those free tools that empower people to be able to empower others, would stop.

So, that's one example of how we can look at any energy exchange flow and work out how the current of Chi is moving through it. If anything is out of balance, we need to address it.

You can use the same list to see how this model is working in your business or your personal life. Identify where the blocks are, the debts are and how to clear them out.

At the moment, the out of balance Chi flow at Ascension101 is that the output of final "product" is about 10,000 times larger than the input of Chi from the end receivers of the product. This creates a buildup at the receiving end, and starvation in the previous ones.

This limits our ability to get 2.a, 2.b on the list, which limits 2.c (in our case, delivering the message of empowerment to billions of people rather than millions). The question is, how do we increase the Chi entry percentage from number 2.d, so we can increase 2.a, 2.b, 2.d? The limitations are simple programs and agreements. Programs like "ascension information has to be free!", this translates in "free to receive" only. At the moment, it does not translate into "free to produce or deliver" due to our present social structure. In fact, there is nothing "free" on the planet except what we all bring forth from our own imaginations. And even spending time imagining things takes energy (food, water, a location to be safe enough to imagine things, etc.). And it is only because we at Ascension101 have at some level subscribed to those programs, that they affect us.

Time to hit the Processing!

One of the highest vibrational number 2.c products on the planet is "inspiration". But we rarely send money to those who inspire us. I send money to those who inspire me because inspiration is is the breath of life. It is more important to me than food and water. The reason is that inspiration is pure Chi, Life Force. With inspiration we can move mountains, remove all obstacles and achieve whatever it is we want to achieve in life. Writing this article, for example, has inspired me to process all my subscriptions to programs that say we cannot receive Chi back from 2.d, or generate our own from 2.a! And that is myself generating 2.a :D

When we look at 2.a, we see that there is our limit as 3D existence. Once 2.a is freely available to everyone on the planet in unlimited supply, then we can achieve anything. The question is, how do we make 2.a unlimited? And just having the intention to find that answer, is an amazing expansion of awareness.

If you have some brainstorming ideas about this topic, I would love to hear from you. Post on the comments below!

When we brainstorm, we create a co-creative intent to find solutions, we not only tap into our own individual sources of rmation and inspiration, but also tap into the global sciousness, our guides or entourage, Source, and Higher Self.

Tools:

1. Clearing Your Wealth Lines

2. Journey Into Manifestation

3. Limitations Why Do We Create Them

2. Reconnecting With The Spirit of Money Exercise (Free)

How do your LIMITATIONS serve?

Last Friday, we hosted a Brainstorming session here at ascension101.com. It was really awesome, ideas and viewpoints were aired, and amazing expansion of awareness was experienced.

As I sat with the information that had come in before the call, during the call and after the call, I saw a pattern. It didn't matter what subject matter we were looking at, the questions all had one thing in common:

LIMITATIONS

I'm going to give you some examples, and if any of these trigger you emotionally, or make you want to argue how wrong I am and how right you are, take a look very closely because there are programs running in you there. You see, knowing that you are right and I am wrong is a perfect example of our different viewpoints, but wanting to make me wrong so you can be right, that's a program triggered to defend itself.

First example: **Money** is pure, brilliant, chi. But we react to it with rejection, this rejection was programmed in by the cabal. How? By placing **PROGRAMS OF LIMITATIONS** on it.

Think about it. Is it money that you hate, or desire, or feel disgusted at? Or is it the lack of money you or others have? The difficulty of receiving limitless money? The fact that those who don't have it are castigated on the planet?

Do you see the pattern?

Second Example: **Health** is wholeness, completeness, and we CAN be 100% healthy at any moment. Yet, most of us have chronic health issues. Why? Because they either serve us or serve those whom we have given our power to. **How does it serve us**? IT LIMITS US. Think about how your sickness or condition limits you. And see if those limitations have a purpose.

Third Example: Power. We ALL limit our personal **power**. Why? Why don't we just create the environment and life we want in an instant? Why do we sometimes self destruct? Imagine having all the power on the planet. **Does it make you afraid**? Afraid of messing up? Afraid of being lost to the ego? Afraid of being attacked?

Fourth Example: **Linear Time**, a lot of people are talking about time banks, but these are even more limited than money! These quantify your minutes and hours, and give these value. Not pure chi, but time. As we are not yet in a non-linear time existence, time banks are a huge **LIMITING system**.

Fifth Example: Free Energy, we BELIEVE as a society that it is not possible. YET, there has been technology patented for decades now that can generate it. We limit our energy as a species because it serves big corporations to make us think it is limited.

So, why do we do this?

This is my thought: We limit ourselves to provide us with a way to experience life in bite size pieces. We limit ourselves completely when we are walking a path that our higher self does not agree with, forcing us to change course. We limit ourselves to have a limited experience, which existing as individual beings is by default.

Our limitations are like the controlling factors that shape and form our passage and experience through time/space. And THAT is why chronic illness don't go away, that's why our income is limited, that's why we don't reclaim all our power, that's why we still subscribe to a past, present and future.

IMAGINE

Identify a LIMITATION in your life right now.

Now, imagine for a few minutes, what your life would look like without it.

Stay in that LIMITLESS imaginary time/space for a while.

Now imagine every human being on the planet without that limitation.

If any fear popped up, process it, remember, fear is the bricks that build the walls of limitation.

Let's stop messing about and become limitless yeah?

Mass Media Changing Paradigm? What?

I have been **looking** at the past months of media released information with regard to what is happening on the planet ,and I was surprised to find that major outlets are now being used to release information which was previously reported to be "tin hat looney bin conspiracy theory crackpot fantasies".

They way this information is being released is **highly controlled** and minimized by the medium it is being presented on, or invalidated by the comments released with the information. As well as limited in the scope of the information. Sometimes, the data released is talked about as though it's going to happen some time in the future. But it is seeping through.

A while back, Al Gore spoke about chemtrails on a major network show, but referring them to some future crazy plan.

We also had some mainstreammedia covering the Citizens Hearing on Disclosure, but emphasizing how the participants had been paid a lot of money to sit through it.

At the start of 2013, I saw the coverage of the harmful effects of fluoride in our water, reported by Fox News. A step in the right direction? Tiny step, but at least some of the information is being delivered to the **sleeping masses**. This is always good news to me. Plus it is an article I can send to all my conservative friends and relatives, as it was released in their media network.

My satisfaction comes from the fact that the Fluoride being harmful information is now being given to the sleeping masses. it is still limited as they don't mention **decreased IQ** or the damage to the brain and pituitary gland, and that it disconnects us from our capacity to connect with our inner Source. But at least it is a step in the right direction.

I also did wonder about the **cabal's ulterior motives**. Not so much of the publication but the reversal of health concerns of fluoride by a governing body. The most negative view is that they want to add something even more debilitating, or perhaps **DNA manipulative**, that is incompatible with fluoride, to our water supply. And the most positive is that we are finally seeing a shift in the puppeteers that reflect the higher planetary vibration.

The same train of thought went through my mind when I watched Iron Man III. If you haven't watched this movie yet, do so. Not because it's entertaining, and has a great sense of humor, but because in the movie (and in movies I and II also), they blatantly reveal the false flag creation process, the reason behind wars (commercial), and in Iron Man III the false creation of a terrorist to create and feed the "war on terror", naming the real false terrorists created by the cabal. Fascinating.

Yet, it is released in the format of a fantasy film, where nothing is real, it's all science-fiction.

After watching Iron Man III I was of two minds, again amused that the information had been blatantly released to the sleeping masses, and at the same time KNOWING that one of the major rules of this planet is to **LET PEOPLE KNOW** what is being done to them, and if they do not respond by saying it is not acceptable, it is carried out, or continues to be carried out.

That's one of the reasons why my website and FB pages have not been taken down. The pages are completely vulnerable. One person in the government, clicking one button, can take both sites down in an instant. Yet my channel of information, and thousands of others out there, are not taken down. Why? Because we serve the purpose of letting the masses know what is really going on. Whether they choose to click on that information, or visit the site, is another matter.

The times when my sites have been taken down, are when a certain flavor of **information is released.** But the sites are then fully restored a few hours later. What is that information? That **YOU are the CREATOR OF THIS REALITY**. That your consent and you not consenting, rules the world. FYI if you do not make a choice, that is considered a consent to what is happening or proposed.

What can we do?

If you are physically actively minded, write to the network and producers of these shows and films to give your **positive reinforcement** on their covering the truth, and at the same time encouraging them to cover more information. Send the information that is accurately, albeit minimally, covered in mainstream media to all of your sleeping relatives and friends.

If you are mystically minded, **simply "look"** at the mainstream media outlet energetic structure, and collective consent for its role in lowering our vibration. I do not consent to have the human collective's vibration lowered, and therefore my vibration lowered, through the mainstream media.

We **humans** are addicted to drama. If you think you are not, think about this for a minute, all futuristic movies that have made it to the box office have a really negative, cabal ruled planet Earth, where enslavement, disempowerment and little value to human life are rampant. Now imagine a movie that shows planet earth that is beautiful, clean, where everyone here is actively **consciously** and powerfully **manifesting** their perfect life on **this Earth**. Where there is no power over others. No dark motives. No threat and no fear. Any first reactions of thought? Don't censor yourself or make yourself "right" right away. What comes when looking at it honestly? Perhaps it is a thought of "it's not going to happen in my lifetime", or "it's boring", or "we need darkness in order to see the light", or "we can't do it". Take a look at any barriers to that reality happening. Both that future Earth, and the present day movie being created for us to see, and be excited about seeing it.

What possible plots in that world would inspire millions of people to pay to watch it in the cinema or buy the DVD? What plots would send you to the cinema to watch it?

Sit with it. Let's think of plots that would do just that, that don't require an opposing faction to try and destroy the Earth, or enslave humanity, or have a hidden evil reason that allows the planet to exist and are exciting and stimulating to watch.

WTF is happening?? July 2013

You may have noticed that **the energies on the planet** are going a little wacko at the moment. It started near the beginning of June, and it is set to continue and increase until around October or November.

Last year, when people were talking about huge physical changes happening in our Paradigm in December 2012, I kept feeling that nothing would happen at a physical level, but that in the summer of 2013, something was up.

And here we are!

A few weeks ago, I was driving down the street, and very suddenly I got the distinct feeling that **Gaia had began her physical expression of higher dimension**. That the planet consciousness was going from holding space at an energetic level, to holding 5D at a physical level.

At the same time, the **polarized energies of light and dark**, which have been battling on the planet for thousands of years, increased their output to mind blowing amounts. This is causing all sorts of extreme behavior, reactions, beginnings and endings for the people of the planet.

The following weeks, and now into July, there is a sense of **observation and experience without judgment**. This last piece, the no-judgment, is very important and this message has been coming in strong from various individuals, situations and also downloads. It also includes feeling judged, or wanting to be judged in a positive light.

This "battle" between light and dark is very real. It is increasing every day. **Gaia** can be interpreted to have **"taken sides"** to the light end of the spectrum. And is now going to start physical manifestations of this "side taking". I'm not really sure how this is going to pan out. We might fall into fear, thinking that Gaia is angry and we are going to see lots of disasters around the planet. And maybe we are right. But the thought that crossed my mind was, well, we are inhabiting Gaia sentient material, our own physical bodies! Just imagine, everyone on the planet has a physical body, which is sentient, which is an elemental of the planet Earth. Which is directly connected to Gaia.

We, as a species are becoming more and more aware of how we "work", how we "function". The more aware we become, the more able and empowered. We are able to see how we, as a divine, eternal, being, can have a chosen (by us) limited experience. We become conscious of what those limits are, we choose what they are, and thus morph and **transform** our lives accordingly.

If you are interested in exploring how limits are constructed, work, how we can use them for our advantage, or remove them, get the talk "Limitations - Why Do We Create Them?" as it goes into great depth about it. Or you can simply read the huge library of articles at ascension101, as just about all the articles deal with one or more of our limitations and how to become aware of it, and process it.

So, two very important movements forwards for our species this month, one is becoming aware of how we construct our experience via boundaries and limitations, and the other is not to judge those boundaries! Not to judge ourselves, others, or wanting good or bad judgments for ourselves or others.

What can we do?

- I will be launching a free to join, global experiment in consciousness in a few days. This will be totally awesome. So stay tuned!
- Don't judge yourself or others, and don't wish for judgment whether positive or negative.
- Reconnect with Gaia (great free meditation to do this is in the Tools section of ascension101) and give her permission to express at a higher vibration.
- Take off your shoes and walk barefoot for at least an hour per day. It doesn't really matter where, but outdoors is best, wherever the sun has been hitting the ground.

- Enjoy stuff! Eat tasty food, smell the roses, play games, go to a park and roll on the grass!
- Watch a sunset or sunrise this week.
- Find things to enjoy about other human beings in your environment. It could be the way they look, a smile, clothing, it doesn't matter what it is. Just find something to enjoy about other human beings.
- When people, or even yourself, go a little "crazy" around you this summer, don't fret and (again) don't judge. Simply observe.
- Smile :)
- Take time off from the internet, tv, radio and other media outlets.
- Release attachment to result.
- Step outside the box of limitations.
- View this time like you are stepping into the most amazing experience of your life and allow that amazing experience to manifest.

Remember, the energies are going crazy at the moment, both ends of the spectrum are increasing their volume up to max. This will blow a lot of fuses and a lot of minds. At the same time, this can be a time of great enjoyment and **joy/light/love** (because of the light and Gaia energy increase), so don't let the dark end of the spectrum suck you into the drama. Enjoy this time!

The Original Architects, Creators of Our Species...

You have no idea how excited I am to be able to share this information with you. I invite you to look at it with a sense of sharing a story, dream, myth, novel or memory.

This topic is something I have been looking at for years now, and the information has been coming in bits and pieces all this time, the latest piece arrived as I was preparing for my monthly class over at AWAKEN Academy: Ultradimensional Incarnation.

This class was an exploration into the ultradimensional aspect of our DNA, and how, by activating it, our psychic abilities increase. Part of understanding the Ultradimensional aspect of our DNA requires looking at where our DNA originated. While preparing for the various aspects explored in the class, looking at the origin of our species revealed one tiny bit of further information that is amazing.

For a few years now, I've been aware of a species I call the Original Architects. As I mentioned in the class, they are not THE original architects of universe, just the ones who started the ball rolling for our own species, the Human Race. I could see that they created a humanoid species out of Gaia's DNA material. That the species they created was One with the planet. It was made of matter, Earthly matter. Most individuals who are educated on "alternative" human history of origin, will know about the Annunaki. I will talk about the Annunaki role later on in this article, but one thing to know is that they are not the Original Architects. The Annunaki came, much, much later.

The reason why the Original Architects would create a Gaian humanoid species is, from what I can see, anything from scientific curiosity, entertainment, their own expansion of dimensional experience by creating bodies they could incarnate into, or the creation of their own species (think of it as a non-linear time chicken and the egg question).

The reason they created us, perhaps, will be revealed when we "hatch" :)

The first humanoid species they created was different to us in many ways. They were physically more "solid". They had a larger Gaian DNA percentage than we do now. Their form of communication was experiential and whole, not verbal and fractured. Their decision making and nature were linked intrinsically with the planet and every other species on it. Their individual and collective mind worked a bit like those huge flocks of tiny birds that sometimes can be seen in the sky, moving like an intelligent cloud, fast, making fascinating shapes, never two birds flying into each other.

They created us to be flexible, our DNA wide open (a bit like open source programs on the internet). Then they withdrew their presence. Others came and altered our DNA, our natures, our roles, and our "reason to exist". Others added their own DNA to our mix, and placed programs and functions with it. The Annunaki come to mind, creating a slave species.

And this is the bit that arrived now: The Original Architects always knew that other species would come and "play" with their creation. That enormously different species would add their DNA to the mix. That high vibrational species would be called to incarnate here. And all this was part of the plan. A type of intergalactic and interdimensional open source cross pollination.

It feels very much like they are of "one mind with us". Like not only are they observing from somewhere or sometime, but they contain all our experience, our thoughts, and more. Yet, they are not attached. They don't seem to be attached to us like we might think a parent would to their own child.

The strongest energy I get when I feel their sense of us, is surprise, or delight, that something worked beyond their wildest expectations. Or even that we can sense them and know they exist and what they did.

This article probably poses more questions than it answers. And that's because it is simply a tiny bit of information which you can play with. As an exercise, I would invite you to "pretend it is true" and follow this data back to them. See what happens. See if you get more data. Even if it is "pretend".

Feel free to add your seeing in the comments section at ascension101.com, or twitter me at https://twitter.com/inelia ;)

It's Time We Picked Up the Ball - Call to Action

During 2013, and beyond, we have been inundated with fear campaigns from every media source known to modern society. From television and radio, to alternative news, internet sites, advertisements, global mood altering technology, chemical infusion via water, chemtrails, and food, you name it, it's being done.

Everywhere we turn, we are told that there is "badness" happening. If we want to stay pure of body and mind, we have to work very, very hard, switch off the TV, radio, filter our internet consumption, drink distilled or filtered water, treat our food to clean pollutants, stay indoors during heavy chemtrail spraying, do regular purification and cleansing routines... the list goes on and on. But all that, all that effort, will have no effect if we stay in a state of fear.

That's where our own impeccability and integrity come in. Why are we going through so much effort to cleanse ourselves and stay pure? The reason is very important as it will dictate the results. If it is done because we are afraid, then no matter how many salt baths we take, or what we ingest, we are playing right into the low vibrational game field.

If we are doing this because it makes us feel good, vibrant, filled with life, energy and capacity to do, then we are in the right track.

If I drink alcohol, I get a buzz, then I get fuzzy, my capacity to drive my car goes to zero (although I would say I am perfectly capable), my capacity to make good decisions is lowered, my capacity to care is gone. In other words, living in a "drunk" state creates a certain life, that is different to the one that I would create sober. It's not very functional, it needs people to take care of me, drive me places, make food, look after my child, and all sorts of things. In other words, I can live like a child. Not responsible for anything, unable to do, and a weight on those who love me, on society, and on myself. As long as I can get a drink, stay buzzed, I won't give a shit, so all is good in that world for me. It is full of physical pleasure, satisfaction and child like "look after all my needs" energy.

And this is how most of the humans on the planet are living their lives. By choice, in a state of drunken irresponsibility. It is us, the human collective, who have chosen this path. Not the "White Man" taking over "native lands" by killing everyone... but the natives co-creating the destruction of the planet by liking the alcohol and dropping the ball on being the planet's caretakers and instead going into a drunken stupor. Anyone who has Native blood running through their veins, or lives close to Native People in the Western world, knows what I am talking about. We have at least one relative or friend who is an alcoholic or drug addict who has wreaked havoc in our or our family's life. The alcohol and drug problem is horrendous. It hurts. Yet, this very poignant example is not really about Native People or White Men. It is about us. It is about each person reading this article. It is NO LONGER about who is to blame, who feels guilty or is guilty, it's not about anger, fight, flight, fear, attacking or defense. It's not about giving away our power or our authority to the Native Shaman, our Spiritual Leader or the White Government. **It is about us realizing that we are POWERFUL and can create any reality we want, and can do it NOW.**

How is that?

WE are the native people of the planet. No matter what race our body is, no matter where our original soul evolutionary path, our soul's home, is, we are HUMAN now. We embody a body of EARTH. Created of Gaia's earth and water. We resonate with the caretaker energy. WE, reading this article KNOW that we are here to co-create a pure, clean, healthy, abundant, and free world. We KNOW it. We are alive, we breathe, we live, we love, here on THIS planet. Otherwise we would not be reading this material, we would have unsubscribed from this website.

CALL TO ACTION

So, what do we do?

1. We acknowledge that we are all actively co-creating the world we live in today. No one to blame. No one to allot guilt to, including ourselves.

2. We know that no matter what pollutants and fears get thrown our way, we don't have to ingest it or be affected by it.

3. We process our fear, our guilt, our anger, our blame (of ourselves and others), and our judgment.

4. We become the planet, person, being, we aspire to experience in our own lifetimes. This is an act of choice and intent.

5. We move in small steps, guided by the energy of integrity and impeccability, making daily choices of words, actions, thoughts, and emotions that are aligned with that Earth we want to experience.

6. Take action in our local area, write, speak, do, what we know co-creates the world we know exists within us all, and do it from a place of non-judgment.

Refuse to ingest the drug of drama, fear, hate, anger, judgment and complacency, and join with Gaia in BEing your true self, your sovereign empowered human being that you were born to be.

Are you ready? I am :)

Time to Turn You ON - How to step into your POWER

By first exploring where we think we are not powerful, we can then tap into where our power lies as an individual.

The most expansive questions we can ask ourselves as human beings, and often the first questions we ask when we first awaken, are "Who am I?" "What is my mission?" "How can I become/express my highest self?" "Why are we here?" "What is this planet all about?"

One of the most poignant things to find out is that we limit our own capacity to see the answers to those questions through energetic, mental, emotional and perceptual restrictions. We RESTRICT ourselves. And why do we do that? For at least two reasons, one is so that we can play a limited game, within limited parameters, and the second is a fear that if we become completely unrestricted, we would harm others.

All these restrictions reflect the fear we have to our own personal POWER.

What is power?

Power is the ability to do, and it is CHI.

The more ability to do we have, and the more Chi, the more "powerful" we are. Both in our own life and in society at large. As an example, money is a representative of Chi and ability to do. If you had 20 Billion dollars in the bank, would you be able to do more than you are able to now? This brings money back from all the energetic wrappings and wrong-nesses that it has been painted with, to its most simple role: representation of power (chi and ability to do). The program of self gratification vs empowering our collective experience is very prominent when we look at what we would do with all that power.

We are taught over and over again that power corrupts, power is abused, it will take us over and rule us, power is BAD. Who teaches us this? People in power. Now, in these previous two sentences, replace the word "power" with the word "money" and you will start to get a real feel for how we agree to be disempowered, even in the "new age" networks: *We are taught over and over again that money corrupts, money is abused, it will take us over and rule us, money is BAD. Who teaches us this? People with money.*

The fact is that the relationship between our manifesting power, our wealth, our capacity to do and our Chi, is often equal to how we feel about power and how we feel about money. And that's NO COINCIDENCE.

We are taught to fear and reject our own power, and to feel money is evil, from the very beginning of our lives. We are taught this by those very same people who are themselves in power because if we realized, stepped into, and used our power, their power would be shown for what it is, nothing more than smoke and mirrors. Those same people have created a financial model which is indeed nothing but smoke and mirrors which diverts all chi, money, and power directly to them.

Who are "they"? They are every single being you have placed in authority over you. Anyone who can tell you what to do and you will do it even though it feels wrong. Anyone who you have given the capacity to remove stuff from your life without your "consent", such as a job, electricity, water, shelter, food, communication, love, comfort, joy... Anyone who you feel is to "blame" for your suffering, pain, distress, or the suffering, pain and distress of others.

"They" are our OWN creation to stop us from being powerful. It is like a self feeding loop.

So, where does **YOUR POWER** lie?

Where your own curiosity, joy, inspiration and passions are ignited. A combination of what you are "good at" and "love doing".

Take a look around your room right now, or if you are in a public space, take a look at your clothes, and what you have in your pockets, backpack, handbag or other personal items. Look at the browser history in your internet program.

There will be themes popping up. A color, a style, a historical period, a technology, a question, a theory, a skill, something will be more prominent than other things.

For one, the interest you have in your own expanded awareness (ascension) and growth. You are here to BE awake.

Now look at the people you are surrounding yourself with in your personal life. The ones you share most messages with, emails with, conversations with, time with. These are the people who are reflecting back to you the reality you are creating, the power you are using, and, very importantly, the power you are suppressing.

Grab all the communications you have had with these main individuals the past five days. Analyze the topics covered, the words you and they used most, and the main energy direction (was it raising your and their vibration, or lowering it?).

Now, this bit of the exercise is interesting: imagine all those individuals having absolute power over reality. Having power and chi unrestricted. Now you will get a very graphic idea both of where your own power lies, and where you are restricting yourself of your power. And yes, agreeing to restrict others too.

Useful tool for this exercise: Fear Processing Exercise

Related article that you might want to read: How do your LIMITATIONS Serve?

Related tools that support the Ascension101 Staff:

Advanced: Rules of Engagement

Beginner/Intermediate: Limitations, Why do we create them?

Thank you for your unwavering support!

"Everything we do, everything we are, rests on our personal power. If we have enough of it, one word uttered to us might be sufficient to change the course of our lives. But if we don't have enough personal power, the most magnificent piece of wisdom can be revealed to us and that revelation won't make a damn bit of difference." Carlos Castaneda

Looking Ahead - 2014 in View

I've been feeling very "quiet" in my own thoughts since we began 2014. However, the sound from the human collective has become really, really loud. It is as though everyone is now capable of transmitting their thoughts, emotions and creations in a much more empowered way.

This "power" is basic **chi and ability to do**.

I speak a lot about power. I also speak a lot about how to get one's power back. You see, we are all powerful, it's just that some of us use that power ourselves and some of us give it to someone or something else to use. But, we are still incredibly powerful.

As I look around at our world, I am at peace in that I know that every single thing that is happening, has been agreed by us as a species, and also by the planet. I also know that we are transforming. We are moving into a more aware, more connected space with our brethren and our environment.

It's almost as though we have gone full circle, from being completely connected, to being completely disconnected, to being connected again.

I don't remember the last time I felt alone or lonely. And that's not because I am in particularly close relationships. It's more of a state of existence. When I was quite young, I did want to experience that "alone" feeling, where we don't know what the environment is doing, or other people are thinking or feeling. But that experiment in awareness is long gone for me, and now I am always accompanied.

Yesterday I noticed something very interesting, fascinating in fact. I noticed that the energy I constantly feel from the human collective, the "noise" or "company" that everyone on the planet generates by simply existing, was near identical, if not identical, to the energy of the Sun as it touches our skin. I was so surprised! It felt one and the same. The sun is where all our life force, and energy comes from. If that is the same as our collective, then that's a very interesting concept.

Looking at last year, on a physical level, 2013 wasn't really that harsh. But energetically, as many of us can attest, it was like a never ending marathon. This coming year 2014, is going to be pretty much the same, only more intense. Some of us will feel this energy as harsh. Others will be in nirvana, others in hell.

Two things that came up in 2013 for us as a species stand out above all else, one was the very clear "choice" each human has on what happens in their lives, has become known. In other words, how we, moment to moment, have the choice on the reality we manifest moment to moment. The second was "integrity". Integrity is the following the highest personal resonance at all times, being "true" to ourselves above all social and cultural programming, contracts, promises, or attachments.

This year things are so different for us. Our conversation on the 26th of January explored this in more detail. But to give a sense of what is happening, it's the same as how fast (for example) mainstream commercial companies did a 180 turn around from supporting monsanto to widely displaying their non GMO products in huge advertising campaigns. As each person on the planet starts choosing what they think, feel, want, and thus manifest what their reality, the collective agreement effects build up and become powerful.

At an individual scale, we are in a process of having to look deeply into what it is we want. Yes, there are billions of sleeping human beings, who's power is being manipulated by fear, instant gratification, and dramatic distractions. But, the choice, and action, of one awake person, can overcome that of hundreds of sleeping ones.

We are coming into the moment of collective awareness. Collective communication, and the sharing of everything we are, think, want and feel with others. With everyone.

Information being disseminated on the internet at the moment on the amazing similarity of the egyptian eye, and the pineal gland. The pineal gland as been linked to extra sensory abilities, including telepathy and empathy. The collective router perhaps? At the same time, the all seeing eye is used to depict the Illuminati, creating a very distinct "repulsion" to this symbol by the alternative media and practitioners. This repulsion is very likely done on purpose, just like the repulsion to being wealthy and thus stopping us from being effective in affecting our planet with our present financial structure.

Think about the results of everyone on the planet having a fully functioning pineal gland. There would certainly not be any secrets, or lack of integrity. There is a lot of personal and media attention on how private our interaction is in life, on the internet, on the phone, even in the privacy of our own homes. Yet, at a human collective level, there is no privacy. Think about this for a moment. If you knew that everything you did, thought, felt and wanted was seen and experienced by thousands of other people, would you continue as you are, or would you change things?

Let me know! Write comments, share this post, and allow the communication to continue.

Have you wondered what is behind the oppression of our feminine side?

It's easy to fall into the victim/aggressor cycle when we think about the oppression of our feminine side. Not only the suppression of our own, personal feminine traits, whether we are men or women, but the physical and often brutal oppression of women and feminine men around the world.

It's easy to fall into rage, anger, frustration, fear and hopelessness when we open our eyes and look around to what is happening all around us. How we tell our boys to "be men", and not cry, run, laugh, play "like a girl". How we program our girls to be passive, helpless, submissive, beautiful, and compete for the attention of men (which until recently, and in many countries still, is vital to their physical survival and the survival of their children).

The oppression of women did not come about coincidentally, or through the survival of the fittest. It is a program that has been brutally imposed by all of us, on all of us, for thousands of years now. And it's coming to an end.

If you are familiar with my work, you will know that I will tell you "you are an eternal divine being, powerful beyond measure, the Creator of this reality". Know that this is true. At this time, we are, some of us are, on a bridge between a reality where the suppression of women was necessary to keep a certain light/dark paradigm alive, and a reality where that paradigm, the old paradigm, is no longer in existence. All we need to do, is become conscious of various key aspects, or anchors, that keep the old paradigm real, and decide to dissolve them.

By becoming conscious of where we hold those anchors in our own energy fields, our own minds, our own bodies, our own belief systems, we become the pioneers, the path-makers, for the collective dissolution of one of the most insidious and enslaving programs known to man.

We can recognize these programs, which are usually related to our beliefs about men or women and in particular sex, when we feel, think or sense an emotion, thought or feeling that is "not allowed". Something we automatically suppress. Something we have been taught it's evil, bad, naughty, not allowed. Something which, at the same time, has been placed in our bodies of energy by exposure, design, or purpose. It keeps us from expressing our full power, because we become afraid that this particular thing will surface when we are powerful and cannot be stopped.

But here's the thing: humans are one of the few animals on the planet that do not react from programs alone. We are one of the few species that can want, think, feel, desire, and be programmed to do something in reaction to an external stimuli, but CAN CHOOSE to do something else instead.

And when we allow ourselves to feel, think, sense, desire, or fear, whatever it is, but not react to it, and instead simply OBSERVE that energy in ourselves, the program DISSOLVES.

I invite you to observe yourself in the mirror, and imagine, believe and know, that you are the opposite sex to which your physical body is presently in, for at least 10 minutes every day for a week. I also invite you to observe someone close to you, whether a spouse, work mate, family member, or friend, and for at least ten minutes KNOW they are the opposite sex to what their body is. You may need to start with a couple of seconds to begin with, and build it up to ten minutes in both instances.

Another exercise is to read the next sentence and watch your reaction to it: "Inelia Benz is a powerful, highly influential, and fearless woman". What do you feel? Think? Sense?

What about these combination of words: "powerful woman", "highly influential woman", "fearless woman".

Now read the following and watch the difference (if any) "The Dalai Lama is a powerful, highly influential and fearless man". Any differences?

Now the word combinations: "powerful man", "highly influential man", "fearless man".

Interesting huh?

As you do these exercises, watch and observe your reactions, whether emotional, mental, egoic, physical, or energetic. Keep a journal and be amazed.

When we move out of the programming, we can take action at a social level. The oppression of our feminine side results in more than the subjugation of women, it is also in part the reason why the majority of human beings accept war, abuse of animals and lack of empathy toward living beings and the planet as a whole by men and women alike.

When one awake individual **(YOU)** dissolves his or her programs of oppression, she or he creates an energetic map, a resonance, that starts activating the feminine side of hundreds of other individuals. And when we act at a social level in the redefinition and treatment of women, animals, and other brutalized beings, we do it from a place of **fearlessness and impeccable integrity which is undefeatable**. We no longer "save" them, or add to their victimhood by feeling they are victims. Yet we literally stop what is happening because it does not fit into our chosen reality. How we do this? It's up to us! We rally and organize with others, and use the social and personal tools at our disposal. But FIRST we liberate our own selves, our own bodies, energy field, minds and emotional bodies of those enslaving programs.

Let's put our egoic survival instincts on hold for the next few months, and lets dare to act in breaking this link in the chain of enslavement. Let's let our feminine side out of her cage! What do you say? Are you game?

The message is clear - YOU are POWERFUL and they don't want you to know it.

You are powerful and they don't want you to know it. Who are "they"?

"They" are the individuals who project authority onto themselves, and make the rest of us think we need to hear things from them, get their permission, or pay them dues for living on the planet. Why do we give them all this authority over us? Because we have been taught to from day one to do so. And because if we don't, we are told we will die, or worse, we will suffer.

Now, let's not fall into the victim/aggressor cycle here. "They" exist because we all agree to have them there. The majority of us find it easier to have someone manage the majority of our lives, tell us what is "real", what is not "real", give us "official information channels", and tell us how to live our lives.

When I first became a public person, a man told me that he did not like that I would look at vibrational lines, situations and events, and simply state what I was seeing with full authority. He suggested I add the words "in my view", or "my opinion is". In other words, he wanted me to step down from my personal authority. Why? Because it threatened him. You see, any of us can be in full control and use our personal authority, but others will see and react to it as they do to "formal" authority, that it is something imposed on them that they have to accept without question.

However, I don't have any attachment or allocate any importance to whether a person "believes me" or thinks that I am "full of BS". Why? Because I speak my truth, my reality, my seeing. And I fully accept that their seeing can be different. And that's OK!

You are POWERFUL and they don't want you to know it. This fact is true.

Power-full. Full of power. Full of Chi, full of ability to do. It means you can completely reinvent yourself with one strong personal decision which you follow through with a change of mind, thoughts, words and actions.

Enough of us realizing this fact, can literally change the planet and how we experience life on it.

Often, when speaking with advanced spiritual seekers, I will tell them that their lives have no meaning and no importance. That their search for spiritual perfection is meaningless. That their daily lives are irrelevant. Most, not all, freak out. Why? Because it is part of this physical existence's game to have a meaning and be important. We may value watching soap operas or football on TV as little meaning, and reaching enlightenment as a big meaning. But it's simply grades of meaning. Both are false Gods.

Meaning, and the search for it, is a distraction. The fact is, you are an eternal, divine all powerful being, and the rest is just a dream. We do like to give our dreams meaning though, right?

And by realizing that meaning and importance, whether ours or someone else's, is just an illusion, a distraction, a link in the chain of enslavement, we can truly step into our POWER.

Power= the ability to do = Chi

We value our lives, and the lives of others. And this is also a key element to living our lives powerfully. When we start valuing without judgment through meaning (whether ours or society's), our lives begin to morph into something completely different. When we value without agendas, we are free from the agendas of others. When we put what matters to us under the microscope of our conscious awareness, we can manifest matter (physical experience) which we choose by design, and not unconscious or programmed meaning or importance.

Why has meaning and importance been given so much attachment? Because all one needs to do to distract a person, a society, a planet, is to give it a focus of attention on the small self, the ego, the present life or something else, and call it "meaningful". And if you want to break that person or society, all you have to do is to take that meaning or importance away.

A real life example is: Telling someone, "I love you because you are beautiful", this sentence has meaning and importance on beauty. As opposed to telling someone, "you are love embodied". This second one is simply a statement of fact without importance or meaning. And feeling it, knowing it, is called "unconditional love".

Another example would be: Driving an expensive, sporty car because it makes you feel young, sexy, important, and lets others know you are wealthy. As opposed to driving it because you love the experience of luxury, the sound of the engine and the fast speeds. The first is meaning, the second is pure experience.

A while ago, I switched off the universe of light/dark experience. But a few milliseconds later, it came back like it had never been switched off. So I did it again. And again it came back. I wondered why it kept coming back, with all its imperfections, wars, suffering and enslavement of consciousness. The answer was very, very simple - the human collective is not done playing out this scene yet. The unraveling of meaning, importance, individualism, separation and conquering is not yet complete. Each person has to reach that realization by themselves, or it won't be done.

I invite you to switch off the paradigm of meaning and importance, and step into the paradigm of consciously chosen high vibrational experience of the present moment, and conscious creation of high vibrational reality for yourself and others.

This information, the information contained in this article, is dangerous. It is filled with reality shattering energy and data. It is here to challenge your reality construct and it is being expressed because it is time you stepped into your power. If now is not the time for you to fully step into your power, you would have stopped reading this article on the second paragraph and would not be reading these words. Or, you will have a blank in a few minutes when you try to remember what it says.

et's share this information far and wide!

More empowering Reality Construction information on: Rules of Engagement Talks.

Why You Might Want to Ascension101 Yourself this Spring

I have been in personal conversations, and public ones, with a LOT of individuals the past couple of months. And one thing has come very clear: Information Overload.

This Overload is not just about what we see, hear, read and perceive, but it is also energetic data and fields of energy which are very, very intense right now.

The Sun is "hyperactive", our Earth is also going through some very interesting energy fluctuations, in fact the entire Solar System is doing so too.

We, as a species, and as individuals, are picking up on ALL of this. And it manifests as "there is too much information, too much stuff coming in", the desire is to sit in stillness, quietness, and simply have some time to process it all, reach that inner place of balance and quietude where we can relax and breathe easily.

So, what do I mean when I say **"Ascension101 Yourself"**? And why **this Spring**?

It is VERY simple. It means redo the Ascension101 Course. I know that many of us have done the course multiple times already, our copy a permanent resident on our MP3 players. And every time we do the course, something new comes up for us to use we hadn't even heard the previous times. This time it is a tool that will help us "tune" all our bodies (mental, physical, spiritual, emotional and energetic), into the new Song being played on this physical reality we call Earth, which is really ramping up this Equinox. And this is the intent we can use while doing the Course, to Tune IN to Gaia, Sun, and the Universal Mind quality of vibration for this period in linear time.

This period of linear time calls for us to take the next step. The step in fully, and consciously removing all programs that are not serving our intent, and building new programs that will serve Us and not another person's, entity, or organization's agenda.

Stepping into our POWER, and raising our vibration happens much easily and effortlessly when we are fully "tuned" and reconnected with our bodies and environment (including the waves of energy as they come in).

Expiration Date: December 31 2017

March and April 2014 were marked by many intuitives, astrologers and seers as being a really powerful energetic junction. And, personally speaking, I've felt it in my own life. I've been down with a massive headache since the equinox in March.

When these things happen, I have a look at not only why they happen, but how they serve. How am I responding? Am I reacting? How is this debilitating condition serving me? Serving something, or someone, else?

What came to mind, is that my personal work here has an expiration date. The request I received to go public was not permanent, it was until 2017. This is the main reason I accepted it. And therefore, the likelihood that A) I am being taken out or B) this is the end of the world as we know it, is highly remote, if not impossible.

This is what allows me to breathe easy when I receive YET ANOTHER doomsday email, article or prediction. The financial system was about to collapse any day now in 2010. Probably 2009 too. And huge earthquakes, solar flares and [add your global disaster here] was about to hit "next month" since 2008.

Aliens were about to make first contact (officially), since ... well, the 60s.

Life on the planet was going to end, and thousands of people were going to be lifted up into a higher dimension in their light bodies or their personal, and very expensive, merkabas, on December 2012.

The energetic work-up to the next "event" is highly stressful at a human collective level. And it permeates not just the collective consciousness of the alternative media and those who are awake, but the sleeping masses too, who are then also targeted with fear of financial collapse, disasters, war, police brutality, helplessness, corruption, and much drama via mass media outlets.

The human collective manifested individuals like me, those who are not here to play the game, but to facilitate the collective's choice of changing the game, for a reason. And the reason is that you want a different experience of physicality.

Whether the collective wants a high vibrational experience of reality, or chooses to be dumbed down into sleepy unconsciousness again, it really is up to the collective. Everything that happens to our human experience is a choice. Most of the time it is an unconscious choice, or choice made by our or other people's cultural or social programs, but it is still a choice.

Become aware of the programs, and you become aware of your choices.

But let's return to 2017. Many individuals have asked me why 2017. What will happen in 2017, will I die then? Will the planet end? Will the game end? What's going to happen? Well, I can tell you one thing, the human experience game will not come to an end for millions of years. It will shift, change, and become something different, but will still be the human experience. I can also tell you that I have no idea why 2017 is a key year. I have a sense that the window of opportunity for individuals to step into their power will end. But how and why it ends? I guess we need to wait and see.

I have many highly awakened and enlightened friends. People who in other cultures and other times would be considered avatars, Buddhas, enlightened masters, gurus, and world renowned philosophers and teachers. Now they are, Jenny down the street, little Tom's dad, Aaliyah the realtor, and the list goes on. There has NEVER been so many conscious and awake individuals on the planet as there are today. Think about that.

Most awakened individuals feel alone, and that they are the most awake person in their own environment, so it feels like a nasty world out there. And then he or she goes into the internet to find out about others of similar awaken-ess, and they find that the world is about to end next week. So yeah, it's frustrating.

But here's something that might help. This very moment, this moment when you are reading the word "word", this time in linear time/space, is unique. It is also PERFECT. You, and billions of other human beings have created this moment to be exactly as it is right now. Listen to the sounds around you. Feel the quality of the air on your skin. Hear what other humans are up to around you. Look at the screen where these words are being projected onto your retina, for your mind to interpret. NOW.

This moment is PERFECT.

YOU are perfect. It has taken how many years for you to be in this moment? How many programs? Dramas? Story? Importances? Queries? Awakenings? YOU are here now. And YOU are the creator. Step into that knowing, and allow the present moment to unfold. Feel its vastness, its completeness, it's busy-ness. Feel its beauty, its noise, its quietude.

Most importantly ALLOW IT TO EXIST. Allow YOU to exist. In this moment SEE YOU.

You see, looking at the world ending next week, or what's going to happen in 2017 is a simple strategy of distraction. The tool that allows others to pull you out of your personal power, the power of the person, which exists outside of linear time and can be felt and exercised in the eternal NOW.

LOOK AT YOU NOW.

I see you :D

The World Ascends next Saturday at 5pm Eastern... Don't miss it!

If you know me, you know I'm kidding :)

If this is the first time you've heard about me, then walk with me. This is my website and you will find here a place that is not about the end of the world, end of society, or end of sanity but instead a place of empowerment and inspiration... and a lot of sanity actually. None of the "this is it! Next month the [enter your social or global structure here] ends! Or [This is it! this -enter astrological date here - means ascension is here!]... unless it's a stunt to grab your attention :)

In fact, we can guarantee that our species will still be around, and functioning pretty much as it is today, only much saner, for at least another 5000 years. And if we are wrong, we will say we are very sorry and close the website down.

OK, seriously now, here is something that is really and truly happening, this very moment, even as you read these words. The BS is ending!

BS is coming to an end. Many people, especially those who based their entire careers and fortunes on BS, are being exposed. Inhumane acts, acts of cruelty, unfairness, lies and lack of integrity, are being aired and exposed in public.

And yes, by BS I do mean "bullshit". Although I do like the politically correct interpretation of BS to mean "belief system". It works either way.

Many awakened people are against the internet. And the internet is translated into all things technology, the computers we use, the wifi in our homes, streets and offices, the nasty stuff being done to manipulate the alternative media, the mainstream media and all the other media. I myself refuse to put cellphones against my head because it literally "burns my brain". Have you tried doing the "fake" cell phone popcorn experiment? I haven't but my head does feel like it's being nuked when my cellphone is against it - like the popping corn illustrated in those videos.

But, I personally like technology. I like the internet. I like computers. When I was 4 years old, my mom asked me what I was going to work at when I grew up, I looked down that timeline, and told her that I would be clicking lots of letters on a flat surface, and that my words would appear magically in a flat picture frame in front of me with lots of colors and pictures. She frowned and walked away shaking her head. At the time I realized two things, one was that I would be writing, and the other was that my work environment had not been invented yet.

The internet has given us the opportunity for us to communicate. For me to write this article, and for you to read it.

It has also, with smartphones, brought us what is happening around the planet uncensored. It is the main tool our species is using to wake up. The main tool for individuals to say "this is insane!! STOP IT" when they see a war, a child starving or abused, an animal treated with cruelty beyond words. It is the tool being used by citizens around the world to take back their power.

And more and more dramatic insanity comes to light, crazy stuff! At the same time, a switch clicks in our minds, our "knowing", and we just KNOW what is real and what is not. What we want in our lives, and what we don't. What we say yes to, and what we say no to. We KNOW it. We might get triggered and fall into rage, or sadness, or hopelessness, but we KNOW that those things are just WRONG. They do NOT BELONG to our species or our nature.

Yet, they are being carried out by other humans. All insanity, all cruelty, all nastiness, is being carried out by other humans.

So, what gives?

No, we are not being manipulated by an external force (at least not unwillingly). What is happening is what has been happening for the past hundreds of years and is accelerating. We are becoming sane. We, those of us who are still reading these words, have CHOSEN to move away from a physical experience that is unconscious, painful, filled with fear and suffering. And we don't agree with others having that experience near us, or with our consent, or ON OUR PLANET.

We are moving away from pain, fear and suffering, and into empowerment, awareness and consciousness.

The entire social system is doing so. A quick look at history will show how much we have progressed. A few hundred years ago, we would have been stoned to death, or burned alive, for writing or reading these words, the words in this article. Now, these words are free to travel the world, go into millions of individuals homes, phones and screens and be read. And the power is with you to either close these words down or trash them - ending their journey- or agree with these words, share them, "like" them, repost in your blog and discuss them.

YOU decide from that place of KNOWING what is TRUE. Not me, not someone else. YOU are the person who is changing the world for the better.

THANK YOU.

Recommended Talk: Rules of Engagement in the New Paradigm.

So this is how the Human Collective Feels Like

Before I sit down to write an article, what I do is to be silent for a while and tap into linear thought structures. Thinking linearly is actually quite hard for me, but necessary in order for the article, or message, to make sense and be effective. And be short enough for a person to read in one sitting.

Today I failed miserably to get into linear thought, and the result will be something much longer than my regular articles. What you are about to read originates from various consecutive viewpoints (I managed to pinpoint a few so that I could convey them in words), while looking at one topic. These viewpoints (the points I managed to bring into thought form, and from which we can look at the topic at hand) don't appear to be related, but they are. Instead of waiting for me to become structured enough to be able to write in a linear fashion, I decided to invite you in on the process itself by requesting your presence during the "gelling" of thoughts as they come into existence in our fractured linear structure reality.

Why is linear structure reality fractured? Because linear thought, human word language, and linear time are "bits" of attention placed one after the other so we can digest them more easily and make sense of what we are experiencing without getting overwhelmed. The moment we separate one whole experience, or seeing, into words, we fracture it. But a sense of it still comes through, and if we are open to it, we can fall into the whole experience of the timeless and structureless reality from where it came.

So this is how the Human Collective Feels Like is the title of this article. The reason I chose it is because it most accurately explains what I have been perceiving and experiencing the past week.

For reasons known only to Gaia and the universe (mystery always adds interest to our minds), I was given the opportunity to spend a full week in Costa Rica with my daughter Daniela at a 4 Star private club holiday destination. I would like to thank the individuals who made this possible.

With no internet to speak of and an energetic break at a time when I have many projects, tools and other items on the works that will accelerate our collective expansion of awareness, created an environment that I don't often get the opportunity to enter: rest.

The first four days I spent in a strange state of physical discomfort (my body can't take air travel right now), with a massive migraine and extreme exhaustion manifesting as physical lethargy and sleepiness.

Meet Elena of the Healing Hands...

All beaches in Costa Rica are public access beaches. Which means that when you leave the private hotel property and step onto the sand, a dozen or so individuals will descend on you to sell you something. Tours, timeshare, day trips, jewelry, and in our case, massage therapy on the beach.

I have met thousands of healers. And a few of them have touched me with healing intentions. The touch in all but two of these individuals have been extremely painful and energetically uncomfortable. The reason is probably that the majority of healers still use their personal energy, which is full of their unresolved issues, history, structures brought in from hundreds of lifetimes, or a structured energy bundle they have learned as a tool to heal with. This doesn't mean their touch is not effective, it just means that for my physical and energy body it translates to pain.

In my life, there have been two individuals who have not caused this uncomfortable pain, and one of them is one of the ladies who provides tourists with massage therapy in Papagayo Beach, Costa Rica. The moment she touched my hand to lead me away from the other sellers, (which the others respected as my attention focused on her), I knew she had "manos que sanan". In English this translates badly as "hands that heal". I don't remember where I learned that term, but it is an ability that is often passed from parent to child, although it can skip one or more generations. It means that the person has direct access to Source energy, bypassing all structures, egoic or otherwise, that the person might carry with him or her in everyday life.

She massaged the back of my neck as she told me the therapy method they use, natural oils, and theory behind the structure and its execution. I felt no pain.

One of her partners joined us and she too massaged my back and neck as we stood there chatting about cost and schedule... man was that painful.

When the second lady left, I turned to Elena (not sure if that's how to spell her name, it might be Helena), and said, "you have *manos que sanan*, did you know that?" She gasped and said, "how did you know?" I told her I knew a little about these things and could tell when someone had them. And that I had only met one other person on the planet who had them in my 47 years here.

"My hands have been blessed," she said. "When I was a small child, my grandmother demanded to see me on her deathbed, so I was brought to her. She told me I would work with my hands and then asked me to put my hands against hers, I felt the energy, a transfer, and it was done, she had blessed my hands. She died immediately afterward."

"People don't know it," she continued, "but we heal hundreds of tourists here every year. They come for a massage, but we heal them. They come hardly able to walk, and leave straight, full of energy and able to walk."

She told me she was in tripadvisor, with 5 stars, but I wasn't able to find her there. I am not tripadvisor, but I know an exceptional individual when I meet him or her. And Elena is exceptional, unique. If you need healing, I suggest you invest in spending 7 days near Papagayo Beach, find her and book an hour per day for seven days (she has her tables at the beach access to the Occidental Grand Papagayo Hotel, off route 255 which is on the North West Costa Rica coast.

So this is how the Human Collective Feels Like

The next day (our second day in Costa Rica) I spent half an hour under Elena's care. And it helped with my exhaustion and opened a point out of space time where I could experience the human collective without the burden of "stuff".

Years ago I shared an experience during my first public interview which talked about a very dark being on Earth, possibly the "black pope". It was an experience that happened in the "astral" or "mystical" realm of awareness. I had been requested by Source to work with a very dark person at a psychic level. To hang out with him, and write his doings as a book. After working with him for a few weeks, during one of the sessions, I found myself outside a vast mansion. There was another man outside the mansion carrying crosses, books, and other paraphernalia, a psychic, with the intent to give front to the person I had been working with. I looked at the psychic, and knew he would be destroyed if he entered the grounds, the reason was obvious, he was afraid. I communicated to him to stay where he was, not to go in.

I stepped into the grounds, and found my way into the mansion, all the time I could feel the energy we know as evil all around me. It was in part of the location, like the air we breath. Like a color. I remember thinking, "so this is how evil feels like against my skin". There was absolutely no judgment on my part. No expectation, no curiosity as such, just the experiencing of what we know as "evil".

When working in the mystical realms, I interpret houses, or buildings of any sort, to be the person's life. I worked my way through the rooms, feeling through the energy as it became thicker and thicker. Eventually I found the man I had been working with, he was sitting on a throne. He looked at me, and I looked at him. He was pure, perfect, evil. I sat next to him and simply observed his perfection, the perfection of his energy. Allowed the experience to be felt. Suddenly, and unexpectedly, he conveyed a request for "clemency". As soon as he did that, I felt pure source energy passing through me directly into him. He then transformed from the darkest energy I had ever experienced, to the most beautiful, pure light. I was really surprised and shocked, and as I reentered my physical body, I felt a few minutes of judgment and "unfairness" to how he had been simply transformed without "paying the price" of what he had done to our planet, our species and all those innocent children and people. But that judgment passed quickly as it was simply an egoic shadow reaction from my human construct called Inelia.

So this is how the Human Collective Feels Like

I swam in the ocean. Every environment on the planet, including the human collective, sings a different song. It is all very busy, extremely busy, with constant and multiple communication to and fro. The ocean is one of the environments I find most comfortable. Water and salt does purify the busy-ness, and also buffers us from the heavy load coming in from the human collective.

Sometimes, when we spend too much time in a room that smells of apple pie, for example, we no longer smell the apple pie. But someone stepping into the room from the outdoors, will experience the full aroma of the apple pie, the warmth of the room, and the joy and comfort that apple pie brings to most hearts.

I spent a lot of time swimming in the sea, watching the fish, snorkeling and enjoying "apple pie comfort".

Everyone who has ever been to a holiday resort will know that it is heavy with human stuff as most people on holiday take holidays because they really need a holiday. And this resort was no exception. It was quite full, and very heavy.

As I stepped out of the ocean, the energy of our collective would hit full blast. But instead of being painfully heavy, due to the opening outside of space/time I was able to simply sit with it, look at it, and experience it. **So this is how the Human Collective Feels Like.** It is simply a color, a note, a feeling against our skin. A symphony of busy-ness, emotions, experiences, importances.

That's when I heard it. It was a simple request from Source to sit and simply observe and experience the Human Collective. And this is when I want to ask you something. The request is not just for me to do this you see, but for you to do so too.

Can you sit and experience and observe how the human collective feels like?

If you got a reaction, emotional, mental, or otherwise when you read that, please process it. Use the Fear Processing Exercise, and change the word "fear" for whatever you are feeling or thinking.

And then step back into the exercise, and experience what the human collective feels like. And simply state over and over again:

This is how the Human Collective Feels Like

When you can be in the experience of feeling what the human collective feels like without any judgment whatsoever, no desire to heal, take action, do something, experience something else, connect with something, but simply be in the room and experience the human collective, then we have accomplished the request.

During the holiday, we went out to sea in the hope of seeing dolphins. I didn't get to see any dolphins. They were busy with their scheduled activities, something about a pod of yummy fish that was swimming past at that time in a different location (to mine). They knew I would understand.

They obviously have no idea how childish and petty I become when it comes to being rejected in favor of a pod of yummy fish.

This is how the Human Collective Feels Like

I don't know why we are being asked to do this exercise. There is no "outcome" involved, or wanted, from my perspective. If the wish of an outcome was to enter my mind, judgment would be involved and the exercise would have to be restarted.

Let me know what you experience!

In My Defence

If my life is in danger, or someone in my environment is in physical or psychological danger from an aggressor, I will defend myself, or them, without question. But when it comes to defending my integrity, my name, my work, pride, or anything else, I will simply walk away even if affected by it.

Sometimes, I do get affected, there is an emotional charge to being "betrayed" by someone who professed their friendship, for example. Or someone who goes behind my back and speaks against me so that they are liked by others, while pretending to be my friend and supporter. Or someone who would viciously attack me on the internet (often anonymously of course), in order to feel important, or get some attention, or because my power and influence threatens them. It does upset me sometimes. But instead of reacting to that upsetness, what I do is process it, the disappointment and pain, and continue on my path.

It's hard though. When we receive a negative energy of engagement in the form of insults or attacks it often incurs a cost. This cost is the effect it has on the "small self".

And I DO have a small self. It's not very influential in my life, but it does affect me at times. It wasn't always there, but at some point in linear time I created it in order to understand what others are going through in this life. Most of the suffering, stress, pain, fights, and conflicts we experience are due to the small self in us and/or others.

Take a look at a conflict you are in right now. Step back and see if it has any bearing to your physical survival. If it does not, then it's about the small self.

Some cultures will teach that people should kill to defend their pride, their honor or their family's honor. Or be severely punished if they dishonor themselves or their family. But what is honor, and pride but an egoic projection of importance?

Often, we use the story of all the physical, emotional and psychological attacks we have received throughout our lives to validate our own brutality.

The nature of attacks

Most personal (non life threatening) attacks have very basic patterns. Three of these patterns are:

1. The making oneself right by making the other wrong.

2. Validating oneself by invalidating another.

3. Reacting to an unconscious (or conscious) fear.

In my experience, number one is the most prevalent in our society. It is, in fact, encouraged. We find this being used in politics and debates of all sorts in science, religion, and social organizations and think tanks around the world.

More than once, I have received messages and emails "demanding that I respond" to some claim or other that I am [enter comment making me wrong here]. Or that I defend or validate my views on things. I don't respond to or answer these messages now, but have done so in the past due to giving in to external pressure. I tend not to give in to external pressures these days.

Recently, a friend of mine told me that he has seen that the more powerful, confident and capable I appear to become as a publicly known individual, the more vicious and insidious the attacks get. This is simply a reflection of number 3 above. People are afraid of influential individuals. They are afraid of power (and with good cause), and are afraid of being conned. The energetic attack (at a mystical level) has also increased tremendously every month since I accepted the mission to become publicly known so as to deliver the message of empowerment to the masses.

How we deal with mystical attacks is pretty much the same as we deal with overt attacks. We process any effect they may have in us, and we move on. Retaliation, defense, or "justice" is irrelevant. and would only feed into the attack and the lowering of our vibration.

322

If we spend any time defending, attacking our attackers or getting payback, we are simply feeding the aggression cycle. All that energy is much better spent inspiring and empowering others.

How does observing our defenses empower the planet?

Conflict and war, at any level, lowers our human collective vibration. It doesn't matter whether you are shouting at your dog, or shooting bullets at an enemy. The energy of conflict goes against our nature and it is only there through heavy programming.

The past week, as I was recuperating from long hours on airplanes, I watched several shows on TV. I was shocked at the normalization of violence. And the brutality of the violence depicted.

In one of them, a film about a gangster family in witness protection relocated to France, showed children and adults being brutally beaten up by the protagonists. It was supposed to be funny because the kids and adults who were brutalized had said something wrong to the protagonists, or done some minor wrong to them. In another show, an extremely popular TV series, the level of violence was simply incredible. It included rape, sexual abuse, brutal murders of children, men and women, and extreme psychological abuse. All "normalized" in some fantasy time and geographical area.

Reality TV is popular because it is conflict driven. Violence of many kinds are depicted, even physical fights.

And it doesn't stop at TV shows, most computer games are about killing other people, creatures or monsters.

But here's the thing, the programming to be and act from a place of aggression and violence cannot succeed unless we subscribe to it. Once we see that it is simply programming, that it is indeed an attempt by a faction of the human collective to walk a low vibrational and highly addictive path, then we can simply switch that programming off.

How do we switch it off? We make a list, and observe all the areas where we feel wronged, where we are defending ourselves, where we are attacking others. We observe each item on our list until we

323

see the larger picture. Until we are no longer energetically affected by the conflict or attack. Until we no longer "want to do something about this", to bring it to justice. But remember, if it involves you or someone else's physical or psychological survival or well being, do get yourself or the person under attack away if possible and if not possible, then defend, act and protect. Why? Because survival of our person is different to the survival of our small self.

Do note that aggression and conflict are highly addictive. They are dramatic, and we love drama. Drama and conflict do not exist outside of the small self. The fact that they do not exist outside of the small self is often the reason why we hold on to the small self so strongly.

Our reality, our planet and species, still supports low level experiences such as war, conflict, drama and such. This is a fact. Our species is empowered with the choice. It is up to us whether we want to hold on to those low level games or not. That's why there is such heavy programming happening via our media, culture and religions, to hold onto the small games. We are exposed to them and the effect is the same as someone being exposed to crack cocaine for the first time. We either become totally addicted to it, refuse to ingest it, or "recover" after being addicted to it for a long or short time.

We can help our species to drop the addiction by observing it within ourselves, and empowering others to enable them to observe it within themselves. Just observing, without any intent, expands our awareness on the facts behind this addiction at a global scale.

Do share this article with anyone whom you feel will benefit and be empowered by it, send to your lists and reblog. The more of us who act by sharing this information, the easier the load will become and the faster our species will expand in awareness.

Inelia Benz

Recommended further study for this topic is the MP3 "Limitations - Why do we create them" by Inelia Benz

Falling in Love.

Abstract from the Love, Sex and Soulmates in the New Paradigm Talks. Edited for publication as an article:

Falling in Love

About our social program of love, and how romantic love affects our lives at an energetic and evolutionary level. Here we will explore how to increase the pros and remove the cons.

There are energies and programs around falling in love and we can see all the positive sides about it, because there are lots of positive sides about this, and we are going to be able to have a look at them and structure them. We can also look at the negative sides around falling in love, and how we can process those, because they are all energy packages, they are all programs.

Even the words, 'falling in love', talk about a fall, "The fall".

You fall in love.

When you fall in love, the person's awareness field shrinks into a tiny little space, so it's a falling in awareness, they can't think of much except the other person, often they can't eat or sleep very well, they're in a state of euphoria or fear, depending whether the other person is also in love with them or not, and they can't really do things very well.

They say 'love is blind' too, so there is another saying that really embodies what is happening here.

The person will not see the faults in the other or will quickly forget them or disregard them.

And we also have the honeymoon period, the time, space -it sometimes can last up to two years- that the person doesn't see the dirty socks on the floor, or doesn't see the farting or the burping or the constant talking or really that the other person has absolutely nothing in common with them. Because they are in love, so they don't see anything else, they just see "Oh my gosh! I love this person, this person loves me, I want to be with them all the time, I love their energy, I want to be in their energy". And all that type of thing, the physical effects of course, apart from not sleeping, can be very much a sense of a physical satisfaction.

Basically when we are in that state there are various programs that kick in, one of them is the thought of, starting a family, and it doesn't really matter whether you are heterosexual, homosexual, or asexual, everybody will, all of a sudden, if they meet somebody that they want to spend time with, even if there is no sex involved, all of a sudden, lets adopt a child, or they start getting people into the house, or pets. They start getting lots and lots of pets, or even just one pet and it's "their baby".

It's like that, "ok we are safe now, we can start this", and that's also a program.

The falling in love and the romance behind love is quite recent in human history.

It was first registered by a sociologist, or the historians, that on the mythical, Greek and Roman stories, they would have stories about Gods and Goddesses falling in love with humans, and we can really go into that as a completely different subject here! But we won't go in there.

It was very unknown or not really part of the human construct.

During the industrial revolution there were lots of novels written about romance and falling in love and everything, and that's when it really started to kind of impregnate the societal program around falling in love and mating and being a partner for life type thing; because before that yes, I mean people would fall in love but it wasn't necessarily what made them marry each other and have babies and create that whole structure.

Marriage was very much to do with alliances, survival, and all that type of thing. And we're going to go into that as well later in the course.

So what I'd like us to do right now, -this is the first exercise and I hope you have a pen and a paper, or you can open a little notepad in your computer, if you are listening through your computer- we are going to do a list.

So we are going to make a list about what we relate to our belief system or what we think it means 'to fall in love'.

So first of all, "do I want to fall in love? Yes/No"

And, "do I want the other person to love me back? Yes/No"

So we are going to write those down.

Then, "what does that mean exactly?"

I'm going to say a few words to get you started okay?

For example:

Does being in love/falling in love have anything to do with belonging?

You belong to the other person, your heart belongs to the other person.

The other person belongs to you.

The other person's heart belongs to you.

So you can write those down and just start looking at those energy constructs yes?

Owning and belonging.

Does your body? So we move from the heart to the body.

Does your physical body belong to the other person?

And, does the other person's physical body belong to you?

So this is just one item we are going to be looking at, have a look at those energies.

And how these translate into, "we are going to own a home together", "we are going to own a car together".

Do you see how it veers off and goes into the social structures there?

Another program that you might want to look at, another energy that might be there, is the safety.

Safety

The program that says, "with this person I am safe".

Or sometimes it's the opposite, "with this person I am not safe".

"Is this person safe with me?"

"Is this person not safe with me?"

And here we go and look at the energies of fear how those can be all intertwined with falling in love and being in love. Sometimes the euphoric energy is because for the first time in our lives we feel safe. We feel safe with somebody else, we are able to be ourselves without any danger of attack.

You know if you start getting charges, emotional charge around it make or put a little star around the word, and you are going to go back and have a look at these. Process all the energies around all the charges that come up, these are programs that are being triggered.

Now the next thing about falling in love is very related to safety but it's actually slightly different, and it's security. So do you feel that once you find the one, or when you're living with that person that you really want to build a soulmate relationship with or you want to look at and see, what are the energies behind this security?

Security

Security in building something. Security in building a relationship with this person.

Which also then translates very, very easily into the security of going forth in life.

Moving away from your nuclear family into the new, starting your own family, even if it's just a couple.

You get more security to buy a house, you have more security to go out into the workforce.

Have a look at security, the security to start something.

See these are things that normally we wouldn't think would be related to falling in love, but they have all kind of intertwined with each other.

Another one is comfort.

Comforting.

You are with somebody because it provides you comfort.

It's like a very physical type of comfort, but also emotional.

Comfort.

When we imagine, or we look at, or we're working in a relationship that's already there, we think about comfort a lot, we think, you know, I'd like to be able to come home or be home and be in a situation that's supportive, comfortable. You don't want to come in and have arguments, those are very uncomfortable.

And then we go into things like company.

Often individuals will get into inappropriate relationships and really fall in love with individuals who are really not compatible, because they are wanting company. They want somebody to do things with, to go to the cinema, have hobbies, have a farm with.

There can be all sorts of things.

Or just hang out with and just, you know? Have really deep conversations with, somebody who gets them.

Company.

And of course, there's the physical company.

Being hugged, being kissed, being made love to and with, at a physical level, our bodies, our physical bodies are in deep need of physical contact, they need to be touched, they need to be kissed. That's a human program.

We don't live in isolation, when we do, we have emotional problems, often as a physical body we have problems, yes?

And society has taught us that as adults we can only hug and kiss individuals who we are sexually involved with.

In other societies individuals will, upon meeting with strangers, kiss them on the cheek, once or twice.

In some cultures they even kiss each other on the mouth, even men.

And even there, you get to have that contact. When you meet people you know, you shake hands, kiss, hug.

Physical bodies need and love to be touched.

And often we will get pets because then, they go on our laps. And dogs in particular are so loving.

Physical contact, that's physical company.

And often when we fall in love, we're looking for nurturing, to be looked after.

Someone who cares.

The whole romantic thing, we think about the man who brings flowers and writes poems; we think of the woman who will do all sorts of different things.

Immediately the focus changes, you know I don't know if you noticed the focus changing there, between what the man would do for romance and the different things the woman would do for romance.

And that very much brings in the belief system of what romance is, which is actually a creation.

But it all comes down to one thing. It comes down to nurturing.

That person cares about me, they did something special, just because.

Just because they exist.

Acknowledgement.

So these programs are all intertwined with falling in love.

And at the same time when we do fall in love, we're blind!

Because love is blind, right?

We can't see any of the other things.

Like, "Oh well, you know, this person doesn't really spend much time with me".

"They have no interest in what I have interest in, she doesn't build cars".

"After a period of time, I will go back to my mates and start building cars, and you know, she will be there, she will have my dinner ready when I get home".

These things start happening. And when do they happen?

It's when - another saying that everybody knows - the honeymoon period is over.

There's a period of time that on average is two years - and often marriages only last two years these days- which is the honeymoon period.

And the being in love period.

If the couple don't graduate into, from falling in love to loving each other, or being in love to loving each other, there is a shift in energy, if they don't make the shift, often what will happen is that they will have a really unhappy and uncomfortable marriage after the two years are up, or they will divorce.

And let's have a look at that difference. Let's have a look at the difference between falling in love, being in love and loving each other, it's actually quite significant, something quite important.

Falling in love, again, is when our awareness field becomes extremely small, so we can't see.

Love is blind. The honeymoon period, everything is sweet.

Thus being in love, and falling in love.

Because you are in a field and a field is a construct. You are IN love, you have fallen INTO love.

After the two years, and sometimes this happens right away, you love each other, what does that mean? It means that you <u>are</u> love, and you are expressing love, you are coming from a space or location of love.

I'm going to talk about one that's being really bombarded on to society.

Saved

Falling in love means being saved!

And this one has come in through lots and lots of fairy tales, movies, novels.

The image of being saved and also the image of the savior. So you have for example, Cinderella. She was in a really bad situation there, until the prince, the savior came in and recognized her, saw her, "I see you", and she became the princess, she was saved.

We can think of Snow White, again the same story, she was in a bad place with the evil stepmother: another female had poisoned her and put her to sleep. And it was Prince Charming I think wasn't it? Who came in and kissed her, and his kiss woke her up, she was saved, and awakened.

So these programs have been coming in, one of the things that we investigated, when I was in university; because when I went to university I studied communication and some individuals there had put together a course that was very comprehensive and one of them was about fairytales. And there was another disagreement. For you who have read the article on the sociolinguistics class and if you haven't read it then I am going to give you a little summary afterwards.

But there was another class and we were talking about fairytales, and we talked about all these fairytales where this female is in dire straits, the dragon has her or she's been poisoned by another woman or, she's being abused physically and psychologically by three women, do you see the pattern here?

And then a man comes along and saves her.

And they were saying, the lecturer was saying, well this is all about the man, the person, the individual, this individual, it's not about men and women or social structures, it's about the individual, the individual is in a bad place and their higher self has to come in and save them, wake them up.

But they were ignoring something very, very in-your-face; these stories are being told to children from the time they are born. These stories are being read to them.

They are being programmed into them, if you are a boy you have to be out there saving girls, yes? It's not about the individual at all.

And if you are a girl you have to just be passive, hope for the best.

Often when you take action on things everything goes wrong. You're fooled, you know you're fooled into eating an apple, twelve o'clock comes and all your makeup comes off, you are stuck in a tower and you can't get out.

So the woman, the female is helpless and hopeless, and quite incapable. And it's the male essence that comes in, always empowered, I mean we don't know, we don't hear how he became that powerful, he was just born that way, and saves her.

And we are reading these stories to our children you know and we were brought up with these stories, they're programs.

Let's have a look at religious structures.

Most of the religious icons, or Gods in the present day, are male. Or leaders right? Founders, male.

So we have Jesus, we have Buddha, we have Allah.

And females don't come in, and if they come in they come in very passive, submissive.

The link between "pain" and "falling in love".

334

Very, very interconnected. We have, again, lots of stories in our repertoire. Romeo and Juliet, pain.

And the pain that comes when the blinkers come off. All of the sudden the other person will hurt you, or you will hurt the other. Hurt and pain. And often, when a person is falling in love, it is physically and emotionally painful.

Why is it? Because it is a fall in awareness, it is a fall in vibration. And we think, "oh my goodness, how can falling in love be a fall in vibration when love is everything, we are love".

But you see, falling in love and the whole concept of two people being in love, is a different vibration and I am going to talk about the link between that one and Universal love, and why we call it the same thing. But a fall in vibration is always painful.

And one of the reasons why it is painful is because we have all those programs attached to it. Like belonging, owning, attachment. Lots and lots of attachment.

Worship.

And there we have the program of "giving away our power" that has been really, really used by religions.

We love Jesus, we love the Virgin Mary. Those are the ones I can say because those are the ones I am familiar with.

We love the Guru, we love the cult leader, and a lot of the time it is very similar to falling in love. That feeling of falling in love. And because love is blind, that's when all the other stuff can come in. "Well, if you love Jesus you will do this, and you know Jesus said that", but if you did a bit of research you would find out he didn't say that.

The link between falling in love and playing a game.

We get bored on this planet often. An individual, a divine being, an eternal being, will get bored and needs games. And all of life really, I see all of life as a game. Everything we do in it is a game. There's players, there's a game board, and there's the game, and different games co-exist as well. And falling in love can be that.

I had a friend who, as a young woman, she said, the only thing she likes about love is "falling in love". And what she likes most about falling in love, is making the man fall in love with her. And she used the words, "making the man fall in love with her".

And she said to me, "I don't care who the man is. Whether he's married or anything. If I want to, I can make him fall in love with me. I will do it."

I said, "and then what happens?"

And she said, "well, once he's in love with me, I lose interest."

That was her game. She just wanted someone to fall in love with her. That's the game she was playing.

People don't realize it but the game can be, "I want to fall in love", "I want to be in love". That can be the game.

The lack of self love. This is a key for the whole concept of falling in love to work.

The illusion of lack of love.

We are going full circle now, to "the fall".

What does "the fall" mean. If we look at historical stories or records about the fall, in Western society we can think about the fall of Satan. He fell, that was a fall. We also think about Eve. One of the things I read on the internet that I thought was hilarious is, "did Eve fall or was she pushed?"

The fall is all related to the illusion of lack of love. The illusion that we are not love.

And here we go to the real urge behind falling in love. Let's have a look at this program.

We are in a state at a collective level that we are separate from each other. And also, we are separate from Source. Those two programs are very powerful and very necessary to have a dual experience of light/dark, very necessary. If you don't have that illusion of separation, you cannot experience light/dark.

As soon as the person becomes, is able to see that they are, light/love. Then all the programs around falling in love and being in love fall away. They're no longer there. They are light/love.

They are Source.

And the urge, that huge urge to meet that special somebody and fall in love and be in love, that urge is the misinterpretation, or the program that we were programmed with as children, and growing up on the TV, movies, everywhere, novels, the program that says: "this is the only way you can merge". The merging, the becoming complete, when you hear these words related to love, romantic love and falling in love all the time, "I am now complete", "my other half", "I am one with", "I have merged with".

And it is true, it's not a falsehood, it happens.

But it's the desire, ultimately, it's never satisfactory because the desire, the real desire is to merge with Source, to be complete, to be who and what we really are; to break away the illusions of separation. That is what this whole structure we're stepping into is.

And at a physical level, and at a 3d level, sometimes the only way to have a taste of that wholeness and completeness is to merge with one individual. Physically, emotionally, mentally, and energetically.

And of course if you are asexual and you don't have any interest in sexual contact with another person, either male or female. But you still have the other, you see, you still have that program that says the only way you can have this, this merging, this being complete is if you mate with somebody else, you partner up with somebody else.

And of course, you know, the majority of the population is either heterosexual or homosexual, an asexual person has very little choices with regards to whom they feel that connection with.

And they will be in a relationship that requires them to have sexual intercourse when they don't really want to.

Yes the hugs and kisses, often. They put up with it.

In a not so far away time in linear time, and even nowadays in many societies if you are homosexual, you couldn't have that merging with somebody of your choice because the sex part was tied into it.

So what is the difference between falling in love, and love/light?

The words that we use like, love light, joy/love/light, to explain the energy of Source, to explain the energy of what we are, the essence, when everything else falls away, what's left behind?

Joy, light, love. That's it.

The difference, we use those words because we don't have any better words but really they are like a shadow, like a tiny little thing. Compared to the real energy that is our essence which we often call Source or externalize and call the Great Spirit, God, Goddess.

But it's us.

One of the words that we can describe to see the difference is "unconditional".

Now let's have a look at unconditional in relationship to falling in love.

Unconditional, if you were in love with somebody, would you unconditionally be happy to let them go so they can be happy somewhere else, with somebody else?

No, that would hurt. You have conditions around falling in love, depending on your culture and the way you were brought up.

For us in the West the conditions are, faithfulness, the conditions are, exclusivity, the conditions are, we are going to be living together, we're going to belong to each other.

All these conditions, it's way, way far away from unconditional love.

Often a relationship that lasts and evolves into something more could be unconditional.

But society makes it extremely difficult to have a relationship of unconditional love.

Fear comes in right away. Because if you think unconditional it means, "that person is going to hurt me" immediately. That person is going to go off and be with somebody else, and that's painful.

Conditional means that you need to be physically with that person, that's conditional.

Unconditional doesn't need to, you have no need.

And this is one of the key words again, so one of them will be unconditional.

The other one is Need.

For as long as you have a need in any of these programs, you are playing the game.

So one of the homework will be to look at these programs and say ok, do I have a need for this? And why do I need it?

And why are we looking at these programs?

Because most of the time we're moving through life with these programs at an unconscious level.

And when we work from an unconscious level we fall into all sorts of bad situations and traps. As soon as we become aware of them and conscious, we have a choice, we have a choice, it doesn't mean, ok so now I'm aware that when I think about falling in love what I'm talking really about is belonging to somebody or somebody belongs to me, so that's bad, so I have to process that away. No, it's not about that, it's about acknowledging and recognizing, "I want to be with somebody who I belong to and I own and I consciously make that decision," because it comes from a conscious decision, you know what you're getting into.

And then when jealousy pops up, because there's a fear of loss, you know where that's coming from.

Often people say, jealousy comes from insecurity, feeling afraid, so that's their security aspect, safety aspect, the person feels insecure that the beautiful woman they have fallen in love with and adore and worship is going to meet somebody if she starts going to college for example, or she gets a new job, she's going to meet and fall in love with the boss, it's always the boss for a woman, right? She's going to fall in love with the boss and leave me.

And for the woman, "oh, he's got a new secretary and she's very pretty, he's going to fall in love with her" it's never the boss for the man. Although nowadays that has, you know, it's coming in to the social structures of jealousy and insecurities.

All these programs that came in about romance, and uniqueness and falling in love that were made priorities in the relationships of marriages and alliances during the industrial revolution came about because there was a need for the female to be faithful seeing as the societal structure left all the property of the man, including the woman (as the woman was the property too) to the children of the man, so the man had to make sure that all the children that woman had were his, genetically speaking. Survival.

That's one of the areas where these programs and the reason why these programs were put in place.

For the woman they had all sorts of laws, she couldn't have a bank account, she couldn't work as soon as she got married so she had to leave her job, she couldn't go to university, she couldn't empower herself. She couldn't even vote.

So for her security it meant keeping that man. Divorce was a disaster. She would be shunned forever, so she had to put up with everything. And make sure that he didn't divorce her, so that yes, any women who he might go off with were enemies.

Falling in love is filled with these programs.

When you are sitting in contemplation, or meditation, after you do your meditation or contemplation.

Remind yourself, sometimes it's good to have a little piece of paper next to you that you can read afterwards so you don't have to remember through your meditation to do this at the end.

And have a look and say to yourself, "My intent is to uncover all the programs around falling in love and being in love", because this is today's topic.

We are going to cover all sorts of different topics in the next few days [this pertains to the days during which this course was recorded and those topics can be read and/or listened to in the full course].

But today's topic is about falling in love and being in love, so any type of program, it might even be, "That person doesn't even exist". Or, "Those people, those individuals whom I can have an unconditional loving relationship with, do not exist."

And all the other programs that we talked about earlier as well, have a look at the intent and really have a look and examine in your physical body. The programs in your physical body, very important, very, very important. A lot of them are just physical body programs.

In your soul level programs. Those are ones that belong to you, again the sense of separation and all that stuff.

Have a look at the programs there, again, the intent to uncover them.

Belonging, owning, attachment of any sort, the need to merge physically, energetically, emotionally, at a soul level with another. Safety, yes? Security, comfort, company, nurturing, the intent to look at being in love, falling in love, loving and being joy, love, light.

Have a look at and see what programs might be running, from a social point of view, in your field.

You know like the ones from fairy tales, the ones from religion, the ones from the romantic era, yes? Novels, movies, that type of thing.

So yes, have a look at those, and have a look at them for the next 21 days, just sit with the intention of uncovering and seeing, and then being able to process, keep a journal.

The abstract above came from the Love, Sex and Soulmates in the New Paradigm Talks by Inelia Benz

Alien UFOs exist - And this is why the government won't let you know about them.

The ONLY reason why we have not been "formally" told by our government that our species is in constant contact with Extraterrestrial and Ultradimensional Aliens is because of POWER. **Power over others**, power to do, power to own and sell new technology. The reasons why Alien species have not made their presence commonly known to the human masses is because of PERSONAL AGENDAS and our own blindness. There are agendas that benefit them, and our shadow governments, to keep us in the dark. And it's not because most of us plebs would panic and kill ourselves. Nope. It's about us plebs having access to technology, knowledge and awareness that would make each person unstoppable and uncontrollable. And our own blindness, well, we refuse to see them.

ETs and UlraDs DO exist. They are all around us.

A while back I talked about how I wanted to develop a methodology of teleportation. One that could be used by everyone on the planet, to travel anywhere they wanted to go. About half the responses I received to this possibility were from people telling me not to discover or disseminate this information. Why? Because, according to them, it was going to be used to abuse power, for criminals to pop up inside their bedrooms and rob or rape them. Basically, they were firmly against the dissemination of this technology due to fear. Plain and simple.

I am no stranger to UFOs, I have seen them various times throughout my life, and usually in highly populated areas. It has occurred to me that most people wouldn't see them unless one points up to them and says, "look! there's a UFO up there!" and they would then see it. But often forget about it a couple of days later.

We are extremely good at limiting ourselves. Our own limits define our spectrum of reality, the things we become aware of, and the things we remember. The main reason is collective agreement of the reality we presently choose to live in. And a holding on to whatever importance and games we are heavily invested in.

One of the limits is about our true history. Where we came from, our origins, our nature, our abilities, capacities, and power.

As a collective, what was impossible 100 years ago, is now common. Change in reality happens all the time, and something that did not exist, or was impossible one moment, is possible and completely normal the next. We do this as a society. Each society having it's own limitations, awareness of surroundings, beliefs about men and women, family, power, and all the rest. Even some countries in the West have fully embraced the knowledge and knowing that ETs and their crafts exist. But in the USA it's stilled officially "laughed at". Because the alternative would be for the shadow government having to share all the technology that has been reverse engineered by the shadow government and private enterprises. It would mean that suddenly, we could all have small devices in our homes that would provide enough energy to run a regular house for hundreds of years and more.

But the more people who become aware of something, the more it becomes "normal" for us as a society, as a species, and the faster it manifests in our daily lives. Anyone over 30 will remember the days before smartphones, for example, or even cell phones! They were just a fantasy depicted in sci-fi movies. Now look at us.

Another interesting bit of information that is being "discovered" around the world is that our history goes way longer than the few thousand years we thought we even existed. And to support that information as true, all sorts of highly advanced cities and pyramids are beings discovered around the planet, in the Oceans, Poles, inside mountains (which were all thought to be natural formations) and other interesting locations.

So, what do ETs, UltraDs, UFOs and Teleportation have in common? Simple. It's "vibration", or resonance. Looking back at the moments when I have seen UFOs, and the times when I was able to spontaneously teleport, the common denominator was vibration, or resonance to a certain frequency of vibration. Think of it as a camera changing focus, or a radio changing stations. The moments in which UFOs appeared, they seem to be responding to an energy, feeling and a mind set, that I and present individuals were feeling. It is almost like certain ET technology is designed to respond to us. This is clearly seen in key locations on the planet where people gather to UFO watch, or with those individuals who have learned to "call UFOs" at will. And at least one UFO technology appears to use teleportation through time and space to make themselves present in our 3D awareness of the world. Keep in mind that there are multiple races of ET, and UltraDs around. Not all friendly, or unfriendly, so use your discernment and process your fear (which can be used against you).

This is just the tip of the iceberg. The fact that our shadow governments refuse to share this technology with us, that we are not educated on the use of teleportation or expanded awareness communication, CANNOT stop us from "discovering" these methods and technologies ourselves. The more of us look at these topics, these possibilities (even if we think they are farfetched), the more of us look toward these possibilities, without judgment, the faster and wider the door will open for us to access the technology and abilities. All we need are numbers. More individuals looking. We are extremely powerful by ourselves, and even more so when we join in intent.

What do you say? Want to look in this direction with me? If so, share this article with anyone who you think would also be willing to join us in cracking this topic wide open and stimulate a change in our society that has ETs, UltraDs and their abilities and technology (including teleportation), as something completely "normal" in our culture, society and species.

A short comment by **Ilie**, our webmaster:

"This is an amazing article and, in my opinion, one the very important ones on the website. It is about power and keeping us under control. And we allow it, by accepting not to look at these issues and dismiss them instead.

Technology that would make everything super cheap (or even free) would end the slavery and the money paradigm virtually overnight. The so called "global controllers" would become obsolete as they cannot control a happy human that has the tech to provide for himself or his family.

It is my hope that our readers will take this to heart and really understand the implications of this article.. Apart from raising our own awareness as a being, I think this is the most important thing we need to be looking into right now. The tech is here, the ETs are here, but very few individuals demand access to it, and of those few even fewer are doing it from a place of self-empowerment.

The ETs, Advanced Tech, Self-Empowerment and High awareness are very deeply connected and working / looking at any one of them will likely help with the others as well."

If you haven't already we recommend reading the book "Interview with an alien" and also understanding the "Rules of Engagement in the new Paradigm".

A physical action toward a solid intent shifts us quickly into a different more resonant timeline

We work on ourselves, find empowerment tools, and shift our awareness because we want CHANGE. We want change to our personal lives, our perceptions and lifestyle, and we want to see a larger, global change in our species.

For that change to happen, there are various factors we can work on:

1. There's the original intent, what we want to see.

2. Then there is a period of processing our fears, belief blocks and disbelief at the possibility of the change. This may include any judgments we have about the current situation too.

3. After that, we release the attachment to ways in which to get the result we want to see, as well as limitations of the result (opening ourselves to "that or better" type energy).

4. We now process "blocks" that come up in real life that seem impossible to overcome.

5. That's when we make the decision that yes, this is going to happen. And more than a decision, we are now living in an energy of "knowing".

6. We then "feel" the new reality as existing now. We sense it with our physical and emotional bodies as being "real". Not something wanted or something needed, or something we are going to achieve at some point in the future, but as an actual reality NOW.

7. And now, we take action in the physical world.

Let's create a real life type of experience example. Say, a person, let's call her Sam, wants to get a new job but has huge financial and emotional ties with her present work structure:

1. Sam realizes she wants a new job and move on with her life independently of her present workplace.

This is the original intent. A new job.

2. She is afraid to lose something secure and then a new job not working out. She is also afraid of whether she can manage financially to support herself and her children, and pay her husband alimony. The job market is so bad right now that she feels at her age, she will never get a new position somewhere. She is also afraid to lose the friendship she has with her co-workers and supervisors. They take turns hosting bbqs every two weeks, and she is also heavily involved in their golf league. And the job is not horrible. Some days, she actually enjoys it.

Her fears are loss of security, income, being too old for the job market, loss of friends and social activities. She judges the present job as being "good enough" and perhaps it's not such a good idea to make the change. She sits down and uses the Fear Processing exercise to dissolve her fears, and the Firewall exercise to process her judgments and "made do" energy. She now decides she will go ahead and start looking for possible positions.

3. She strongly feels that she must get a new job where she can use her creative art skills more, within 20 miles of her home and that pays $90K per year.

Although a good starting point, she makes sure to add "or better" to her "list". As well as releasing the attachment to location.

4. As soon as she has moved to a point where getting a new job is something she really wants to do, her supervisor retires and she is asked to take over as department supervisor. Her work hours, and administrative duties, increase. Her house is found to have termite and she is now forced to take out a hefty loan for the treatment and repairs involved.

She sits down after her daily meditation and scans the energies that have manifested the physical blocks. Are they ways in which her environment are reflecting that she should not move jobs right now?

Or are there fears or social beliefs she did not get to the bottom of? Or is it a push from her higher self to radically change her life now? She decides it's a mixture of fear and a push from her higher self to get out now. She processes her fears, and emotional reactions to her new workload and financial burden.

5. She now KNOWS that she is getting a new job and that it's going to be an absolute improvement to where she is at right now.

The energy of Knowing, as opposed to wanting or wishing, or needing a new reality is radically different. For example, we know what color our hair is, we wish/want/need to go on holidays more often.

6. Now, when she goes into work, she totally feels her new experience. The satisfaction, the use of her creative, artistic, side, the shorter hours, the larger paycheck are not longer wishful thinking, they are real.. She feels secure, appreciated, satisfied, happy and complete. People compliment her smile all the time now and feel her self confidence and ... she's wearing much nicer clothes!

When we make the shift, it happens in the present. It happens where we are. Soon after that, our environment starts reflecting our new "reality".

7. This is when she writes down an honest, heartfelt Resume, that truly reflects her personality and interests (**physical action**). She checks it for resonance, makes sure there is no fear, neediness, or attachment energies on it, and clicks the send button to several companies around the world. Then she gets afraid that she will be rejected, her true self be discarded and thrown in the trash. She processes those fears and realizes that there is absolutely no attachment to any results, or any job. She's happy, content and satisfied. She KNOWS her perfect job exists, it's just a matter of vibrationally matching its timeline.

Program-free physical action is very important. And when we do it, often fears or misgivings pop up, that's when we process those fears and misgivings in earnest.

This example could be translated into many life situations. Moving house, getting a love partner, leaving a love partner, changing one's physical appearance, starting a new hobby, reaching enlightenment... you name it.

I will be discussing and expanding on this topic on our new Empowerment Platform WalkWithMeNow.com MP3 for July 2014! But don't worry if you are not ready to join the Empowerment Platform, the MP3 will be released to the public a week later.

I feel guilty...

So, I wake up this morning and find myself feeling guilty... oops what did I do???

Guilt is one of those dissonant energies that are widely promoted by the popular media, religion and cultural and social programs. BIIIG TIME. Why? because it lowers our vibration and sucks us into the victim/aggressor cycle.

My first thought was, "what did I do that's so bad to wake me up with buckets of guilt?" I spent several hours allowing the feeling of guilt to exist, express, grow... and nothing. I had no idea why it was there, or where it came from. I did see that it had overtones of victim/aggressor energy, and fear.

When I was a young kid, at some point I decided I wanted to experience life as a regular human being experiences it. This was mainly because I had no grasp of why people behaved in the way they behaved, or held on to dissonant energies way past the time they were triggered. The decision was immediately carried out, and I was able to experience many strong, human emotions, conflicts, decisions, I suffered (held on to pain past the moment of its usefulness), and so on. But it was artificial, and even at the darkest pits of despair, I was observing, learning, knowing it was artificial.

One of the first acts I did as a kid, when I was able to "experience" being human, was to remove a personal guilt by removing the memory of what I had done/experienced from my mind. This cascaded into forgetfulness, the vail fell across my eyes. Before that, I had complete recall of every single moment in my life. I could quote from a random page of a book I had read several years earlier. After that, I couldn't remember what I had for breakfast.

Some decades later, the usefulness of "living like a human being" died off, and I stepped into my natural self once more, but with several programs still in place from the years of "being human". This means that often I don't know what a particular dissonance is about, where it comes from, or what triggered it, but have a sense of what it might be by it's "description".

This morning the feeling of guilt was in my field, in my body, and I could not figure out where it came from, what "I had done" to activate it. I thought about the last thing I was doing last night, and remembered I was working on an article on war. In that article I talked about a veteran I had met a couple of weeks back. And I thought, that must be it, I don't know how to contact him (he was a guy I talked with in a cafe), to ask permission to share his experience. I thought, "I don't have his permission, therefore sharing his experience is wrong".

I deleted the article. Nothing. The feeling was still there.

There are two adults living with me in my house, so I basically told each one that I was feeling guilty and didn't know why, did they have any input. One went into a huge dialogue about how guilty he felt about something or other. The other simply had no idea.

I thought, maybe I'm feeling someone else's guilt? Is this something in the collective?

Bingo!

The resonance of the find went through my body immediately. There is someone feeling guilty in my field of awareness. Then I received a strong, "I am so sorry." But... sorry about what?

The victim/aggressor overtones picked up. And as I was looking at those, I saw the person behind the mask.

Then I got it. It was nothing more than a mystical play of agreement. This is when energies are overlaid in a person to cause them to think they have done something or something will be done to them, or something is about to happen to them. Often what follows is an actual act of doing something, or being the victim to something, that corresponds to the energy being overlaid. The reason is that the person "believes it", and therefore it is a "yes, go ahead, this can happen in my life". The unconscious agreement to the act being done on the person.

352

My entire life there have been attempts to suck me into the victim/aggressor cycle, where I would be either taken out or disabled enough to make me ineficient in delivering the message of empowerment. And many times I was sucked in big time, for many years.

I fell for it today, I was running in circles for hours. And if I hadn't identified the ultimate "intent", I would still be running around, perhaps in fear that someone was about to do something horrid to me. And it was that last attempt, the attempt to make me fearful, that gave the game away. You see, I am not important. If I fail, someone else, actually hundreds of people, will continue delivering the message of empowerment. And even at my most stupid/ignorant times of my life, I survived all these attempts, and lived to deliver the message another day. Now, today, although not the wisest person on the planet, I am not taken in so easily.

We are all connected. And if I had not processed this situation, anything I wrote, anything I did, expressed, would have had a layer of "wrong doing" in it. Anyone who is waking up, or is sensitive to energies, would have picked up on it and felt that I was guilty of something. So, the implications of how I deal, or not deal, with what pops up in my life are broader than just me. This energy would have quite effectively polluted the message of empowerment that I deliver every single day.

The reason I have decided to make this very personal journey public is because it clearly demonstrates how dissonance can make us spin into the wrong paths.

YET, whether that dissonance is from an external source, or whether we did indeed do something dissonant ourselves, we can step out of it in a moment. There is NO POINT keeping the feeling of guilt after something we did. Instead, see it as a red flag. It is your body, your higher self, your emotional body, your energy body, your mind, telling you there is a huge dissonance between your true self and your action. Process it, and move into a more resonant Self. The more resonant we are in ourselves, the broader our awareness, the more we can step into our power without fear. The more we can be that person that others can map to. The person who is wide open, transparent, empowered, and living in complete resonance.

Come and explore this and other topics at our Walk With Me Now Empowerment Platform.

Moving into Resonant Timelines - Upgrading Relationships

Abstracted and edited from this MP3 Talk by Inelia Benz, which is ready for download.

"Today, I want to talk about how a physical action based on a solid intent, on a solid clear intent, will shift us very quickly into a more resonant timelines.

Shifting into more resonant timelines, or manifesting the world of your dreams, and also basically shifting your reality, are all very closely related if not the same thing.

I've talked about manifestation many times before, and the methodology that we can use to manifest things quickly in the physical universe. I've also talked about how to reconnect with our environment, which is also part of the same thing.

Today I want to talk about the subject in more detail and from a slightly different perspective. Once we look at the creation, or manifestation, of our reality from different perspectives, we start to get a complete view, or more holistic, more empowered view. And with that more empowered view, we are able to manifest things quicker and more easily.

The example I want to use today, is that of relationships. And I am not just talking about love, sex and soul mates, like I have done for my course at Ascension101. I want to talk about all the relationships and in particular the relationship we have with each other as a human species. How we connect and reconnect with other human beings. The way in which those connections are either positive or negative to us, not in a judgemental way but in a resonance way.

When something or someone is very resonant with our own vibration we feel very comfortable around them and we can do great things together. And resonance has to do with equal vibrations it does not mean that both persons have to be high vibrational for it to happen, there can be resonance within low vibrational situations and beings as well. But what we are aiming to do is to create a more resonant environment and more resonant relationships with those vibrations which we want to achieve, the changes we want to see in our lives. And normally those changes are for more positive, higher vibrational experiences.

So let's have a look at why it is important for us to be looking at relationships right now. And why I'd like us to talk about the moving of ourselves into more resonant relationships.

Since the solstice of 2014 (in June) we have entered a period of time where relationships are up for us to look at and morph. The way in which we communicate with others and with ourselves has to be really looked at right now.

Everything we do has to do with communicating with ourselves and others. Everything is in relation to each other. When we raise the vibrational signature of our relationship with other individuals we shift the world, we shift the nature of our species and the nature of our common co-creations and human experience at this time.

This period of time where we are looking at relationships I think will probably go for at least 12 months if not longer. So it's, obviously, an ongoing thing as we shift paradigms, but is really really up for us to look at right now. And these things come in waves, so it's really intense right now. So you might be getting a lot of people going through some drama, for example, with individuals going to rage and other things and then we will also find that you will be getting moments of "I'm done with this person/relationship/situation". So all those are indicators that this is the perfect time to start addressing our relationships.

So let's have a look!

Most of this call is going to be very practical with exercises and items for us to work through.

The first thing I'd like to address is the intent. So let's have a look and see a relationship that we want to change.

It could be a relationship with a significant other, it could be a relationship that is based on the workplace or in our family or somewhere we live. Have a look and scan your relationships and see which one would you like to see improved. Which one needs an upgrade?

Once we have identified and located that relationship we can start the process of looking at blocks and fears and disbeliefs about the possibility of ever changing what's happening with this other person.

In this MP3 we are going to upgrade a personal relationship and a group relationship step by step. Are you ready?"

The Splitting of the Worlds - Coming to a planet near You!

In 2011 a separation occurred in the human collective. Those who wanted to have a fear free, empowered, aware, awake reality of physical incarnation, and those who didn't. Gaia has actively been pushing for a physical separation that is done through time, three generations, and is trauma free and gentle. We, the human collective, however, have been pushing for a fast and furious separation.

Various people, and environments I find myself in, have mentioned WWIII, and other doomsday scenarios. I am presently in various conversations via email, txt, physical and at WalkWithMeNow.com, about this topic.

It appears, very strongly, that a fast physical separation of realities is being chosen by our collective. How this comes about, well, that's what we are playing with at the moment. What we are deciding on.

Most of the people on Earth will interpret and manifest the choice depending on what is real to them. What choices they see as real.

One thing to remember is that no one chooses for us, or chooses us, there is no chosen people. No targeted people. It is each person who chooses for themselves. If you are working on yourself, you have chosen an empowered reality, it is that simple.

I've lived through close encounters with doomsday timelines before. And that's certainly one way we could do this, but what I sense now is a strong "collision" with a timeline of vibrational **physical** separation.

This may play out in war and violence and billions of deaths, or may play out in ways we cannot even start to imagine, but are open to "that or better".

What we have been doing, identifying resonance, dissonance, is exactly this. We are splitting the worlds. We are at an advantage in that we do it consciously. But everyone is at it in some form or other. (This months MP3 Detoxify Your Life Now discusses resonance and dissonance in great depth)

It is easy to be sucked into a battle field. The energy of the savior, the martyr, the soldier, the warrior, the commander, is strong is some of us here. But it implies a lowering of vibration, as all war and conflict is low vibrational by nature. If you do feel pulled in, to save, protect, others, I would suggest to examine the energy of the "guardian" instead. Not the weaponized guardian, but the guardian like an impenetrable wall energy. No consequences to who tries to trespass, just an impossibility of getting through.

We are bridges for people to pass through into the new paradigm. But it appears that soon, many of us will become a wall to stop the old paradigm from polluting the new. A wall that is so clear, so awake that cannot be infused with, manipulated, or corrupted by programs or judgments, or temptations.

Or maybe not :).

The physical separation is really up on the human collective mind right now. I would say, for now, just observe it.

As I observe it, and this is something that is coming out in the *Interview with a Psychic Assassin* book, there is a third option manifesting. It's is so outside of our reality scale that it needs to be observed.

Basically, light and dark can and do exist without the other. In fact, that's the only way they can exist. We can see both because there is both existing separately from each other in our world. There is also a reality where neither exists.

And something that is just appearing in our awareness, is a reality where they both exist as One. Not light and dark making grey, but making a color that is not in our spectrum. Not a reality where they neutralize or mesh, but where a new element emerges.

The urge to separate to different realities seems to be somehow related to the emergence of this new vibration. It is almost like if we don't separate now, we will be all gobbled up into the new element and that is so unknown, so different, so "not human" that we are pushing our choice hard now. Do you feel fear? Fear could be a pull to familiar surrounds.

Do we feel a desire to find out more? A way, perhaps to explore where other's have not gone before.

The only way we can stay clear, and keep our choice conscious, is to actively pursue resonance, and actively not engage in dissonance.

Journey's Beginning...

Well, you know it! Things are changing. The world is shifting, and it's shifting VERY QUICKLY. We find ourselves in a situation where the clear distinction between those who are awake and aware and those who are fast asleep is becoming more and more obvious by the day.

At a mystical level, the energies on the planet have never been so intense. They have also never been so polarized, or so clear cut.

For me personally, the past few years, and in particular the years I took on the job of being a public voice of empowerment, have seen my role changing from moment to moment. And in the past few months a massive change has come about in the core of the type of work I am required to do.

And the first step in that new journey has been taken. I am now in Europe. Next year I will be traveling the length of North, Central and South America. Why? What for? To touch you.

Up until this summer, my work was very simple. Be the voice of empowerment. Deliver as many tools as possible, as simple as possible, to as many people as possible.

And then it changed. The winds of change began early in the year (2014) and it brought about Walk With Me Now (walkwithmenow.com). A platform where I would make myself available energetically and online to as many people as wanted to come. Little did I know that this was but the first step of a massive change of strategy by those whom I work for... YOU. I have often said that most of the requests of things for me to do come from the Human Collective, or Gaia, or the Planetary Council. All these are different aspects of each and every person on the planet.

We are each other and we are our environment.

What does this mean for me, Inelia Benz? Well, it means that one on one connections, first virtual as it is in Walk With Me Now, and now through meeting individuals in person, is paramount and doable. Why? That will be revealed to you in person, not because it is any great mystery, but because it is about connecting one on one, person to person, reconnecting as an aware, intelligent, expansive and empowered collective.

When I first looked at this possibility it appeared to be impossible for me. The logistics, the travel, the amount of energy spent, and what for? A few minutes of physical contact with individuals around the planet. It made no sense to me. Plus I was not really able to do it either physically or energetically.

But the human collective, and Gaia, and the Planetary Council, does not ask things lightly, nor does it leave things for me to sort out on my own.

This past month has seen a massive change in my personal circumstances. I am no longer required to live in California (which was a very heavy job in and of itself). And I now have the support to be able to travel and meet individuals around the world. And touch them.

As soon as this change happened, we organized a few, very small meetings in Europe. The only one we have open at the moment of writing this article is the one in English and French, in Barcelona, Spain for the 20th of November. There are only a few places left, so if you want to experience this new opportunity to meet in person not just with me with other individuals who have also chosen the empowered reality, do come to it.

This new strategy is not going to last forever. I will not be available like this for very long. When I look at it, I see it lasting the rest of this year and for most of next year (2014-15). Nothing has been decided for 2016 just yet, and as I have often mentioned, I have no idea what is going to happen in 2017 but I am only booked for this job until then.

What does it mean for you?

That's up to you to decide. I'm here. And if you want to find out why our meeting in person is "important" right now, then we can get on with it and find out together, because to tell you the truth, I have no idea. It is a strong and powerful request from our Higher Self, and I am saying, "yes. I'll do it."

Will you?

Dealing with Friends and Family during Holiday Season...

It's December again, and most of the planet is going into deep religious mode. This will cause several things to come into our lives and energy fields. One of them is the cultural tradition of spending time with individuals whom we would normally not spend time with.

A second one is the reestablishment of the giving away of our power to a third party in order to be "connected" to our Higher Self, God, Divine Consciousness, Source Energy, Goddess, Gaia, and/or any other manifestation of our own divinity. In other words, our "disconnection" from our core self is strengthened.·

This causes several things to manifest at a social level. We have the highest rates of suicides of any month around the world, for example. Desperation and the sense of "lack" gets amplified. Indulgence and addictions get triggered.

What does this mean to us energetically? Well, it's like a big heavy, and low vibrational wave going through our own emotional, energetic, mental and physical bodies. It can trigger the savior energy in us, or perhaps also the martyr or even victim energy.

So what can we do?

Well, first of all, we learn how to deal with our sleeping relatives and friends. I have a youtube about this topic which I would highly suggest you watch again here:

Dealing with Sleeping Friends and Family:
https://www.youtube.com/watch?v=tdhBv6eALxE

Secondly, set up an alarm in your phone or clock every two hours or so, and when it rings simply observe where and when you are. Ask yourself, "am I here and now?" and see how comfortable you are in the here and now. If there is deep discomfort, then take action to move into a situation or place that feels more resonant to you. Make sure to do this without putting others "wrong" and you "right". Without judgment of yourself or others, simply shift your place, location, space, and vibration.

For the next few days, I would also suggest you do the Reconnect With Gaia's New Paradigm exercise once a day. You can find the exercise here: https://www.youtube.com/watch?v=RkYQnVFjEyQ

Whenever we shift vibration, especially when we go from a low vibrational situation to consciously shifting to a personal high vibration, we are transforming and morphing the entire human collective "agreement" of what happens during this Holiday Season. The more of us that have the intent and actively and consciously move and shift from the "given" Seasonal programs and media campaigns into an empowered and joyful state of being, the faster we will achieve the reality we want to experience on this planet :D

Next year I will be concentrating on making myself available to meet you on a personal basis through events around the world, as well as expanding on our mystical and energetic work knowledge base. You can, of course, get in touch with me personally any time at our online WalkWithMeNow.com platform.

Interview with a Psychic Assassin - Inelia Benz's newest novel is here!

IT'S HERE!!! My latest novel "Interview with a Psychic Assassin" is now available in electronic format. Instant download available on my website.

I write novels to impart otherwise inaccessible information which expands our minds and knowledge base on how Earth has been run. What also happened with this novel was that my life transformed completely during its writing.

My personal life transformation was a complete surprise to me. What I can say is that now I live somewhere different, my environment is highly and completely supportive and nurturing, and I am now in the most incredibly loving, equal, honoring and amazing love partnership of my life. So incredibly amazing that it is way beyond anything I had ever imagined. And that energy, that transformative quality, is embedded in the book.

Since its publication, I have received hundreds of comments and messages that also reflect the transformative energy which the book carries.

My feeling is that this can be an ordinary novel, just a run of the mill novel that one reads and then remembers, or not, for the rest of one's life. But it also has the energy and capacity to expand and transform a person's life as much as that person allows, wants or intends. Free will at its best. Doors are opened for us to walk through throughout the novel, but it's really up to us whether we want to walk through them or not. We have full control over the experience we have during the reading of the novel. And then we read it again, and find out there are hundreds of other doors which have magically appeared, and that reflects a massive growth of awareness.

This experience is traveled through a fantastic, or what some might call a science fiction journey. The main character is Ramona, who was recruited from her loving parents by a secret world government agency to be educated at an elite school for gifted children. Only this school's true purpose is to create the perfect assassin. Using technology and skills learned from alien captives, occult orders and super soldier programs, Ramona became their most deadly of weapons. Until she received a target from them that she could not kill.

What was meant to be a straightforward interview quickly turns into a dangerous and mystical adventure into the depths of creation.

Some things just cannot be killed.

If you have enjoyed "Interview with an Alien" you will love this new novel!

Looking Ahead - 2015 in View

In January 2014, I wrote about how the human collective felt much more powerful. What this meant is that it didn't matter if individuals were awake or asleep, they were more able to do, affect and influence themselves, their surrounding and the people in their lives and environment.

In 2015 I feel very strongly that we must take responsibility for our power. We can't expect the sleeping masses to take responsibility (ability to respond) as they are in a cycle of reaction rather than response, but we can't say the same about ourselves.

So what type of things are we talking about?

Well, let me quote from the Developing Mystical Skills for Everyday Life MP3:

"I often hear individuals say that they seem to be getting more sensitive to the energies in crowds, in shops and other public places. Or more sensitive to the energies of people at work, their families and their friends. This is true. But also what is happening is that people around them, everyone on the planet, are becoming more powerful. They become more able to broadcast their energy, to broadcast their thoughts, intents, their fears, their desires, their stress, their joys... You name it, they're broadcasting it, a thousand times more powerfully than what they used to do in the past.

At the same time, they're also more able to influence their environment, including us, to fit into the reality they are creating day by day. Which, unfortunately, is mostly created through programs and external stimuli and manipulation. In other words, they are creating realities that conform with society's rules and the rulers' choreographed designs: programs, belief systems, religions. And mostly through fears.

On the other hand, we are also more powerful. All of us who have decided to wake up at this time. Not only are you more powerful, but are more powerful just by the fact that we can now consciously choose, what we want to do with our lives from our own decisions and not decisions taken from social or cultural programs, from traumas, from fears and from egoic manipulations, whether it's our own ego or other people's egos.

With this power comes a great responsibility. Remember: responsibility is not fault. It's just and ability to respond. But also, it comes with a requirement to become more conscious about how we are using our energy, how we use our thoughts our intents and the emotional bodies.

What does this mean?

Well, it basically means that we are impinging into the energy fields, the mind, thoughts and the creative process of those around us.

If we're not conscious of this fact, we are walking around other people like a baby elephant in a china shop.

So the first thing that we have to look at is how we manage our power. How we manage our energy field and thoughts.

It's not about suppressing or not having any energy field. It's not about suppressing or censoring out thoughts. But it's about management.

Just like when we were babies we learned how to speak, we learned when to cry, when to shout and scream, when to whisper, when to speak normally, when to speak with a smile, when to speak with a pout... It's the same thing. It's becoming conscious of our energy fields, conscious of how wide, how big we're making them, who we are projecting them to. And then learning to adjust the volume, and the size, just like we learned to adjust our voice and our body language when we were babies.

We might call it mystical etiquette."

And this is the thing. Mystical etiquette in years gone by would have been something only seasoned mystics would have known about, or been trained in. Today we all need to get some mystical etiquette under our belts. Not just for our own benefit, but also the benefit of those around us. Learning how to manage our and other people's energies, emotions, thoughts, intents and manifestations is not complicated at all. BUT it's very important.

Why is this so important?

Our human species, our human collective, has taken some really important decisions. The nature of those decisions is who goes and who stays in our evolutionary path. And how that decision is carried out, is by collective agreements and the co-creation of our reality.

Really simple stuff like, for example, if a person subscribes to being vaccinated every few months against one disease or other, then they are giving consent for their immune system to be compromised, their quality of life damaged, and their lifespan shortened dramatically. They do it from a place of fear and also from a place of giving away their power to people who "know best". At the same time, they will widely broadcast, and not just verbally but emotionally, mentally and energetically too, the fear they are feeling about the disease. Fear is a very low vibrational energy, and as they too are more powerful, that energy will impinge in our energy field. If we haven't trained ourselves to identify what is ours and what is someone else's, it can send us spinning down into lower vibrations really fast.

We've all experienced this type of stuff at one time or another. Things we had processed and were finished with, suddenly come back for no apparent reason... well, it's not ours. BUT it affects us because we are connected and are part of the human collective.

My solution? We learn how to manage, work with and positively empower our own energetic, mental, emotional and physical output as well as consciously learning to respond and manage how we are affected by other people's broadcasts and influences. There is a ton of data on my website as well as on the internet on how to do this. This month I have put together some immediate tools and information on an MP3 called Developing Mystical Skills for Everyday Life which specifically address these issues.

"One of the things I noticed was just that there's been this kind of coming of age from The Shift. And I can really see that people who are awake, people who are waking and taking charge of their personal evolution by doing things for themselves that raises their vibration . . . listening to your show and things like this . . . really are stepping in. And the period has started where a person needs to learn how to manage their power because everyone is becoming more powerful. When you step into your power you become more powerful, so a learning and a looking for ways of how manage your energy. . . to manage your emotional body's transmissions, your thoughts . . . your intent . . . all those things . . . I think it's one of those things that started this year. So it's like we graduated from kindergarten, now we have to start real school, you know." Inelia Benz on the Hundredth Monkey Radio Show.

I'm living on a boat with a perfect soulmate... really, I am :)

One of the things that individuals will most often say to me, is that what they respect about me is that I walk my talk. That my personal life is not only open and transparent, but it perfectly reflects what I teach. I use the tools I have developed and/or "uploaded" from our common Source and integrate them into my daily life.

When I have a personal breakthrough, it's something which has come about through directly using the developed or uploaded tools. This is how I know they work, I use them myself!

On the 24th of December 2014, I published my newest novel,"Interview with a Psychic Assassin". During the writing of the novel, and parallel to it's end, I found out that a close friend of mine was in fact my life partner. My life has completely changed since then, for the better.

This didn't happen overnight, or simply because I wrote the novel, or simply because I finally saw him. The novel was simply the physical manifestation of a change that began in 2010, when I agreed to go public and become a voice of empowerment for our human species.

In 2010, I brought into our collective consciousness the Ascension101 Course. This is an amazing foundation for anyone who wants to empower themselves, wake up fully, or simply needs a refresher course to get them back on track after decades of spiritual training. I have since "taken" the course several times. Every time there is more growth, understanding and my life becomes easier and easier. This has caused huge changes in my life, and also has given me the strength and energy I needed to be a public figure. I am a recluse by nature you see, very private and prefer to observe than be observed and prefer to listen than to be listened to. The Course gave me the connection I needed to all aspects of myself that required strengthening and healing.

But what about my personal life? What about love?

For years I was asked about soulmates, sex, love, and relationships in hundreds of emails and Facebook messages.

So, in 2013, I created the Sex, Love and Soulmates in the New Paradigm Course. Even though I personally did not have much of an interest in finding a perfect mate, my Higher Self had other plans. As I always do, I took the course myself. It was really quite amazing to see how all the information fit into my personal life. What belief systems I was carrying, what blocks and firewalls to a fully satisfying relationship I had, and how I was blind to the existence of men who were perfect mates for me. As well as how and why this happens.

Because of the nature of the Interview with a Psychic Assassin novel, before I started writing it, I took the Course units in Sex, Love and Soulmates again in 2014.

At the time, in my personal life, things were breaking apart. I had been asked by Source, Gaia, the Human Collective, to stay, live and work in California for many years. But at the start of 2014, it asked me to leave. In fact it was very insistent that I leave! But by now I had been in California for nearly 10 years, had a life there. Two of my children live there, my ex-husband and close friend lives there. So, I procrastinated moving out. The result was that I got extremely sick for months. There were a couple of close calls, when I nearly didn't make it.

But I stayed!

In September 2014, I had the opportunity to spend some hours with an old friend. A man who lived all the way up on the very tip of Washington State, so we didn't get to hang out very often. We'd originally met in 2011, at one of my public events. He was then very active in most events, volunteering, helping out and even organizing some too. We also became collaborators on a couple of projects, and would often hang out with friends. He was like a brother to me. Or one of the girls. Completely invisible as a man, or possible partner. In fact, the thought was so ridiculous, when someone finally verbalized it to me after a mutual friend's birthday party (they thought we were secret lovers), I thought it was hilarious and also impossible.

Normally, when he left California, he would also leave my attention. When he was gone, he was really gone. And he wouldn't pop up in my attention field until he sent me a text or Facebook message. But this time, this time not only was his visit different (I noticed two things: one that he was a man, and the other that he was extremely handsome), but after he left, he sent a continuous flow of text messages, which meant he did not disappear from my consciousness.

The second day after he left, I looked at all the messages on my phone, and realized that our discourse was not over. That our conversation needed to be had and concluded... All this time, I was writing the Interview with a Psychic Assassin book.

Long story short, some serious fires engulfed the areas around Sacramento, where I lived. My asthma kicked in, and I was not able to procrastinate my exit from California any longer. I packed my car, my dog and drove North West toward the coast. He suggested I travel to where he lives, as the air is clean, cooler and the sea is all around.

Of course I had huge resistance to do that! So I invited him to come with me on my European Tour during November 2014 instead. Traveling with someone will often be a great way to get to know them quickly. Really know them. When you are sharing small spaces 24/7, if anything is going to show up, it will. Plus my public events are really high vibrationally charged, nothing dark can hide!

It's now February 2015, and we moved in together... onto a boathouse. Another amazing surprise is that living on a boathouse on the sea was one of my most cherished dreams. A dream I had actually given up on. When we tried to rent a house, any house, we found really crazy blocks coming up. We realized we were not looking for the right thing. Then his mother said to me, "why not a boathouse?" And I thought... whoa, that is one of my life long dreams. So I asked him if he wanted to live on a boathouse. And guess what! That was his lifelong dream too... figures.

Now I am writing a new novel, one that explores and expresses who and what he is, and the journeys that took us into each other's arms. I'm here for the very first time as a being anywhere in time and space. He's been here as long as time and space have existed.

If you are part of walkwithmenow.com, you know who he is. If not, then you will have to wait until he decides to make himself known publicly. Not an easy thing to do ;)

Language as a tool of enslavement...

Have you wondered why we all spell things the same way, well not quite, as in England we spell things differently as in the States - same with Spanish from Spain and Spanish from South America, but generally it's pretty uniform.

Also, did you know that the structuring of sentences (e.g. some people beLIEve that a sentence MUST have a subject, verb, and no more than one adjective... must all be in the same tense... and same "person")... is a very recent invention?

It blocks the free flow of information and energy behind the words. Not only of writing it, but also of it being received. If the writing has "mistakes" or "errors", a person stuck in the "grammar matrix" will not be able to understand it, or will get terribly distracted by these "errors in grammar" and miss the point, thought, or energy being carried in the piece they were reading. It creates minds that are barren (only in expression), restricted and overall unsure of how to express fully, without mistakes.

I had the good fortune of manifesting two amazing English teachers. One in high-school, and the other at University. They both taught that the best thing a person can do, is to forget all grammar, and any other kind of rule that dictates the free flow of energy and information while we write... including how many commas we can use in a sentence... how long the sentence needs to be... how many times we can use "and" or whatever... and even the rule that says we cannot invent new wordiethings. Also, they taught me that colons (:), dashes (-), semicolons (;), slashes (/) and parentheses (()), belong in mathematical formulas only and have no place in a free flow of expression (they divide and fracture). And... never have a "but" or "and" start a sentence, and especially not start a paragraph! And... to forget all that too and just do what we bloody well want.

Both gave the following example of one of the greatest chapters in English literature, which is a perfect example of free flow of energy (emotion, thoughts, information, visualization): James Joyce's

Penelope (Episode 18 of Ulysses)
www.online-literature.com/james_joyce/ulysses/18/

Here is some historical data on the invention of grammar and spelling for the English language ~ look at the qualifications of the men who invented it to understand the real reason for it: en.wikipedia.org/wiki/History_of_English_grammars

And it basically pretty much reflects why rules were invented for older languages and other modern languages too. Aristotle didn't follow any grammatical rules ;) What we think these days is the sentence's subject (originally "the concept being looked at") which is what the sentence "subject" was based on, has been totally misunderstood: home.mira.net/~andy/works/aristotle.htm

Anyways, I am sharing this with you because language is something that didn't start being dogmatic and filled with rules and structures. A bit like religion... it was hijacked for a while so we could experience separation really well. Now we move on.

It's not about blame, ever. Remember that we are the ones using language and subscribing to things, and giving our power away, and taking our power back... no one can force us to do anything. But I can see that we can easily fall into the victim aggressor thing here. My article is really aimed at making us aware of our choices, and how a divisive, unnatural, structure was introduced into our communication system. It also has really good bits to it, that help us in communicating better, like a standardized spelling system (one we can all understand)... I think is very useful. As we become aware, we have greater freedom to choose to keep aspects of it or discard them.

I invite you to step out of grammar and express as your heart desires! And I can say that because I have a 1st Class Honours Degree in Communication Studies from Dublin City University and got the highest scores ever achieved by anyone on Sociolinguistics... which was taught by the top linguist in the world at the time... how about that for a push on authority hehehehehehehe :O 8) Did it make this post suddenly become more real and something to listen to for you? That's about the programming that says we can only talk about language if we have a degree or two, or ten... or it means nothing. A whole subject in and of itself.

It's OK to ask for help!

In my life, I haven't really "asked for support" for a personal project. The support I request is usually for a collective need, such as the Global Ascension Center, or Ascension101. But for personal support, there was never an opportunity for me to actively ask for support. When I heard how much money it will cost to repair some key areas of our boat's hull (which is our home), the first thing I thought of was, "I'll ask for support from my audience, start a crowdfunder or something like that". Which was soon after blocked by... "how does one do that?" And then I hit a program which said, "asking for help for your personal life is wrong".

When I looked at that program I was really surprised it was there because the individuals who follow my work, and hang out with me, are extremely supportive all the time, and would be really happy to be part of an inflow of energy and well being into my personal life. Yet, every time I look, that program kicks in. It feels artificial and external, but there must be something in my own field where it latches on, or it wouldn't affect me.

So, I asked a bunch of friends at Walk With Me Now to look at this particular program with me. And the energy started freeing instantly. Before I knew it, I was ready to ask!

How come I live on a boat?

You may have heard the news of my moving to Washington State, here is sections of what I wrote before:

> *I had been asked by Source, Gaia, the Human Collective, to stay, live and work in California for many years. But at the start of 2014, it asked me to leave. In fact it was very insistent that I leave! But by now I had been in California for nearly 10 years and had a life there. Two of my children live there, my ex-husband and close friend lives there. And I had nowhere else to live. So, I procrastinated moving out.*

The result was that I got extremely sick for months. There were a couple of close calls, when I nearly didn't make it.

But I stayed!

In September 2014, I had the opportunity to spend some hours with my friend Larry. A man who lived all the way up on the very tip of Washington State, so we didn't get to hang out very often. We'd originally met in 2011, at one of my public events. He was then very active in most events, volunteering, helping out and even organizing some too. We also became collaborators on a couple of projects, and would often hang out with friends. He was like a brother to me. Or one of the girls. Completely invisible as a man, or possible partner. In fact, the thought was so ridiculous, when someone finally verbalized it to me after a mutual friend's birthday party (they thought we were secret lovers), I thought it was hilarious and also impossible.

Normally, when he left California, he would also leave my attention. When he was gone, he was really gone. And he wouldn't pop up in my attention field until he sent me a text or Facebook message. But this time, this time not only was his visit different (I noticed two things: one that he was a man, and the other that he was extremely handsome), but after he left, he sent a continuous flow of text messages, which meant he did not disappear from my consciousness.

The second day after he left, I looked at all the messages on my phone, and realized that our discourse was not over. That our conversation needed to be had and concluded...

***Long story short**, some serious fires engulfed the areas around Sacramento, where I lived. My asthma kicked in, and I was not able to procrastinate my exit from California any longer. I packed my car, my dog, and drove North West toward the coast. He suggested I travel to where he lives, as the air is clean, cooler and the sea is all around.*

In February 2015 we moved in together... onto a liveaboard boat. Another amazing surprise is that living on a boat on the sea was one of my most cherished dreams. A dream I had actually given up on. When we tried to rent a house, any house, we found really crazy blocks coming up. We realized we were not looking for the right thing. Then his mother said to me, "why not a houseboat?" And I thought... whoa, that is one of my life long dreams. So I asked him if he wanted to live on a boat. And guess what! That was his lifelong dream too... figures.

We found an amazing boat - a beautiful wooden trawler-yacht from 1961 designed by William Garden. The price was really low, so we didn't have to get into debt to buy it due to the extensive repairs it needed. Some planks in the hull had dry rot, as did some ribs, and the "house" needed a bunch of caretaking done too.

When we posted our predicament in Walk With Me Now, someone immediately volunteered to help us with the house repairs. So that brought our total bill down many thousands of dollars (thank you Hopi!!)

We started a crowdfunding campaign to repair the hull, which can only be done by shipwrights (expensive) to make our new home sound and safe to be in the water.

We raised more funds than we could have possibly have imagined.

Thank you for your support!!

Not all Greys are Created Equal

In my newest novel "Interview with a Psychic Assassin", I explored the nature of Greys. In it, I mentioned some thoughts about Greys, what they do, their technology, and where they might come from. The discussion, in the novel, went on for about two pages and explored the main character's experience with Greys during her military government training.

Since writing the novel, I have been asked several times about the nature of Greys. I have also received emails and posts saying that Greys are all evil, and sent links to websites that prove it. And some that say that Greys are good, and those come with links to websites that prove it too.

The thing is, looking at the evidence of our interactions with Greys throughout history, we start to see certain patterns that are replicated from culture to culture.

A few decades ago, for example, they were not grey but green. Little green men with big heads, large black eyes, small noses and tiny or absent mouths. In modern culture we see them depicted as made of light, some very tall, some very small, some grey, some white, some blue, some good, some bad.

As our collective awareness field expands, and more individuals are starting to remember interactions with Greys, a huge collection of data is beginning to surface about them.

One thing is becoming clear. There are many shapes, colors and forms of Greys and they are not a new, or Western, phenomenon. What appears to be universally common, is that their heads all look like that of a human embryo.

Another aspect of the Greys, is that they appear to be more of a "suit", than an actual being. It is almost as though their body is artificial, maybe part organic, certainly sentient, but the "driver" is elsewhere. Communication between the Greys and humans is mostly, if not all, telepathic in nature.

The "nature" of Greys seems to vary from shape to shape, and color to color. It is almost as though different species are using these Grey "suits" to enter into our system (solar and dimensional), to interact with us. Some people say their experience is they are treated by the Greys as though they were farm animals, others say that they feel highly identified with the Greys and consider them their real and true family - their human experience being a temporary experiment or mission.

And so far, apart from physical trauma to some of those who have been abducted, they have not used their technology to "invade our planet", or "destroy us all".

In the novel, the main character Ramona at one point says:

"People don't seem to realize that if the Greys were malevolent, considering their abilities and technology, they could have wiped us out completely a long time ago. No question about it"

Yet, there is a lot of fear about the Greys.

From whistleblowers, and government leaks, we have been told, or shown, that the Greys whom the government have captured, or are working with, are not aggressive in any way or form. At least not physically. In fact, they appear to be very physically weak, and carry no weapons.In fact, if there was any aggression, it was from humans.

In popular culture we see Greys depicted as ruthless and violent, as harvesters that eat human flesh, as friendly cuddly and wanting to phone home, and everything in between.

This article is meant to open to the possibility of a broad spectrum of species presently using the Grey "suit" technology to interact on our planet. Who made them? Who is developing them? When are they from? Where are they from?

When I look at them, I see an artificial intelligent biological "drone" as it were, that can house consciousness without trapping it. It reminds me somewhat of our own human bodies, except our bodies feel more alive. Our bodies feel more like highly intelligent elementals that need us (the soul being) to animate them and stay alive. Yet, if we were to take a human embryo before the soul entered it, added some sort of developmental retardant, made it grow to a useful size, included nano technology to allow it to exist in an environment outside the womb, and were then able to remotely "borrow" it to walk on distant times or planets, it would sure look like a Grey.

Just saying ;)

By the way, we are wired to forget what you just read above, so I would say go back and read it again, see if you saw it all, or forgot some already.

Project, Joy or Duty? Let's take a closer look at relationships

Our human species is all about relationships.

What are these relationships? The relationship we personally have with ourselves, the one we have with our environment, and the relationships we have with every single person who touches our life.

Some of those relationships are nurturing. The nurturing relationships positively influence us, put us in a state of joy, and we usually talk or think about those individuals in highly positive words.

Other relationships are toxic. Toxic relationships poison us, put us in a negative state of mind or emotion. We usually talk or think about these individuals in negative words. Or we find ourselves making an awful lot of excuses for them, or validating their actions with "understanding" where they are or they came from. These poisonous relationships will usually bring a lot of drama, whether directly or indirectly, into our lives.

By making a simple two sided list, and putting everyone we have a relationship with in it on one side or the other, whether at work, home, social groups, online, or school, etc., we can start having some clarity on the patterns we are falling into. Obviously some people won't fit in either or will fit in both ;) Remember, this is just an exercise where we put the "main" energy we detect or share with the person recently. It may have been radically different a year ago, or it might be very varied, changing all the time.

At this point, if there are people in the poisonous side of the paper, it's important NOT to fall into judgment or guilt ourselves, for having these relationships, or the people we are playing these low level games with. This little exercise is not about judgment, or even action. It is about becoming conscious and aware of what is happening in our lives.

Of course, sometimes action becomes very clear, and we go ahead and do something about it. We make a schedule to spend more time with the individuals in the nurturing side of the list, and less with those on the poisonous side of the list.

And here is where it can get a little bit complicated. Often we believe that there is nothing we can do about certain relationships, that we can't change them, or move away from them, or have more of them. This is because when we have a relationship it's not always clear why we stick around in it.

So look at your list again, and mark down those people whom you have either chosen to keep having a relationship with, or feel you cannot end the relationship with.

Next to their name, place the following words, depending on what category they fall into:

Joy: this is where you want to keep a relationship because you have an enormous amount of fun and joy when you hang out with this person. Afterward you feel inspired, satisfied, happy and energized.

Project: this is a relationship you have because you feel you are a positive influence on the other person, or the other person has a positive influence on you. Often it will come down to a feeling that you want to help the person change or better themselves, or that they are changing or think they are making you better themselves.

Duty: this is where you put the people whom you feel you cannot stop having a relationship with. It could be that you are married to them, work with them, they are an underage son or daughter that you are responsible for, a parent you are responsible for... in other words, people that you believe you cannot stop interacting with.

Again, this second set of categorizations is not necessarily to do something different with the individuals, but simply to get to know why you are hanging out and interacting with another human being. If you fall into judgment or guilt yourself, or judge them or make them guilty, process that before you continue with the next bit.

Are there major patterns here?

If, for example, all the women in your life are co-dependent, dramatic and addicts, then there is a definite pattern you need to address because the majority of the women on the planet are independent, joyful and free of addictions.

Or, for example, all the men in your life are absent, control freak, aggressive workaholics, then there is a pattern there to look at because most men on the planet are independent, joyful and free of addictions.

If, when you read the words, "most women/men on the planet are independent, joyful and free of addictions", you think to yourself, "I never met one", then there is definitely a reality filter happening that you need to address. The reason is that the only common denominator among all those men or those women whom have very similar patterns and personalities, is you. If YOU are different to the group that appears to be all the same, it's not because of your gender, age or demographic. It is because you are simply different to the people you are able to see. We only see what we think is real, if something is not real to us, we don't see it.

Another really good question to ask ourselves is: "Am I required to put on a mask to interact with this person?" But that's a full article in and of itself. Still, it is a way in which we can see how genuine and visible we are to others ourselves.

By becoming aware of the patterns and type of individuals in our lives, we can then make conscious choices on how to proceed with those relationships.

You are the common denominator of all your relationships. Therefore, you have absolute power to change, clarify, engage, encourage, remove or nurture them. Cool huh?

Postscript

I hope you have enjoyed this book as much as I enjoyed writing it! What happens between today and 2017 is unknown to me, but it fills me with excitement and inspiration.

Do keep in touch through the ascension101 site, and if you are ready to start manifesting a new way of interacting and co-creating together, join us at walkwithmenow.com

Do know that by purchasing this book, which you didn't have to because it is all published for free on the website, you are supporting me, my family, and the ascension101 team.

Do know that you working on yourself is not just helping you, but the entire human species… and all our ET cousins too!

Hugs

Inelia Benz

Made in the USA
Middletown, DE
10 July 2017